Walking Wounded
Inside the U.S. Cyberwar Machine

Michael A. VanPutte, Ph.D.

Lieutenant Colonel, U.S. Army (retired)

The offices of the Secretary of Defense, Director of National Intelligence, and Secretary of Homeland Security reviewed this manuscript to ensure it did not contain any classified or sensitive Government information and have no security objections to its publication. The redactions throughout this book are information these government agencies censored without explanation. This review, however, should not be construed as an endorsement of the author's views.

I appreciate your suggestions, comments, and criticisms.
You can reach me at michael@mvanputte.com or my website at www.mvanputte.com.

Update version: August 5, 2017

Dedication

To three ladies: Linda, Ashley, and Brianne.

Contents

List of Illustrations

Foreword

Want to learn how to pick a lock?

What was your initial reaction to that question? How would you feel about a lesson on how to hi-jack communications, guess people's passwords, and exploit computer software?

Initial reactions to these questions almost invariably fall into one of two categories. Some people react with curiosity: "Oh! I always wondered how that worked." Other people assume the person asking these questions is a criminal, or at least up to no good. They don't want to learn the skills or even understand how the systems they manipulate work, because only criminals would be interested in how to pick a lock, and these people being asked this question are obviously upstanding citizens… right?

It isn't inherently wrong to know (or want to learn) how to pick a lock. After all, this is a technology you use and depend upon every day, so wanting to understand it better is reasonable. Unfortunately, the people who respond as described in the second group are falling into the trap of labeling some kinds of knowledge as "bad".

The lock picking questions and skills alone have no intent or morality associated with them. Allowing preconceived notions regarding intent or morality to prevent learning can make it very difficult to make informed decisions later. Buying a lock for your gym locker, home, or bike? Knowing how locks work, their shortcomings, and the different classes of lock types, with their varying benefits and limitations, can come in pretty handy.

I wish I could tell you that most people fall in to the first category and that everyone is open to learning new things. Sadly, it's more common for people to allow their stereotypes and assumptions regarding intent and morality to keep them from learning about the world around them. This second, less curious category of student is unsurprisingly somewhat prevalent in the U.S. Government and military complex. After all, people in the government or military are busy people with lots of important decisions to make, and being willing to question their assumptions takes time. Of course, when it comes to matters of security, a total unwillingness to take in new data that challenges your point of view can lead to disaster. Being able and willing to re-evaluate assumptions is important to strong decision-making skills.

"Today I'm going to show everyone how to pick locks, remotely compromise a computer, crash an unknown software application, and I'm going to show you how to guess the passwords of everyone else in this room." These were probably pretty close to the first words that Mike VanPutte, then a Captain in the Army Corps of Engineers, heard from me in 1999 at the Army War College in Carlisle PA. A year later he would hear more things like this, again from me, in front of a group of officers at the Naval Postgraduate School in Monterey CA.

I wanted to teach these future government and military leaders how to be hackers.

To many people, the word hacker has strong criminal connotations. A hacker to them is some geeky, gangly teenager in his parents' basement trolling people, breaking into corporate computers, and generally trying to cause global thermo-nuclear war. This is a misconception and a perversion of the original definition of a "hacker." A hacker is simply a person who can take a system, be it complex or simple, and figure out how to make that system do things it had not been intended to do by the people who built it or by the people who normally make use of it. Hacking can happen in all types of domains from the arts to the hard sciences. Tinkerer, explorer, maker, experimenter, and inventor: these are all synonyms for hacker, as I use the term. Unfortunately, to many, the synonym for hacker is criminal.

The immediate, short-term goal of lecturing these classes was to teach young officers in the Department of Defense (DoD) some core skills of computer security hacking and how to critically examine assumptions about software and systems. We covered how to pick locks and how to exploit buffer overflows, race conditions, information leaks and object re-use. The more important longer term strategic goal, however, was to identify true hackers within the DoD, encourage them, and hope they would take the hacker way of looking at problems with them into more and more significant leadership positions in the United States Government: Influence them positively early in their career and hope for the ripples of change to become waves years later. This is where Mike VanPutte comes in. While Mike has been kind enough to credit me and a few others for being the ones to open his eyes so he could see how a hacker sees the world, think how a hacker thinks, the fact is Mike was already a hacker. He just did not know it yet.

Mike was one of the (few) people at the time who took in the new information without prejudice. In fact, that's an understatement. Mike ravenously consumed the new information and was very enamored with the different thought processes that allowed him to look at new problem sets, new technologies, and new situations and see them differently from his peers.

I kept bumping in to Mike as he progressed through the ranks over the years from Captain, to Major, to ultimately a Lieutenant Colonel (then retired) and fellow Program Manager at DARPA.

Mike was early to the game of full spectrum Computer Network Operations (CNO), a Department of Defense term that is commonly used to cover all aspects of DoD cyber, not just defense. Luckily he had figured out that the more data he took in, without prejudice, the more novel conclusions and solutions he could achieve later. "The key to a great strategy is to have multiple options," is how I have lived my professional life. Mike has made use of this strategy as well.

Even people who may think that they excel in challenging assumptions and thinking critically usually have a significant blind spot. Most blind spots stem from the fact that it's easy to challenge assumptions that other people make, but it can be downright frightening to challenge your own beliefs when new information comes to light. People of all walks of life and intelligence level can fall into this trap.

Mike spent a lot of his professional life in the U.S. military, both as a soldier and a civilian. This is an institution that rewards, even requires conformity and homogeneity. Free thinking, exploratory tinkering, hypothesis challenging, and other characteristics that I looked for in the people I trained were not typically the most rewarded traits in the DoD. Being in this environment most likely impeded some of Mike's ability to explore and critique, but the fact that Mike not only survived, but flourished, implies that the attributes I'm describing were more of an asset than liability.

Both Mike and myself have both been honored with the highest medal that can be bestowed by the Office of the Secretary of Defense upon a civilian. We are very different people; one of us comes from a long military career followed by civilian service, the other a long haired liberal-leaning hacker. What we have in common is that we fall into the first category of people: curious, open to taking in new data, and trying to never ascribe intent or morality to context-less information.

Because of this, I'm very much looking forward to consuming the information presented in this book. I know that Mike has been in unique positions within the U.S. Government, seen a wide range of situations that many people have not (or are only beginning to), and has had to operate within that strict, constrained military environment. I will be evaluating this book as I read it. Where did Mike take in new data and come to novel conclusions? Where is Mike possibly closing off new data or taking a shortcut to his conclusions? Perhaps more importantly, I will be attempting to evaluate myself the same way as I read this book. My hope is that should there be new information presented that is at odds with any of my core beliefs and assumptions, I will have the strength to not only evaluate the new data but to evaluate and challenge my own beliefs. I hope you, the reader, are ready to approach this book in the same way.

Peiter "Mudge" Zatko
-Hacker, Coder, former DARPA Cyber Programs Manager,
Director of the non-profit Cyber-ITL

Preface

"Those who cannot remember the past are condemned to repeat it."
- George Santayana (1863-1952)

On the lush hills overlooking Pearl Harbor on the island of Oahu, Hawaii I gazed at Camp H.M. Smith, the headquarters of the U.S. military forces in the Pacific. Every year I came to Camp Smith to take part in the two-week military exercise the Pentagon called Terminal Fury. Terminal Fury is a vast war game with over 3,000 military service members, government officials and defense contractors connected by a web of electronic communications systems for planning large-scale military operations in the Pacific theater. As U.S. military forces in the Pacific theatre—called U.S. Pacific Command or PACOM- play the war game they are forced to react to challenges thrown at them from another 300 people whose role is to dream up a myriad of simultaneous crises from major military battles to humanitarian support for tsunamis.

As with every military exercise Terminal Fury has a group of players play bad guys and poke holes in the U.S. Pacific Command's beautifully laid out plans. Locked in a special vault on Camp Smith, these players try to anticipate what the Pacific Command will do and outsmart the good guys.

Instead of playing everyone's actions on a battlefield, decisions are fed into a giant computer game. Like the 1980s movie "War Game," the computer tracks the actions, supplies, and health of every soldier, airplane, and naval vessel in the game, plays both sides actions, and calculates the results of every choice and action.

Every year the generals and admirals tell us the goal of the two-week war game isn't to win; Pacific Command designed Terminal Fury to exercise the plans and stress the leaders in the Department of Defense Pacific region. Terminal Fury forces leaders to rehearse and refine their plans on the shelf against a skilled and adaptive adversary, to see how well the good guys can make changes on the fly, to create new plans against unanticipated scenarios, to discover shortcomings, and to train the leadership within the command.

But just between us—everyone is trying to win.

And in December 2004, a group of hackers mercilessly attacked, outwitted and outmaneuvered everyone in PACOM.

Preface

Trouble in Paradise

It was December 2004 and I was a U.S. Army officer assigned to the Joint Task Force – Computer Network Operations in Washington, D.C. Our team was a small, tight group responsible for protecting the vast Department of Defense computer networks and directing the attack of foreign nation's computer systems. In our defensive role we monitored the military networks and met with vendors and the rest of government. We knew all the latest cyber threats, and we reacted to every new virus and hacker attack.

My leadership wanted to know how well PACOM could defend their networks against their potentially hostile neighbors in the Pacific Rim. One dreary Washington, D.C. day my boss called me into his office. "I want you to lead a team to Hawaii. Monitor everything related to U.S. Pacific Command's use of cyberspace during Terminal Fury." My commander went on, "Unbeknownst to the rest of the Terminal Fury players, the leaders of the U.S. Pacific Command have requested we send a group of government hackers to break into U.S. Pacific Command's real computer network and see how far the hackers can get inside their networks. I want you to see if PACOM's cyber defenders will detect the hackers and to evaluate how the defenders react."

We gathered a group of ████ cybersecurity experts to play the hackers. The ██████████████████████, is the ultra-secret Department of Defense intelligence organization that eavesdrops on other nation's communications and networks and develops technology to protect our communications and networks from foreign eavesdroppers. PACOM leaders had asked that the hackers act as motivated foreign cyber hackers. "Our mission is to probe and penetrate the PACOM military networks," the lead hacker told me. "PACOM leaders have tied our hands. They told us we have to play 'fair' and only use common hacker tools available to anyone on the Internet and none of our 'special toys,'" referring to extraordinary and highly secret cyber tools developed to break into foreign nation's networks.

My group was giddy with anticipation as we left the cold and gloomy Washington, D.C. for the beautiful island of Oahu. Oahu is magnificent in December, especially after living in Washington, D.C. and spending 12 hours a day in a windowless secure military facility. Once we landed I sent my cyber warriors to military bases around Oahu. "Let me know how the organizations defend their networks from hackers," I told them. Then I met with the hackers.

"Our goal is to gain access to a new Navy command and control application used to track and manage all the Department of Defense warfighters worldwide," said the hackers' leader—a tall guy in his thirties, wearing jeans and a polo shirt. "We discovered this computer program has a *bug,*" an error in the computer code, "allowing anyone to take over the system if they can obtain access to a machine running the program."

"Department of Defense engineers know about the bug?" I asked.

"Oh yes, but U.S. Pacific Command's leaders are confident the system is safe behind layers of Department of Defense cyber defenses."

The hackers proved them wrong.

Reconnaissance Pays Off

Like all hackers, they cheated. "We don't break the rules," the leader said. "We just don't play fair." People expect others to behave like they do — to think and act within the bounds of "normal, acceptable behavior."

Good hackers don't think like the average person. Another hacker had told me "When you're driving down the street, you may see double yellow lines in the middle of the road. Instead of thinking you're prohibited from passing, hackers just see paint on the road; they can pass if it's in their best interest." Hackers use the same philosophy when they try to push computers to their limits and beyond, like the mechanic who tweaks a car for an extra mile per gallon.

The leader explained, "We use the common hacker process. We've been searching PACOM's public websites and compiling a dossier of personal information on PACOM employees, including the military projects they are working on. Using this information, we searched their personal website and social network sites. This research allowed us to discover their friends and their interests." He smiled.

"Next we examined the network traffic leaving the Hawaiian Island military networks. By examining the network traffic we could determine the unmaintained PACOM computers."

Computers come with open doors in them, called vulnerabilities. At first no one knows about these open doors, but hackers work until they find them. Once found, hackers can use them to get into a computer and establish a foothold on a network. From one little foothold, hackers can then move to other computers and steal information off all the computers or damage the computers.

Another hacker continued the explanation. "Commercial vendors sometime publish patches or updates to close the doors. Hackers take these vendor patches apart and figure out exactly what they changed. Then they tell the entire hacker community that the door exists. If the system administrators don't maintain their systems by quickly applying these patches to their computers, their doors are left open and vulnerable to hackers."

He was referring to a technique hackers use to examine the communications leaving computer networks to determine the version of operating systems and applications used on computers on the network. By researching the version information hackers can determine weaknesses in the systems running on the network.

The leader finished the explanation, "By understanding which versions of software is vulnerable we can look at the network traffic, determine the version of software running on PACOM machines, and know which are not patched and have their doors wide open; these are the targets we attack."

On the first day of the 10-day exercise, the hackers and I- armed with the information the team of hackers had discovered- gathered in a corner of the vast exercise control center on Camp H.M. Smith. The hackers' weapons were basic commercial-grade desktop Dells, similar to what sits on your desk at home, and a phone to speak to the █████████████████████.

And the game began. On the first day the hackers sent *phishing* emails to Pacific Command employees. In a phishing attack a hacker sends emails to victims containing subjects that the hackers created to entice the recipient, making the emails appear to come from friends or coworkers. Email is one of the least secure methods of communications and often hackers can make email appear to come from anyone. The hackers had gleaned the subject of the emails and the fraudulent source of the emails through their previous research of the recipient's interests and friends.

The ████ targeted these employees, not because of what they do or who they know, but because they work on one of the previously identified unpatched and vulnerable computers. Besides innocent messages, the emails contained viruses that would infect their machine and make them vulnerable to further attack, bypassing the layers of security tools installed on the Department of Defense systems.

On the second day, the hackers searched all the computers they had compromised for words like 'password' and 'account.' One team member exclaimed, "I found the jackpot, a treasure chest of government and personal account names and passwords stored in a spreadsheet. Let's see what we find." The hackers enjoyed using the account names and passwords to read senior military leaders' emails and download sensitive government presentations and personal documents.

By the third day of the exercise the hackers were deep inside PACOM's network and 'owned' many individual computers, meaning we had access to their computers and could do whatever we pleased to their computers. The hackers and I were reading the commander's email. We were reading senior officers' travel itineraries. And we knew the location and mission of all PACOM's military forces. The computer network was like a soft-boiled egg, and once the hackers had penetrated the network's soft outer shell using common hacker tools and techniques they were inside where there wasn't any security. They had bypassed the security the taxpayers had paid billions to create and maintain. Even more frightening, we were invisible.

"Okay, this is fun. Remember, we're on the good guy's team," I reminded everyone. "It's time to let them know we're in their systems and see how they react." The hackers begrudgingly agreed. But how should we alert the defenders we were inside? The possibilities were endless.

On the command and control system we had compromised we noticed a U.S. Navy carrier strike group, complete with an aircraft carrier and its supporting destroyers, submarines, and tenders, steaming toward an adversary's shores. White blips on a blue map. "Well," we thought, "we can't let that happen." With a few presses on the keyboard our hackers caused bright red foreign submarines to appear magically in front of the fleet in every command center across the Pacific Theater.

If someone had discovered foreign submarines in front of our fleet they would have sent an incident report up the chain of command. We believed this lack of confirmation would alert PACOM personnel that something was amiss. "Surely the Pacific Command leadership must know something's wrong?" I pondered. "The cyber defenders will realize their network is compromised and kick us out of the network." I called the rest of my team and told them, "Stay alert to observe the reaction to our recent network activities."

Instead, we watched in growing amazement as the white blips of the U.S. naval vessels slowly turned to the right. *Blip, blip, blip.* It was a slow, graceful arc across our computer screen, away from our ghost submarines.

We burst into laughter. We gave each other high fives. Our hackers had penetrated computers, gotten into the network, jumped to other machines, created phantom submarines, and now turned a U.S. Navy carrier strike group.

Then it hit me. We had just turned a carrier strike group.

"This will hit the fan," I exclaimed. Here I was, a U.S. Army officer with a bunch of hackers. Typing on a keyboard had manipulated the Navy into changing the direction of a U.S. Navy carrier strike group. Military leaders don't like to be manipulated, especially not the Navy by a lowly Army Major.

It hit the fan.

That evening we conducted our daily report with the Terminal Fury exercise staff in what the military calls an "after action report." We explained passwords we had discovered, the systems we had penetrated, sensitive mail we had read, presentations we had taken, and information we had changed. Then we explained that we had compromised the Navy command and control system and injected false "bandit" submarines, and how PACOM had not detected our mischief. The surprise was palpable – no one had realized a couple hackers could get this far and could influence military operations.

The next day U.S. Pacific Command ordered us to report to Admiral Thomas Fargo, the 4-star Navy Admiral and supreme commander of all U.S. military forces in the Pacific theater. He was not happy. He sat stiffly at the table.

"What happened?" he asked.

We explained how we planned and executed our activities.

"I get it," he responded. "You control *my* network and *my* systems. Now stop whatever it is you're doing before you bring the entire exercise to its knees."

That was it – the hackers had defeated PACOM.

Our team had made so many changes to the information in the Pacific Command's systems that any more changes would threaten the rest of the exercise. Once U.S. Pacific Command had discovered hackers in their system, the military leadership had panicked. "What else do the hackers know about? What else had they changed?" With a few keystrokes, hackers had caused the senior military leaders to lose confidence in the military information systems that control the mighty U.S. juggernaut and they didn't know what to do. We discovered that when hackers compromise a command and control network and inform those using the network that they were compromised, they force military leaders into inaction. The command didn't have a plan to respond to a catastrophic cyber event and they would not improvise one.

Back to the Beltway

"Our work here is done," I told the hackers. We all shook hands, packed, and left Hawaii. While sitting on the plane and thinking about the concrete and traffic of Washington, D.C., I thought, "The Pentagon will surely investigate this situation. They will realize that if our team of hackers can break in and change the course of a Navy strike group in three days, using only common hacker tools, then any motivated hackers could." Surprisingly, the whole situation stayed quiet for a while.

The PACOM staff was outraged that the exercise had exposed significant vulnerabilities in the Department of Defense network and the command and control systems. But before Terminal Fury, the ▮▮▮▮▮▮▮▮ had agreed with PACOM to not to tell anyone about any shortcomings they discovered. Government organizations won't permit the ▮▮ to assess their security if the ▮▮ will blab to the rest of the government how insecure they are and embarrass the leaders. That's how generals get fired.

However, rumors soon ran throughout the Pentagon that a group of hackers had compromised PACOM systems during Terminal Fury. PACOM leaders decided this was too serious to keep quiet, reversed their prior position, and reported the incident to the Pentagon.

Lieutenant General Robert Shea, a Marine in the Joint Chiefs of Staff responsible for coordinating warfighter communications across the Department of Defense, called me to a meeting.

"How did this happen?" he wanted to know.

"Sir, our ▮▮ hackers used commercial computers and common hacker tools to break into U.S. Pacific Command's sensitive networks and systems, steal information, and control their command and control system," I answered. Then I told him the rest of the story.

"What are we going to do about it?" he boomed. He wasn't angry with me, but at the realization there was little real security in 'his' networks.

"Sir, our networks have marginal security. Our system administrators can't maintain the systems they have. The system administrators responsible for maintaining our networks are overwhelmed, don't have the tools to do the job," I explained, "Sir, our warfighters are provided with multimillion-dollar communications and command and control systems that an average hacker can break. Except for the ▮▮▮, our military members are forbidden to use hacker tools to evaluate our networks, while anyone else can download the tools freely from the Internet and use them against us. Although the ▮▮▮▮▮▮▮▮▮▮▮ certifies our systems 'secure' they prohibit anyone from discussing when hackers penetrate these same systems. Our policies of keeping our failures secret prevents senior leadership from understanding the hacker threat, resulting in more uninformed decisions that expose more vulnerable systems and data to hackers. Those on the front line see this activity every day and have their hands tied by the bureaucracy. The 'system' is broken."

He stared at me. It was clear he had never heard about this. He dismissed me from his office. Soon he called a meeting at the Pentagon with senior government leaders to discuss our little jaunt through U.S. Pacific Command.

I was sitting behind a general officer from the Defense Information Systems Agency (DISA), the agency responsible for managing military networks and systems. She was actively hostile to the hackers and me at the meeting. She assured General Shea and the other esteem members of the Pentagon staff "There was no compromise of classified networks. This was just a bunch of ████ hackers. The hackers had taken no sensitive information. No one from outside the Department of Defense had ever compromised these networks. Clearly, the ████ must have used secret information or special tools. The networks are secure. Case closed."

I was aghast. "I can assure you we acted as common hackers. We can't tell if anyone has already compromised our networks because, as the hackers showed, we aren't monitoring the networks." I retorted. "We aren't doing basic security practices like patching machines, installing antivirus software and running intrusion detection systems to monitor our networks. The tools [that are purchased by DISA] are vulnerable to amateur hackers. We are hiding behind a myth of security."

There was stunned silence. The DISA general swung around to stare at me.

"Thank you," she said icily. It was military officer speak for "shut the hell up."

A few days later she called me into her office. She stared at me for a minute. "Do not speak at future briefings at the Pentagon," she said. The meeting was over. Others were allegedly brought in to fix the insecure networks. I moved on, but something kept gnawing at me, always in the back of my mind…

A few years later I would get a sense of déjà vu. By this time hackers had escalated assaults on government and contractor networks and unbeknownst to the public these networks were hemorrhaging government and personal information daily. In the midst of these daily attacks, two disgruntled insiders demonstrated to the world the lack of security on the government's most sensitive networks by their wholesale harvesting and publishing of our most sensitive government secrets. Little had changed.

Acknowledgements

I would like to express my gratitude to the many people who saw me through this book; to all who provided support, talked things over, read, wrote, offered comments, and assisted in the editing and proofreading.

I will always be indebted to the many people who have helped me understand cyberspace and cyberconflict. I would not have finished this book without the hours of discussions with my good friends and cyber visionaries over the years, most notably Larry Blankenship, Thomas Sammel, Bink Skinner, Chris Hartley, and Richard Guidorizzi. I credit the good ideas to them, and the bad to myself.

To Frank Heidt, the amazing man with an even more amazing ponytail (who opened my eyes), Mudge (who taught me how to think), Michael Zyda (for being a great life coach and friend), Cynthia Irvine (for teaching me to be a scientist), and to Al Tierney (for providing a contrarian view).

I also have to thank the many mentors throughout my career who dragged me kicking and screaming to where I am today. In particular Tony Tether (for giving me a chance), Bob Minehart (who was responsible for me staying in the Army), Gerald Wilkes (who wouldn't let me leave his office until I made a huge decision that he knew before I made it), Jeff Brown, (for teaching me to think like an airman), and Gary McAlum (for being a great boss and friend, and being there when I needed him).

Last and not least: I beg forgiveness of all those who have been with me over the course of the years and whose names I have failed to mention.

Introduction

Nam et ipsa scientia potestas est.
"Knowledge itself is power."

- Sir Francis Bacon (1561-1626)

The dramatic rise of cyberspace has presented unparalleled opportunities to improve our way of life. The dark side of this proliferation is an even more dramatic rise in the malevolent use of cyberspace.

The instruments of this maleficence are accessible and inexpensive. A hacker needs a few thousand dollars of hardware to launch a major attack. The skills can be learned at any university or online. Attack tools are freely available online. At no time in the history of mankind have surveillance and destruction techniques become so prolific and available to the public.

At the same time, senior leaders are hampered by noise and double-talk regarding this malevolent use of cyberspace. The media report daily of attacks against public and private computer systems. Individuals, businesses, criminals, and transnational terrorists are launching cyber operations that span a frighteningly undefined continuum. Governments demonize hackers while simultaneously operating their own armies of hackers under the guise of national security.

Decision makers don't understand operating in cyberspace. This lack of understanding forces leaders to speak in colorful yet vague figures of speech. It degrades the policy and legal discussions. It prevents the efficient prioritization of limited resources. And it results is poor decisions on government organization and responsibilities, and the means to deal with issues.

Security vendors sell technology to protect private and public networks that repeatedly fails under the onslaught of creative hackers. Military organizations and defense contractors promote network-enabled technology to defeat adversaries at the speed of light, while hackers compromise their networks. National leaders recognize they need to fix the problem and have passed responsibility, and billions of dollars of annual funding, to the Intelligence Community whose primary mission is not to secure information systems but to compromise them. Previous government employees who could have prevented us from getting into the position we find ourselves are now obtaining lucrative consulting and speaking engagements. These inconsistencies appear to make no sense until you understand what is really occurring.

Introduction

The challenges are many and complex. It involves the way cyber technology processes information and communicates. It involves vulnerabilities in systems and the ability of hackers thousands of miles away to exploit those weaknesses for their own need. It involves senior decision-makers having to decide between telling the community about vulnerabilities in their systems and our government's desire to use the vulnerabilities to enter our adversary's networks. It involves massive bureaucracies that want to protect their rice bowls and a huge, powerful cyber industrial complex that wants to continue a very lucrative business. And, ultimately, it involves our willingness to accept the mythology we've been told and our eagerness to trust and expose vital information to individuals and groups that want to harm us.

I focused this book on the U.S. military's experience in cyberspace. This is because the U.S. military played a big part in creating many of the foundations of cyberspace, was one of the first victims to serious hacker activities, and plays a leading part in our national cyber strategies. However the lessons apply to anyone operating in cyberspace.

Chapter 1 provides a brief introduction on the vision that led to the explosion of information technology within the U.S. military. Chapter 2 discusses the playing field where cyber conflict exists. This chapter introduces concepts regarding networks, computing, and information. Chapter 3 explains the government's transition into cyberspace and the unanticipated consequences.

While cyberconflict may appear a technical problem, it is conflict between people. The people at the heart of this never-ending battle are the *hackers* who operate, defend, and attack telecommunications and computing systems. Chapter 4 introduces the guardian hackers that defend information systems. Chapter 5 introduces the malicious hackers that exploit systems for their own gain.

The next nine chapters arm the reader with insights into key cyber concepts. Chapter 6 introduces the challenges in tracking and identifying individuals responsible for malicious acts in cyberspace. The technology we use to make life easier also enables hackers to hide in cyberspace, and a good hacker will never be identified. Chapter 7 introduces the use of cyberspace for intelligence collection, spying, and criminal enterprises. Chapter 8 discusses how government agencies compete for their piece of cyberspace, how these equities create conflict within the halls of Washington DC, and make us all less secure. Chapter 9 discusses the threat from insiders. Chapter 10 provides an in-depth discussion of destructive and degrading cyber actions.

Chapter 11 provides a number of alternative strategies nations can use when operating in cyberspace. Chapter 12 discusses how our effort to decrease costs and increase convenience in our nation's critical infrastructures now threatens to disable our nation's very foundations. Chapter 13 discusses how terrorists use cyberspace. Chapter 14 discusses the U.S. secrecy program, and how our efforts to keep secrets may make us less secure. Chapter 15 provides a wrap-up on where we are heading, if we can achieve *information superiority*, and what we should do next. I deliberately left out many potential solutions. You understand your needs and at this point I've armed you with the tools you need to develop your future solutions.

As a retired military officer and government leader who taught at the U.S. Army War College, led offensive and defensive strategic cyber operations, and led national cyber research and development programs, the Government required I submit this manuscript for Government prepublication review. It took a Congressional inquiry and 185 days, but eventually the Government approved this manuscript. The blackened-out words and paragraphs are the government censorship due to their perceived sensitivities.

This should be an eye-opening trip. I hope regardless of your background I will challenge you to step out of your comfort zone and rethink conflict in cyberspace. It is my wish that this book will enable the community to begin thinking and talking about cyber conflict in an informed manner and facilitate a more open and honest discussion of the field.

Introduction

Chapter 1. The Vision

"Before a war military science seems like real science, like astronomy; but after a war it seems more like astrology."
- Rebecca West (1892-1988)
Europe in Arms

"The coming of the wireless era will make war impossible, ... because it will make war ridiculous."
- Guglielmo Marconi (1874-1937)
Nobel Prize winner and inventor of the radio
Technical World Magazine, October 1912

Hyperwar

While the Vietnam War is often described as a "low intensity conflict" in rain forests, mountains and swampland, it was more devastating than any previous military conflict. During this conflict the United States dropped more aerial bombs than in Europe during World War II, including jelled gas napalm bombs that burned at 2,000 degrees Fahrenheit and defoliants that destroyed concealment and food crops. The U.S. also incorporated heavy use of helicopters for the first time to move troops, supplies, weapons, and the wounded. While people often attribute the North Vietnamese and Viet Cong with fighting irregular guerrilla warfare using modern infantry weapons, the Chinese and Soviet Union supplied fighter interceptors, anti-aircraft artillery and surface-to-air missiles that cost the U.S. nearly 10,000 aircraft and helicopters. The U.S. experimented with guided weapons to increase their aircraft and crew survivability and probability of destroying targets. These *smart* weapons had little real impact in Vietnam, but their potential seemed obvious.

The Soviet Union used the two decades the U.S. was focused on jungles to advance their tactical weapons and forces. By the 1970s the U.S. lagged behind the Russians in both sophistication and scale of conventional military forces, with Warsaw Pact armored forces over twice that of NATO. If the Cold War ever became hot, the Soviets could use their numerical advantage to sweep rapidly across Europe. Pentagon strategists believed nuclear weapons were the only means to defeat a Soviet invasion of Western Europe. However, stopping an invading force by destroying any allies' cities with nuclear weapons didn't seem like a good idea. Pentagon planners also assumed this first-use of nuclear weapons would most likely result in a massive Soviet retaliation and escalation, conceivably devolving into a global nuclear war. The U.S. had to find a better way.

On October 6, 1973, an Arab coalition led by Egyptian and Syrian forces surprised Israel in what would be called the Yom Kippur or Arab-Israeli War. Massive Egyptian forces crossed the Suez Canal and invaded the Israeli-occupied Sinai Peninsula and Golan Heights. The invasion took place on Yom Kippur, the holiest days in Judaism, which in 1973 occurred in the same Muslim holy month of Ramadan. An attack on both holy days caught the Israeli leadership by surprise.

The Arab forces primarily used Soviet equipment while the Israelis used Western equipment. The war was short, bloody, and eye opening. Perhaps the most significant technical surprise was the Russian 9K11 Malyutka anti-tank guided missile — what the U.S. would call the AT-3 Sagger. The Sagger was a small missile that a soldier could fire and guide into a moving target using a small control box connected to the missile by a wire. This revolutionary new technology allowed an Arab infantryman to attack and destroy or immobilize expensive and limited Israeli tanks and armored vehicles. The Russians credited Saggers with destroying over 800 Israeli tanks and armored vehicles during the three-week war. It would become the most widely produced anti-tank guided missile of all time with 25,000 missiles shipped per year during 1960-1970s.

The Arabs also used night vision devices that amplified the ambient light on the battlefield. These devices allowed the Arab tanks to see much farther during the night than the Israeli tanks and to fire earlier and more accurately. Arab spotters could also see Israeli forces sooner and at farther distances, allowing them to direct their artillery fire onto the Israeli forces before the Israelis could see the Arabs.

The Israelis' stopped the Arab coalition and forced them to the negotiations table through the use of superior military leadership, military weapon proficiency, and ability to maneuver on the battlefield.

After the war U.S. military advisors swarmed across the battlefield, examining the new technology and its devastating effects. They realized that technology would generate much more destruction in the first battle of the next war than in previous wars and this new lethality would decide the result of the war almost immediately. Visionaries within the Pentagon began to believe that the lethality of anti-tank guided missiles and other conventional weapons might make a war in Europe winnable. However, the U.S. would need to transition from fighting on a battlefield "frontline" to fighting two simultaneous battles— a traditional close battle of forward fighting forces and a deep battle in the enemy rear area where their supplies and reserve forces reside.

From this vision the Pentagon developed requirements for advanced military technology. These requirements included the ability for U.S. forces to target Soviet military support services, suppression and counter fire capabilities, air defense forces, and reconstitution capabilities. Military planners knew this vision required U.S. military forces to see deep into the Soviet's rear area and to attack their second echelon forces. U.S. forces also needed new command and control systems to synchronize and win a decentralized battle. The U.S. needed new ways to experiment and train with new tactics and to revolutionize leadership to enable decentralized execution in a highly mobile battlefield, as well as advanced training facilities to cultivate this new philosophy.

Visionaries soon saw the potential for battlefield capabilities that could revolutionize warfighting, not just amplify its destructive power. This fusion of warfare and technology would result in vastly more intense and destructive battlefield – a hyperwar. And the hyperwar was built on information technology.

The Vision

Chapter 2. The Perpetual Struggle

"Change does not roll in on the wheels of inevitability,
but comes through continuous struggle."
- Dr. Martin Luther King, Jr. (1929-1968)

"To err is human,
to blame it on a computer, even more so."
- Robert Orben (1927)

The Power of Information

Life is a struggle.

Since the dawn of time, life has been a struggle for limited resources and competing ideologies. Since the beginning of humanity's struggle, communication and information technologies have enabled individuals and groups to collaborate, understand one another, and build a community. Some of the most significant technological revolutions were improved means to copy, store, process, and transport information. The Bi Sheng Chinese printer developed between 1040 and 1050 and the Gutenberg press developed in 1450 created societal revolutions by enabling people to share information and ideas between leaders, scientists, and the common people. Information enabled them to make better decisions and increase their ability to accomplish their goals in the struggle.

Today information technologies allow people to acquire, store, share and manipulate more information and thus make decisions that are more informed. Computers may also manipulate mechanical devices from home security systems to dam control gates, increasing a user's ability to perform mechanical tasks from miles away with a few clicks on a keyboard. Cruise controls and automatic pilots led to autonomous drones and robots controlled by computers that operate in hostile environments on our behalf.

All of this technology has the potential to generate and amplify power by enabling people to make informed, rapid decisions and to perform mechanical activities remotely. We are in a period of human history when information and information technology defines the way we live our lives and our lifestyles. Information technology has changed how we communicate, how we buy and sell, socialize, are entertained, commit crimes, and fall in love. Information has become the currency of this *information age*.

The Digital Super Highway

In the 1960s, a telephone call required a temporary but dedicated connection between two phones, called a *circuit*. The telephone systems technology was called *circuit switching*.

At the same time, most computing was done on large computers. Computer *users* worked from dumb terminals that were little more than a printer or screen and a keyboard. Often a user would connect a dumb terminal that spoke the same computing language as a large computer over the commercial circuit-switching telephone system. A user may have had several dumb terminals in their office, each needing a dedicated phone line to each individual large computer that performed work. Since most large computers could not communicate directly with other large computers, copying information between the computers was a manual process using tapes, cards, or retyping the information. At the same time, telephone connections were unreliable. When a circuit broke between two computers the computing would stop, and the user would have to redial the large computer, reestablish the connection, and restart the computing from the beginning.

Throughout the late 1960s and 1970s the U.S. Department of Defense research and development agency- called the Defense Advanced Research Project Agency, or DARPA[1]- had an idea for a revolutionary new way to communicate.[2] The plan was both brilliant in vision and simplicity. DARPA envisioned communications without semi-permanent connections between two points. Rather, everyone would connect to a network of numerous permanently interconnected devices. A computer would divide a message into numerous smaller messages called *packets*. The computer would transmit each packet into a network and the network would forward the individual packets through special computers called 'routers.' The routers would 'route' packets toward their destination using the best path that existed at that moment in time. When all the packets arrived at their destination the receiver would reassemble the original message by ordering the packets into their original order.

The scientists created standard communication instructions called *protocols* that act like a common language to allow any computer to send, receive, and reassemble packets from any other computer. The scientists then wrote software that used the protocols to run on routers and computers. Now any computers on the network could share information with any other computer on the network regardless of the two computers' make, model, or vintage, provided they used the agreed upon protocols.

The protocols didn't care about message content; they forwarded any message to its destination. Scientists envisioned that developers would build applications that would send their packets to the network, and the network would take care of getting the packets to their destination. The network became a postal service that accepts and delivers postcards regardless of the message's content. If a message is too large to fit on a single postcard, the message is divided into separate postcards and sent to their destination, where they are reassembled. Websites, email, and videos are all handled in this manner across the same network.

Telephone links were unreliable during the network's infancy, and the scientists didn't want someone to decide how to reroute traffic around communication outages.[3] The scientists designed this new network without centralized management of the network. When a connection between routers broke the existing routers would automatically reroute packets around congestion and outages using the best route that existed, resulting in a very resilient system.

Scientist called this technology *packet switching* and this network ARPANet, short for Advanced Research Projects Agency Network.[4] Later, the Department of Defense turned ARPANet over to the National Science Foundation as NSFNet. By this time organizations were connecting their internal networks (*intranets*) to this bigger network to share information. The NSFNet soon became the *Internet*.

The engineering decisions made by the early scientists helped to create a very robust and adaptive network and led to the explosive growth of the Internet. When devices and networks are added or removed from the Internet, the Internet reorganizes itself and continues to operate. The common protocols allow developers to build complex applications that can communicate with any other computer on the Internet. This led to a tremendous growth in new applications that could communicate with other applications. The result was inexpensive, worldwide information sharing, communications, and collaboration with relatively little corporate or government control of the technology.[5]

Cyberspace

Science fiction writers, scientists, journalists, military leaders and politicians often talk about *cyberspace*. Some see it as a magical place where we can nearly instantaneously find any scrap of information with a few keystrokes or mouse clicks. Others see it as a dark place where anti-social individuals get lost in impersonal communications and digital interactions. Some see it as a new battlefield without rules that enables them to pursue personal, religious, and political goals. Cyberspace means something different to everyone.

William Gibson coined the term *cyberspace* in his 1982 short story *Burning Chrome* and later popularized it in his 1984 novel *Neuromancer*.[6] Gibson described cyberspace as "A consensual hallucination experienced daily by billions of legitimate operators, in every nation, by children being taught mathematical concepts... A graphic representation of data abstracted from banks of every computer in the human system." While this description is very colorful, Gibson denounced the term cyberspace as an "evocative and essentially meaningless" buzzword that could serve as a codeword for all of his "cybernetic musings".[7]

The Perpetual Struggle

So what is cyberspace? Cyberspace is built on complex, yet inanimate, physical boxes that need instructions to perform tasks and data that represent facts and relationships in cyberspace.

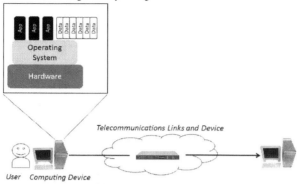

Figure 1 - A Computer's Components

These devices communicate with others using the second component of the system- the telecommunication devices and links that connect devices. These links including fiber optic lines, phone lines, and radio waves traveling through the air that connect our smart phones, microwaves towers, and satellites.

A device has *hardware* and *software* instructions that tell the hardware how to solve problems and perform useful tasks. The *operating system* tells your computer how to perform its basic operations, and *applications* do your work like email, word processing, and browsing the Internet. All of this software and the data it manipulates are represented as strings of ones and zeros, called binary digits, or *bits*.

The third and most important components of cyberspace are the people that use cyberspace to create, process, and store information, improve the efficiency of a workforce, provide for the safety and security of a population, improve the common good of society, generate revenue from goods or services, and entertainment. And they use cyberspace for their own malicious purposes.

So cyberspace is the set of computers and people interconnected by communications systems. The aim of cyberspace is to connect people and computers to enable them to achieve their goals. These physical components exist in sovereign nations, aboard ocean-going vessels in international waters, aircraft, and satellites in outer space. Every computer instruction and piece of data are stored, processed, and transported at any instant in time on a physical device or is being transported through a telecommunications medium. Cyberspace is not magic.

The Great Contraction

Cyberspace evolved from a research project used by government and academic scholars to a worldwide information environment that may be the greatest contribution to mankind of all time. Today, cyberspace connects the world's people, changing how we exchange information, music and movies, create and distribute art, conduct financial transactions, and control power grids and other national infrastructures. Healthcare, education, global finances and commerce, industries, energy, transportation, and public services have all seen revolutionary improvements as they were touched by computing and global telecommunications. Government and corporate leaders have transitioned processes into cyberspace to obtain tremendous productivity and profitability gains. The securities and banking industries use the Internet to transfer trillions of dollars around the world every day, enabling near instantaneous global commerce. The world appears to have contracted as its population is connected through cyberspace.

Cyberspace is more than a source of economic growth — it is an enabler of social change. Education and training over the Internet "has begun to remedy a longstanding and life threatening shortage of qualified health workers in sub-Sahara Africa."[8] Physicians use the Internet to transfer patients' X-rays, computerized tomography (CT), and magnetic resonance imaging (MRI) scans to physicians overseas, who assess the medical condition and provide results the next morning. Regions with access to the Internet receive information, collaborate with others, receive encouragement in tough times, and have an outlet for their ideas, wishes, and dreams.

Cyberspace, synonymous for information technologies, is bigger than the Internet. Today, 'smart' phones send and receive text messages, email, photos, and videos, and are part of cyberspace. It appears every washing machine, refrigerator, automobile, and person will someday be digitally "jacked-in" to cyberspace.

Connecting militaries, governments, businesses, civilian populations, national critical infrastructures,[9] and financial institutions on the same network enables these sectors to efficiently and effectively share logistics, personnel, financial, and personal information. But it comes at a price.

Man made the system, and man makes mistakes.

The Imperfect Network

The decisions of the early ARPANet scientists have some significant security implications we are still dealing with today. Let's look at how messages are sent on the Internet. The original plan was for each device on the Internet to have a unique address called Internet Protocol address, or *IP address*, normally represented as four numbers between 0 and 255 separated by a period. For example, 23.198.108.110 was an IP address for the White House at the time of this writing.

Every message contains a source IP address, destination IP address, and message body.[10] Internet technology doesn't care about a message's addresses or its contents; routers simply forward any messages to any destination IP address. The Internet protocols require the destination to decide if it accepts the message and what it does with the message.[11]

Hackers learned very early that they could put any source address in a message and the Internet infrastructure would still deliver the message. From that insight it didn't take long for them to realize they could send a million messages to a destination using a bogus source address and overwhelm the receiving machine with junk messages without the victim able to identify who was responsible for the junk traffic.

Security wasn't a serious problem when the Internet was in its infancy. The original ARPANet researchers knew each other and trusted everyone on the network. However, security became a major concern as the Internet grew from a research project of trusted peers to a worldwide network of nearly three billion individuals.[12]

Today, the Internet connects nearly every country. It permits near instantaneous communications from homes, schools, cyber cafes, businesses, and governments. It connects people with alternative and conflicting ethics and agendas. Since the Internet doesn't enforce security, we rely on other devices to perform this task.

The Imperfect Machine

The vast majority of the computing systems purchased today are commercial, general-purpose systems. Consumers demand new computers have more capabilities, are easy to use, and allow customers to use the latest hardware, games, and online applications. The vendors that create these systems are motivated by profit- to deliver products that meet or create consumer demand by building computers and the software that operates these computers as rapidly as possible to gain and maintain market share.

Vendors have learned that consumers don't want to re-purchase software so they demand that their systems are *backwards compatible*. This refers to the ability of new computers to operate legacy software and access legacy data files. The result is equivalent to taking old applications and bolting on new functions so legacy programs or data will continue to operate and be accessible.

Consumers also want to change their computers by adding new programs, updating software, and adding new equipment. Software developers have built this *extensibility* into modern operating systems and applications to allow vendors to 'push' the latest 'update' to computers over the Internet to add new functions or correct errors discovered in software.

For example, when a user installs a new printer the computer may not contain instructions that understand how the new device operates. A modern computer will install *driver* software and other applications that extend its abilities and operate the device.

Likewise, the World-Wide Web has turned into a vast multi-media library. When a user wants to access new multi-media, their Internet browser may automatically search for, find, and install new *plug-in* software to enable the browser to deal with the new media.

The result of this demand for convenience and capability is that the software running on typical home or office computers is immense, complicated, and always changing. This complexity and scale hinders an engineer's ability to understand the interrelationships and overall system. The consequence is that engineers create mistakes, called *bugs*.[13]

The computer industry averages one to twenty-five bugs per 1,000 lines of computer code in delivered software.[14] A modern operating system may contain 45 to 100 million lines of computer code, which may result in the operating systems having 45,000 to 250,000 unknown bugs.[15]

However, a computer contains much more than the operating system. Users install, configure, and change numerous drivers, plug-ins, and application software. All of this software may constantly update and change itself with no user interaction. So, if a single complex system can have an unknown number of bugs, then today's computers contain a large, unknown, and changing collection of bugs.

Many bugs are not important or cause minor annoyances. However, some bugs may allow malfeasants to read private information, disable the computer, or install and operate their own applications without an owner's permission or knowledge. The bugs that allow another person to use a computer for their own advantage are *vulnerabilities*.[16]

Additional vulnerabilities exist because of poor management or ignorance by the people who manage and configure business and home systems. When you install a new wireless router or a fancy new television to your home network, these devices come with passwords preinstalled in them. Manufacturers install these *default passwords* to simplify installation and troubleshooting problems. If a consumer has a problem with a device, they can refer to a manual that contains standard procedures to help troubleshoot the problem and often lists the device's default password. Malicious individuals search through installation manuals and compile lists of these default passwords. If they encounter a wireless router or television on a network, they will try the default passwords from their list, which will often work because the owner hasn't change them when they installed the device. The default password may allow the outsider access into the device and perhaps the entire network.

A third vulnerability exists when malicious individuals use tools and technology as designed and constructed but for malicious purposes. For example, a hacker could send numerous emails or other messages to a system to overwhelm the recipient's systems. A disgruntled employee could use their legitimate access to a corporate system to copy or erase corporate information. In these cases the malicious individual uses the essential functions of the system against the victim, and it may not be possible to eliminate these functions from a system.[17]

Advanced and daring hackers may also place vulnerabilities, malware or counterfeit components into products during the design, manufacturing, handling, distribution, and installation stages of the manufacturing process. Vendors may create counterfeit systems to make money and harm legitimate developer's revenue. These counterfeit parts may not be designed and built with sufficient rigor and may fail.

These *supply chain attacks* are a serious threat to the U.S. government since the vast majority of U.S. government systems are created with commercial products. In 2008, the FBI seized $76 million in counterfeit Cisco routers that could have allowed the Chinese access to U.S. government networks. In 2010, the U.S. Missile Defense Agency discovered that the memory in a high-altitude missile's mission computer was counterfeit. The agency said if a missile had launched it probably would have failed. Replacing the counterfeit memory cost the government $2.7 million.[18].

In 2013, the retailer Target suffered one of the largest data breaches in the history of the retail industry that included the compromise of approximately 40 million customers credit and debit card information. Apparently hackers took network credentials from a heating and air conditioning company that provided services for Target. Using these credentials, hackers bypassed Target's network security to access the point of sale systems in over 1,800 stores.[19] Besides the compromise of customer data, the data breach caused the company's net earnings to fall 46% compared to the previous year.[20] Target spent approximately $61 million to respond to the breach.[21]

Many successful cyber incidents have not involved malicious code. While the 2013 Target incident resulted from a vulnerability and malware, other secondary hackers took advantage of the reporting to cause further mischief. These secondary hackers, who may not have had any relationship with the initial Target hack, sent millions of emails masquerading as popular banks. These emails told the recipient that hackers had compromised their credit card information as part of the Target incident. Many of the email recipients did not have an account with the bank or never shopped at Target and therefore ignored the email. Others who coincidentally had accounts with the bank and shopped at Target may have been deceived into believing the emails were legitimate. A duped recipient may have followed the emailed instructions and clicked on a link to reset their passwords. The link took the unwitting "mark" to a hacker's website that resembled the bank's website. The website would request the victim enter their banking credentials to change their passwords, which the hacker would record and use to enter the victim's real bank account and take their funds.

Decade-old corporate applications may also represent a serious threat to organizations. In 2015, President Obama spoke of the recent breach of the Office of Personnel Management systems and subsequent loss of sensitive government employee records and security clearances, noting "Part of the problem [is] that we've got very old systems."[22] Organizations often rely on legacy systems that are no longer maintained but still perform useful tasks such as an old personnel database in the human resource department, a warehouse inventory database, or an investment tracking application. Software developers will attach network capabilities to these legacy applications to enable them to be placed online. However, the original developers may not have designed the application to be exposed to a hostile network environment and the hackers operating there, and these applications may be beset with an unknown number of vulnerabilities that are cost prohibitive to identify and remove.

We refer to the vulnerabilities that allow adversaries to enter or manipulate a system as the *attack surface*.[23] If an adversary can access an attack surface, they act like secret doors that grant the hacker access into the computer. In other words, **hackers don't create ways into computers; hackers take advantage of the ones they find.**

To make matters worse, as we mentioned earlier, vendors built these computers to permit someone on the Internet to push new software onto a computer, often without the user's knowledge. This often means that once an adversary accesses an attack surface, they can send their own software or commands to the victim and make the victim's computer perform any tasks the hacker wishes.

Some experts see this as a technical problem and argue we don't accept these kinds of problems in highway bridges, televisions, or automobiles; and we shouldn't accept them with computers.[24] These critics overlook that an automobile is a machine specifically designed and built (mostly) for one task, where most computers are designed to accept and execute many tasks from strangers.

The amount of malicious activity we see today results from the number of bugs in systems. Some security practitioners state, "… all we need to do is use more secure practices when we develop information systems." While the people who develop our complex computer hardware and software are ultimately responsible for the bugs, they are prevented from eliminating many of the vulnerabilities by the complexity of the problem and drive for profitability.[25] **Functionality may always trump security**. Many secure software development practices, such as managed programming languages, may eliminate vulnerabilities but take many decisions out of the hands of developers and vendors. This may limit development creativity, sacrifice new functionality and technology possibly increasing development costs, and reduce the vendor's market share and profit.

Complicating the problem is that scientists have proven that it's not mathematically possible to build a program or computer that will find all the bugs in computer code.[26] As early as 1984, Ken Thompson also pointed out that no amount of software verification could ensure there wasn't malicious functionality in applications and operating systems.[27] Eliminating all of these bugs can only be performed in limited and expensive projects, that would probably eliminate functionality and extensibility.

Engineers have developed bug searching techniques such as *fuzzing* that help developers discover new instances of certain classes of bugs, however these techniques will not discover or eliminate all bugs.[28] Likewise, organizations can use teams of hackers to break into systems or networks to discover vulnerabilities. However, these techniques only tell if the hacker found vulnerabilities, they can't tell if a system is "secure" from all vulnerabilities. **When hackers fail to break into a system, it means they didn't discover vulnerabilities, not that vulnerabilities don't exist.**[29] And all hackers are not created equally. Hackers with better skills, access, or resources may find the undiscovered vulnerabilities.

Unintended Consequences

Governments and private industries have created vast information repositories connected over highly efficient telecommunications media; **cyberspace is comprised of information concentrators connected via information conductors**. Since information is the foundation of civilization, it's no surprise as cyberspace grew so did the demand for more powerful technology. Computing power doubles every two years, storage capacity doubles every thirteen months, and high-end home network speeds double every 21 months.[30] These rates of change contribute to preventing individuals and organizations from maintaining pace or even understanding what is operating on their behalf.

Since the early 1990s, the Internet has grown from a group of trusted scientists and engineers to nearly three billion people representing over forty percent of the world's population. As participants linked more people, information, and systems they received increased benefits. These benefits encouraged adding more people, information, and systems and greatly increasing the power of the resulting network.[31]

Yet connecting to a network means having a physical connection to everyone else on the network, and the concentrators and conductors that improve personal and organizational effectiveness also make tempting targets.

The rapid growth of cyberspace and increased benefits from being 'connected' has occurred in full view of individuals and groups who perceive that their own political, financial, or personal goals may be at-odds with other cyber residents. If information is power, then reliance on information provides an impetus for conflict, and residents have now chosen to use cyberspace as a place to challenge their perceived adversaries.

The early days of cyberspace tempted spies and curious hobbyists to access the military, academic, and personal information that existed there.[32] Once commerce and banking moved into cyberspace, bringing with them the need to access vast repositories of personal and corporate currency, bank robber Willie Sutton's words to "Go where the money is… and go there often" rang true. By 2013, the FBI Internet Crime Complaint Center (IC3) was receiving 262,813 consumer complaints related to cyber-crimes with an adjusted dollar loss of $781 million annually.[33]

Today the news media reports of criminals stealing personal, corporate, and government information for profit. Amateurs and hobbyists collect information, change information and systems, and deny and degrade systems in the pursuit of personal or organizational goals. Military organizations conduct destructive cyber-attacks and intelligence agencies secretly vacuum all forms of corporate, national, and personal information from cyberspace. Meanwhile, law enforcement agencies conduct domestic surveillance, counter intelligence agencies search for spies, and counter terrorism agencies search for terrorists and their supporters. Online stalkers prey on children, celebrities, and old friends. Terrorists conduct recruiting and share tactics, plans, and someday may conduct destructive attacks. At the same time, we are bombarded by stories of hactivists attacking systems to promote a social or political agenda.

The fundamental challenge we are facing today is that we have chosen to place vulnerable computers with sensitive information on a network connected to people motivated and capable of causing mischief. Today's networked information systems provide antagonists with the unprecedented potential to exploit those who rely on the technology. The increasing connectivity of a worldwide network-of-networks enables a greater number of diverse political, social, economic, and cultural individuals and groups that are capable, willing, and able to take part in nefarious activities.

Information technology has evolved the age-old struggles and created new means to conduct individual, criminal, and state-sponsored surveillance, manipulation, crime, and violence. Cyber conflict is human struggle and ambition projected onto cyberspace — the actions of belligerents in the digital medium where conflicting agendas have transformed information and information systems into the targets, weapons, and battlefield.

The Perpetual Struggle

Chapter 3. Groundhog Day

"We are fighting a war in the information domain,
and our adversaries are outmaneuvering us."

-Vice Admiral Michael A. Brown
U.S. Navy

The First Wake Up Call

By 1986, the U.S. military was deep into transitioning into a high technology fighting force. At the same time, Cliff Stoll was a hyperactive astronomer struggling to make ends meet. When his grant money ran out, he took a job managing computers at Lawrence Berkeley National Laboratory in Berkeley, CA. One day Stoll's boss asked him to look into a 75-cent accounting error in the laboratory's computer usage accounts. Stoll's searched through the computers and discovered hackers had penetrated the laboratory's systems and used them to jump to other systems. The hackers had failed to cover their tracks and created the 75-cent error. Stoll meticulously traced the break-ins to U.S. military facilities and defense contractors, where the hackers were looking for sensitive military information. Through some ingenious tracking and manipulation he helped officials identify and capture West German hackers responsible for the invasion into the sensitive systems.[1]

Stoll also discovered that agents from the Soviet Union's foreign intelligence service, known as the Committee for State Security- or more commonly the KGB, had hired private hackers to penetrate sensitive U.S. military networks. At the time, Stoll noted that the U.S. law enforcement, intelligence, and military community didn't appear to appreciate the interconnections and access to sensitive information and information systems, let alone procedures to respond to cyber activities.

Cliff Stoll announced the first wake-up call. Foreign hackers and intelligence services are very interested in the sensitive information the U.S. places on computers and connects to worldwide information systems. Apparently, the Pentagon leadership slept through Stoll's call, but others were wide-awake.

Desert Storm - Strong Muscles

In the summer of 1991, Saddam Hussein's forces stormed across the Iraqi border into Kuwait. The U.S. responded by creating the largest coalition of

17

military forces since World War II. Hussein refused to be intimidated. "Certainly the U.S. wouldn't invade Iraq over a little country like Kuwait," he must have thought to himself. The Iraqi military was battle-hardened, having fought Iran for eight years in one of the world's bloodiest wars of attrition that left over a million dead. At the time, Iraq was the third largest recipient of U.S. aid. However, on January 17, 1991, the combined forces of a U.S.-led coalition stormed into Kuwait and Iraq and pushed the Iraqi forces northwest toward Baghdad.

People around the world sat glued to their televisions as the vast U.S. information-age technology devastated Saddam's larger industrial age forces in an overwhelmingly one-sided outcome.

In the early morning of January 17, Apache helicopters swooped in below Saddam's radar systems and fired the opening shots. They destroyed air defense systems with laser guided Hellfire missiles. Tomahawk cruise missiles streaked in from ships in the Persian Gulf, their precision guidance systems navigating them down streets to strike government command and control systems and military facilities. Stealth aircraft flew in the skies over Iraq, invisible to Saddam's radar, and delivered precision-guided bombs down elevator shafts of government buildings. On the ground, U.S. Army Q-36 counter battery radar collaborated with Multiple-Launch Rocket Systems to detect the first shots fired by Iraqi artillery, and while the round was still in the air, backtracked the shot's flight to its source and devastate the Iraqi artillery with thousands of rocket-delivered grenades. All the while, Boeing 707 air-to-ground surveillance aircraft mapped every moving vehicle in Iraq. Simultaneously, unmanned aerial drones loitered above the battlefield; untiringly peering through smoke, clouds, and buildings; networked to intelligent control systems that identified and tracked multiple moving adversaries; and sending video images of Saddam's troops to General Norman Schwarzkopf, Jr.'s "head shed." Saddam's forces were entered into computers, identified, tracked, and prioritized for destruction. At the heart of these intelligent systems was the digital network that created a web of interconnected systems and an unprecedented potential for waging "efficient" warfare. After 100 hours of ground war the coalition forces left the fifth largest military force in the world a smoldering ruin.

And the U.S. military fell deeper in love with technology.

Futurist Alvin Toffler proclaimed the 1990 - 1991 Persian Gulf War a *Third Wave War* fought at the dawn of the information age. Toffler coined the phrase to describe the scientific and technological components of the war that for the first time relied heavily on computers and digital communications.[2]

Other military strategist heralded this new form of combat as *hyperwar*. Stealthy aircraft and precision-guided munitions connected via cyberspace could decapitate a national command and control structure and cause an enemy to collapse. All of this occurred because of the advances in technology and the information technology that connected them.

In the winter of 1991, the U.S. technical superiority was complete and overwhelming. Or was it?

Four months before Saddam's forces stormed across the Kuwait border, hackers operating out of the Netherlands secretly penetrated U.S. military networks.[3] For thirteen months these hackers used common security weaknesses advertised on hacker websites and digital bulletin boards to gain initial access into the military systems. Once the hackers had penetrated into the military systems, they used special programs to elevate their privileges from general user accounts to system administrators. With administrator access the hackers now had a higher level of authority and unrestricted freedom in what they could do on the computers. The hackers used their administrator access to add, change, and remove programs and data.

Next, the hackers downloaded and deciphered the system password files and used the passwords to access other accounts and create new accounts. Using these accounts and passwords, the hackers could reenter the government systems at will with no one discovering they had compromised the systems. Once firmly established within the networks, they jumped to 34 other networks and burrowed deeply into these systems. They read "sensitive but unclassified" files and emails. They read personal performance reports, weapons development data, logistics and shipping data. They searched U.S. military information systems for words like "nuclear weapon", "missile", and *"Desert Shield"* and *"Desert Storm"* — the U.S. Department of Defense operational names for the prewar military buildup and combat operations of the 1990 to 1991 Persian Gulf War that was in full swing. The hackers collected information on the Patriot air-defense system, the Navy's Tomahawk cruise missile, and military reserve personnel mobilization. The perpetrators then modified and erased digital evidence of their nefarious activities to maintain their clandestine operations and hinder investigations once they were discovered.

In a bold move, the hackers then approached Hussein and offered to disrupt the U.S. network-dependent deployment to the Middle East for a mere one million dollars. Saddam must have believed this a trick of the U.S. Central Intelligence Agency, and he appears to have ignored the hacker's offer. In the fall of 1990, U.S. government employees and contractors discovered the hacking.[4] The U.S. government never openly identified or prosecuted the perpetrators.

After the firing in the desert stopped and U.S. military forces marched in ticker-tape victory parades, nations around the world discussed two great lessons learned from our victorious desert campaign. First, no one would take on the technically superior U.S. military toe-to-toe on the battlefield. Our cyber-enabled systems were unstoppable in a direct confrontation. Second, the secret to defeating the U.S. lies in cyberspace.

Network Centric Warfare

The U.S. military continued its love affair with cyberspace and information technology. They developed and deployed airborne sensors, intelligent weapons, automated command and control systems, and just-in-time logistics all connected and supported by communications systems that enhance the

19

management and technical capabilities of warfighters and eliminate the shortfalls of a smaller force.

The Department of Defense created a vision for warfare in the twenty-first century known as *Network-Centric Warfare* (NCW). NCW proposes a robust force of independent sensors, decision-makers, and weapons interconnected across the battlefield by information technologies. The information technologies enabled decentralized warriors to "generate increased combat power… to achieve shared awareness, increased speed of command, higher tempo of operations, greater lethality, increased survivability, and a degree of self synchronization." By decoupling sensors, decision makers, and shooters and then connecting the components through an information network, the U.S. military could deliver customized effects on an enemy force at the time and place of their choosing and reduce the force necessary to produce the effect.

A revolutionary new means of warfare was born. The Pentagon believed a force implementing NCW would be more adaptive and responsive. Warriors could use better information, information-enabled systems, and the blinding speed of the computer and digital networks to fight a less bloody war and defeat any adversary. The Pentagon's love affair with information technology was complete.

As time passed the Pentagon applied the lessons learned from commercial industries such as Walmart, Federal Express, and Amazon to automate the military maintenance, logistics, and personnel support systems. Soon NCW included information technology and concepts embedded in all aspects of the U.S. military. Visionaries believed the resulting increased efficiencies would reduce costs and allow the military to operate as effectively as these new information-based commercial industries.

During the 2000 presidential campaign, George W. Bush gave Secretary of Defense William Cohen a mandate to "challenge the status quo and envision a new architecture of American defense for decades to come," and directed the Pentagon cut cold war weapons, enable cross service cooperation, and get everyone on the net.[5] Technology experts promised automation and information networks would offer warfighters the means to reduce the effort, costs, and military force necessary to complete their missions and yet multiply the force they could put apply against an opponent.

They were right.

Throwing Stones in the Glass House

At the same time the U.S. military was creating their decentralized and technologically superior military forces, a secret revolution was taking place within the Pentagon and Intelligence Community. Government leaders began affectionately referring to the Persian Gulf War as the *First Information War*. The news media and politicians told stories of the U.S. launching computer viruses against Iraqi air defense systems via a printer they had snuck into an Iraqi military system.[6] Throughout the Pentagon visionaries started discussing the possibility of defeating nations using weapons in cyberspace, rather than weapons that used cyberspace. Buried in secure laboratories and Pentagon conference rooms, the U.S. love affair with offensive cyber operations and cyber espionage was born.

The Department of Defense became smitten with cyber warfare; bloodless battles where they could force their adversaries to submit to their will through digital attacks against their military, government, and civilian infrastructures and computer systems. The military ran classified workshops and exercises that promoted digital warfare. Military journals were full of articles declaring the dawn of bloodless warfare.

As foreign countries moved into cyberspace, U.S. intelligence agencies discovered the joys of harvesting vast amounts of public and sensitive information from their networks. Personnel dossiers, corporate contracts, personal information, and industrial and military secrets were there for the taking. They must have thought this was too good to be true.

They were right. It apparently never occurred to anyone that their opponents could use the U.S. reliance on technology to do the same to the United States.

Groundhog Day

Other nations discovered the U.S. reliance on technology presented a door into the U.S. military, government, and industrial information and systems. Cliff Stoll's experience with the KGB-sponsored hackers showed foreign intelligence services were running amok through U.S. government, academic, and contractor networks, harvesting sensitive military and industrial information to maintain par during the Cold War. The Dutch hackers demonstrated Department of Defense computer networks were still vulnerable, and hackers could exploit these vulnerabilities to impact military operations. But these penetrations into government and government contractor systems were just the beginning.

In 1994, less than four years after Desert Storm, perpetrators spent two months rampaging through the networks of the "premier command and control research facility" at U.S. Air Force Rome Laboratory. At the time Rome Laboratory collaborated with academic institutions, commercial research facilities, and defense contractors on advanced technologies including artificial intelligence, radar guidance, and target detection and tracking. Hackers penetrated over 150 times and "weaved their way through various phone switches in South America, through commercial sites on the east and west coast, and then to Rome Laboratory" to hide their place of origin. The hackers seized control of the lab's systems for several days, installing cyber bugs to monitor networks and established connections to foreign sites. Similar to the previous incident, the perpetrators used trusted relationships to jump to and compromise other government facilities, including NASA's Goddard Space Flight Center, Wright-Patterson Air Force Base, defense contractors, and private organizations.

Eventually the military detected the attacks. Investigators determined the hackers had taken three years of research costing over $4 million. The government cleaned the hackers out of the networks at the cost of another $500,000. The Government Accountability Office (GAO) noted that there might have been national security risks associated with the attack with at least one hacker possibly "working for a foreign country interested in obtaining military research data." The GAO found that, "at a minimum these attacks are a multimillion dollar nuisance to Defense. At worst, they are a serious threat to national security." [7,8] Yet the Pentagon did not systematically address the threat. Rather, they increased and accelerated their deployment of advanced technology.

Eventually two California high school students were arrested and pled guilty. Their eighteen year-old Israeli mentor Ehud Tenenbaum, known as "the Analyzer," was arrested in Israel and sentenced to six months of community service. Evidence suggested that the trio may have compromised 500 networks worldwide. Although U.S. Deputy Secretary of Defense John Hamre called this "the most organized and systematic attack [on the Department of Defense] to date," senior U.S. government officials dismissed the incident to the news media and Congress, noting that hackers did not access classified information. However, by this time warfighters had a better understanding of the significance of unclassified systems. Informed military leaders understood that when they had connected their systems together, they had put all their eggs in one digital basket. Now critical systems such as the Global Transportation System, Defense Finance System, medical, personnel, logistics, air traffic control, and official e-mail all rode together on the unclassified network.

Solar Sunrise nearly resulted in justification for the U.S. going to war over a mistake in identifying those responsible for malicious acts in cyberspace.

Greetings from the Orient

In 2003, the Department of Defense once again discovered large-scale, successful penetrations in their information systems.

He reported the incident up through the Air Force, which got military law enforcement investigators involved. The Air Force also reported the incident to the military organization responsible for the defense of military networks, the Joint Task Force – Computer Network Operations, where I was responsible for investigating serious cyber incidents.

When a hacker discovers a previously unknown vulnerability they may have the means to break into computers that defenders can't detect or defend against. Since defenders have no time to prepare for the hacker's attacks, this vulnerability became known as a "zero-day vulnerability." A hacker could use zero-day vulnerabilities to secretly break into vulnerable computers and steal information, or create a worm to rip through vulnerable computers.

In this case, we didn't understand who was responsible for the incident but we knew the hackers had the digital version of a skeleton key and could access and take any information or damage any systems on nearly any military network.

Ground Hogs Day

We saw first-hand that the sensors monitoring military networks could not detect new attacks. Most of these sensors operate by comparing network or computer activity with known fingerprints of attacks or vulnerabilities. They can detect known attacks but not new, innovative attacks.

We didn't publish information about the vulnerability to prevent other hackers from using the vulnerability to attack other organizations. Instead, we informed the vendor of the vulnerability. The vendor responded within days by publishing a software patch that eliminated the vulnerability and closed the hacker's door. We breathed a sigh of relief.

In response to this incident we looked deeper into network traffic and discovered more incidents. All around us we discovered hackers within the networks, and as we pulled on one thread they unraveled. The team worked day and night investigating intrusions into military networks. The more we learned, the more we realized hackers were compromising and controlling our networks. Every day we received more reports of military networks compromised by hackers, national attackers, worms, botnets and criminals. As we discovered and cleaned adversaries out of one network, the adversaries adapted and started invasions in other networks. We were playing a cyber version of whack-a-mole.

Cyber defenders focus on protecting networks to prevent future compromises. When they fail (and our technology and processes ensure they fail) they focus on cleaning the culprits out of the compromised networks. For most security defenders the question of "who is responsible" is irrelevant — if it's not authorized then it's bad and must be stopped.

Law enforcement agents understand that cleaning culprits out of compromised networks doesn't prevent future incidents. When prevention fails law enforcement agents view tracking, identifying, and prosecuting hackers as the way to prevent future attacks. Our military law enforcement agents worked tirelessly and called in favors from the rest of the federal government and international law enforcement community, collected and analyzed evidence, and tracked adversaries.

The Intelligence Community did not see a role in preventing cyber incidents. The role of intelligence agents is to create and use sources and methods to inform senior leaders. Often these sources and methods are highly perishable. Intelligence agents know that using or sharing the information discovered through intelligence operations may reveal to adversaries the sources and methods used to collect that information. Once discovers, an adversary will eliminate the sources and methods to prevent future intelligence collection, and cause the intelligence agent to go blind to the adversary's future activities.

While the Intelligence Community was investigating these cyber intrusions, they were leery about sharing any information with those who operate and defend the networks since these security professionals would use the information to prevent future compromises and inadvertently announce to the hacker they had been discovered.

In August 2005, the Pentagon first publicly acknowledged that Chinese hackers were running rampant through military computer systems. Someone within the government had leaked information to the media regarding the intrusions in military systems. A reporter provided the Pentagon with a draft of a proposed article and asked if the Pentagon would like to provide comments before they published the article. My commander directed me to correct inaccuracies in the article. Due to sensitiveness involving our methods of detecting the attacks and the ongoing law enforcement investigations we had to limit details of the attacks. The attacks originated in China, and either Chinese hackers were responsible or other hackers were jumping through Chinese systems on their way to U.S. military systems.[9]

These intrusions were not the first, but they were persistent. Law enforcement discovered that many of the intrusions originated in China, where the U.S. couldn't prosecute the perpetrators. In many cases the Chinese government denied the attacks had occurred and therefore there was nothing they could do to prevent them. The U.S. could not tell the Chinese how they had identified the foreign hackers or they would give away sensitive sources and methods. The hackers learned that when they were discovered they had to cover their tracks, but they could move to other tools and networks without fear of punishment. This activity and situation continues today.

Thumbdrives, Viruses, and Lies Oh My

By this time I was at the Defense Advanced Research Projects Agency, or DARPA, running cyber research and development programs. After I heard rumors of the worm, I inquired with my former workmates and they told me they couldn't give me a copy of the worm due to the NSA's ORCON restriction. However, commercial antivirus vendors were more than happy to share information they possessed, including copies of the worm.

On November 15, 2008 the JTF-GNO published an order banning the use of thumbdrives across the military with no explanations. Military leaders in the field became agitated since they used thumbdrives to move data across networks (insecurely) and some bureaucrats in Washington were telling them how they could do their job without explanation.

The worm was an unsophisticated "very low threat" variant of a year old computer worm that the Finnish security firm F-Secure named "agent.btz." The government had not discovered the worm using the government's antivirus tool or the billion-dollar Pentagon network monitoring tools. They discovered the worm when the malware tried sending information back to its creator.

While the worm was spreading throughout the military classified networks, the NSA leadership was driving to meetings around Washington. The NSA Director, General Keith Alexander, was briefing the President on an out of date and unsophisticated worm. However, his policies hindered the nation's ability to defend itself. The Pentagon was defending cyberspace using Cold War mentality and technology while digital weapons were spreading through networks. The bureaucratic delay resulted in a 14 month cleanup of the worm from Department of Defense networks that became known as *Operation Buckshot Yankee.*

In August 2010, Deputy Secretary of Defense William J. Lynn III published a telling article discussing Buckshot Yankee.[10] Lynn explained a foreign intelligence service had developed a computer program (malware) and copied it onto several USB thumb drives. Hackers have been known to deliberately drop malware-infected thumb drives in parking lots, bathrooms, and offices. They might hand them out at conferences or mail them to victims, advertising they contain enticing programs or free storage.

Military members may have plugged these deliberately discarded thumb drives into their sensitive, classified computers. Lynn noted, "That code spread undetected on both classified and unclassified systems, establishing what amounted to a digital beachhead, from which data could be transferred to servers under foreign control." He went on to say, "Malicious code placed on the drive by a foreign intelligence agency uploaded itself onto a network run by the U.S. military's Central Command," the organization responsible for operations in the Middle East. The malware searched for information on computers and networks and stored discovered information on the thumb drive. Then our trusting service members plugged the thumb drives into computers connected to the Internet. Instantly the malware sent their ill-gotten information to a computer on the other side of the planet.

Mr. Lynne explains how this incident "… caused the most significant breach ever to U.S. military computers… and represents a wake-up call…" for Pentagon officials to expedite cyber defense measures. Lynn's message became the first on-the-record disclosure that a foreign intelligence agency had penetrating the U.S. military's classified systems. He also mentioned that this wasn't "the first penetration."[11]

Lynn called Buckshot Yankee "a wake-up call." But who was sleeping? The NSA knew about the threat from worms and they approved the architecture used on the classified networks. They develop and understand cyber weapons. Or was something else happening altogether?

Buckshot Yankee became the catalyst for creating a new military organization called *U.S. Cyber Command* and convincing the Pentagon, White House, and Congress to place all military cyberspace authority in Cyber Command and under the eyes of the NSA.

Glass Houses

In 2009, the *Wall Street Journal* exposed terrorists eavesdropping on the satellite communications of the Pentagon's Predator unmanned military drones using $26 hijacking software. When a drone communicates to a satellite its signal is directed up and away from the ground and may be secure from interception from the ground. However, when a satellite communicates down to a receiver on the ground, its signal spreads out as it leaves the satellite creating a reception oval on the ground. Anyone within this oval may point a receiver at the satellite and intercept the signal. Terrorists in Afghanistan or Iraq and trained in Iran turned their satellite receivers toward the sky and used simple, commercial, Russian-made software to snoop on the unprotected Predator video feeds allowing them to record and watch the same drone video as our warfighters. The terrorists may have found an inexpensive means to protect themselves from the sophisticated and expensive U.S. military technology.[12]

In 2009, North Korea hacked into South Korean networks and obtained information on *OPLAN 5027*, the joint U.S. and South Korean plan to defend South Korea from a North Korean invasion. This compromise allegedly included the U.S. list of North Korean targets, invasion plans, and post-occupation plan.[13] The North Korean leadership learned, like so many others, that it might use cyberspace to balance the political, economic, or military battlefield with a world superpower.

This was just one of numerous examples of North Korean cyber invasions and attacks into South Korean systems. And soon North Korea would look to the United States.

In June 2010, *New York Times* reported on an apparent Chinese compromise of a major defense contractor network and loss of portions of the engineering information on the Lockheed Martin Lightning II, better known by its military title the F-35 Joint Strike Fighter. Apparently defense contractors placed the designs of the most advanced U.S. combat aircraft on vulnerable machines connected to the Internet where they are physically connected to the nations against which the Pentagon may deploy the new fifth generation fighter. Foreign engineers could use these designs to develop techniques to defeat our military aircraft and build their own. The F-35 is a $323 billion program, the most expensive defense program ever, and hackers may have aided in defeating it before it's ever deployed.

In January 2011, the media reported the fielding of a Chinese "fifth generation" aircraft, the J-20, and in November 2014, the Chinese showed off their newer J-31 stealth fighter. The J-20 appears to have many of the features of the F-22 and F-35 including the same diverterless engine inlet to optimize airflow at high speed.[14] The J-31 appears very similar to the F-35. Some argue the Chinese appear to have developed their J-20 and J-31 based on the stolen F-35 plans. However, U.S. defense contractors may also have benefited from this compromise of sensitive information.

Since 2006, Congress had been threatening to cancel the fighter programs due to the lack of a perceived need. In response to the Chinese announcement, the Lockheed Martin F-35 program general manager publicly stated that the Chinese aircraft creates a "stronger sense of urgency" within the Asian-Pacific nations to purchase the F-35.[15] Lockheed Martin claimed the U.S. needs the F-35 even more because the Chinese developed their stealth aircraft.

It would appear a defense contractor's inability to protect the F-35 plans may have aided the Chinese in creating their next generation military stealth aircraft that now threatens U.S. military pilot's lives and our national security. Yet the alleged theft of the sensitive military industry information also created a business opportunity for contractors by creating a perverse incentive for the U.S. government to purchase a weapon as the result of the previously stolen information. This perverse incentive exists because the government believes it has no recourse. They could scrap the program when there may still be a need or continue purchasing a potentially compromised system.

The apparent Chinese infiltration of U.S. public and private information networks has significantly increased since the revelations of 2003. The Pentagon reported the Chinese alone took 20 terabytes of U.S. government and defense industry information in five years of covert cyber espionage. This information is equivalent in size to half of the printed Library of Congress, or 13 compact discs of information stolen every day for five years. In 2007, General James Cartwright, the former head of U.S. Strategic Command and then the vice chairman of the Joint Chief of Staff, told the U.S.-China Economic and Security Review Commission the Chinese could use the information to identify weak points in computer networks, understand how U.S. leadership thinks, discover U.S. communication patterns, and target valuable information and systems.

While the scale of the apparent Chinese intrusions is impressive, the quality of information is shocking. Pentagon officials note that Chinese hackers have taken not only plans for the F-35 Joint Strike Fighter, but over twenty military weapon systems including the Patriot Advanced Capability-3 (PAC-3) Missile

System which Lockheed Martin claims is the "world's most advanced, capable and powerful terminal air defense missile."[16] It also includes the Army Terminal High Altitude Area Defense (THAAD) and the Navy's Aegis ballistic-missile defense systems.[17] The U.S. government financed the research and development of these weapons to protect the nation, allies, and military personnel from sophisticated foreign ballistic missiles. Now foreign powers may have used the U.S. reliance on cyberspace as the means to defeat these defenses.

We don't know how often foreign hackers access our most sensitive military weapon system information, but we know the threats to our military systems are significant. The Pentagon created a special program to inform the defense contractors, called the *defense industrial base,* of threats to their information systems.[18]

Chinese espionage against this U.S. defense industrial base is a brilliant strategy. The Chinese steal information and avoid the high research and development costs to defeat the technology, while using the information to simultaneously transition from an industrial nation into a world super power and keeping U.S. military might at bay to protect their national security. Additionally, Chinese companies and their government can offer the stolen information and technology to other nations to generate revenue to reinvest into China.

Insider Run Amok

Not all the information stolen from our information systems resulted from hackers breaking into our systems. In 2013, Edward Snowden shocked the world. As a former employee and now Intelligence Community contractor, Snowden had access to countless highly sensitive government documents on the classified intelligence networks. To make matters worse, Snowden was a *system administrator* responsible for managing some of the NSA's most sensitive systems that contained these documents. He claims he was disenchanted with NSA's domestic surveillance and became a whistleblower. Snowden released documents revealing NSA's domestic and international surveillance, and some claim exposing U.S. government violation of its citizen's civil liberties in the name of protecting national security.[19] Snowden also brought to light the potential for an insider to cause catastrophic damage to an organization due to their access to an organization's inner workings and information systems.

Digital Bones

If military power is a nation's muscle, then cyber technologies have become the digital bones that the muscles are built upon. The digital bones are more than computers on the battlefield. Due to the complexity of modern military systems the military also needs cyberspace to support the design and manufacture of military systems before they are deployed.

Today military technology is so complex that developers require computer-aided engineering tools to design systems and sophisticated management tools to plan and track manufacturing. Once fielded, military forces require computers and networks to track and maintain systems, supplies, and repair parts. The military replaced large-scale shipping and warehousing with cost-effective, just-in-time logistic systems that order, transport, and track supplies and repair parts as they are needed around the world. The Pentagon has replaced many of its radios, voice, and fax communications systems with email and digital phones that operate across computer networks. After the systems are deployed the same network is used to sense the battlefield, seek targets, and guide precision weapons to those targets.

In the 1980s and 1990s, military leaders embraced civilian leadership concepts racing through academia and corporations. Concepts such as TQM, or Total Quality Management, strove to collect metrics and optimize business processes. Military schools taught these concepts to senior leaders who then became concept evangelicals in warfighting organizations. Advocates didn't consider the differences in the environments and the threats military organizations face, creating unanticipated consequence.

These concepts strove to increase organizational and program productivity and efficiency by removing redundancy and reducing costs. These goals proved very beneficial in commercial enterprises where driving down costs and product prices may increase market share and profits. However the purpose of the military is to deter foreign aggression and, should deterrence fail, to project combat power on adversaries. The military fights America's wars; it damages and destroys foreign militaries while absorbing attacks from our adversaries.

Efficiency makes an organization brittle in destructive environments. Organizations operating in violent and unpredictable environments require resilience – the ability to absorb adversity and continue. Traditionally military forces have used redundancy to create this resilience.

Since the 1980's, we've modeled our warfighting forces after commercial industry's best practices to improve efficiencies and save money — and commercial industry modeled them on the commercial environment. As a result, military leaders converted warfighters from a resilient but less efficient warfighting force into a smaller, efficient, effective and brittle warfighting force.

Conclusion

For over twenty-five years foreign militaries and intelligence agencies, criminals, and industrial spies have been stealing military, government, corporate, and personal information. Our critical public and private information systems have been bleeding sensitive information — and by the government's own admissions continue to hemorrhage information today.

And this smaller and brittle force is operating and reliant on a vulnerable cyber environment. We've deployed technology faster than our ability to understand the implications or the means to deal with potential risks. The Director of National Intelligence (DNI), as the head of the Intelligence Community (IC) and the principal advisor on intelligence matters related to national security to the President, the National Security Council, and the Homeland Security Council, reported the theft of our military information is "almost certainly allowing our adversaries to close the technological gap between our respective militaries, slowly neutralizing one of our key advantages in the international arena."[20]

To understand the related national crisis we are in, we need to take a deeper look at the technical, social, and political realities. So lets take a short trip to understand the playground.

Ground Hogs Day

Chapter 4. The Guardians

"Defense is the stronger form of waging war."
\- Carl von Clausewitz (1780 – 1831)

"If you want security, you must be prepared for inconvenience."
\- General B.W. Chidlaw (1900 – 1977)

Retrospection

Cyberspace is built on technology and it would seem the natural approach to problems in a technology field is to build better, smarter technology. But technology alone cannot save us.

Cyber defense is about enabling the people who use cyberspace, the *users*, to perform their online activities securely. We've created an entire industry of special hackers, called *guardians*, to defend the *confidentiality*, *integrity*, and *availability* of the user's data, programs and systems. Confidentiality refers to ensuring information isn't exposed to anyone who isn't supposed to access it. Integrity refers to ensuring data is correct and someone doesn't maliciously or accidentally change data in databases, email, or websites. Availability is about ensuring information and systems are accessible when they're needed.

Hackers have been infecting computers with malware since the 1970's, when the Creeper virus infected Digital Equipment Corporation PDP-10 mainframe computers on the ARPANet. Industry responded in 1987 with *antivirus* applications to search for computer code, called *signatures*, which look or behave like viruses the antivirus vendor has seen in the past.

Also in 1987, computer scientist Fred Cohen proved mathematically it was impossible to develop a computer program to detect all possible viruses.[1] He showed it was impossible to create an antivirus, firewall, or other cyber defense technology to detect or protect against every attack. The best guardians can do is to create security tools containing a library of signatures and behaviors they have seen in the past or behaves in a manner someone has previously labeled as malicious and alert on similar items.

Hackers learned they could slip past antivirus programs by creating new malware or minor variants of existing malware whose signatures are not contained in antivirus libraries. They developed applications to make slight modifications repeatedly to previously detected malware until the modified

The Guardians

malware can slip undetected past defenses. Hackers have also developed *polymorphic* malware that automatically changes every time it copies itself to another computer to defeat defenses. The result is malware that may successfully infect a victim and remain hidden until someone stumbles on it.

Individuals and automated security applications report suspicious files to security vendors. However, with the growth of cyberspace and malware these vendors are now inundated with a flood of malware, which has approached up to 60,000 new or minor variants of malware per week.

Vendors have to prioritize the malware they receive based on the damage the malware may cause and/or the number of people or systems reporting the malware. Eventually the malware bubbles up to the top of the vendor's queue and the vendor analyzes the malware, creates a new signature, tests that the new signature doesn't break their security tool, and places the new signature in their commercial signature file they share with their customers. Then the community downloads and installs the updated signature file to their systems to protect them from the latest batch of analyzed malware. During the weeks to months from an initial discovery to defensive systems protecting against an attack the community is vulnerable to malware that is "in the wild" and being actively used by hackers.

This is the *Retrospective Analysis Cycle*. Antivirus products and most other security tools require retrospective analysis. The strength of retrospective analysis is that once a guardian has identified an attack they can add a signature of the attack to their defenses and prevent hackers from successfully using that attack in the future. In this way sharing signatures is similar to sharing antibodies to protect from illnesses. Sharing signatures forces hackers to change attacks or create new attacks to be successful. Operating systems and applications have similar cycles to deal with newly discovered bugs.

Figure 2 - Retrospective Live Cycle

The constant retrospective analysis cycle explains why guardians and users need to constantly update antivirus signatures on office and home computers. But these signatures only help if the victim isn't the first to get attacked and can benefit from someone else's misery through the retrospective analysis cycle.

This back-and-forth battle has created an environment reminiscent of Sisyphus of Greek mythology. Cyber defenders are forever rolling a boulder up a steep hill only to have it roll back down before they reach the top.

Political leaders, corporate executives, and the news media criticize guardians for what they see as the continuous expenditures of millions or billions of dollars for security products, only to have hackers compromise their supposedly protected systems. These individuals don't realize that the security controls are entirely reactive and won't defend against the first instance of any attack since the signature of these new attacks don't exist within the security controls. Guardians must wait for someone to suffer an (often successful) attack before they can create and install a signature to defend against this attack.

In most cases hackers also receive updates and patches from vendors. A hacker can install these on their machines to see if the latest changes from the vendor will detect or prevent their attack tools. These updates also afford important intelligence and feedback to a malware developer by telling them the time they have from launching malware until vendors can prevent future attacks. Knowing the time involved in the retrospective analysis cycle tells malware developers how much time they have to use malware against a target before they need to publish an updated version of their malware to continue being successful.

These patches and updates provide hackers with other critical intelligence. Updates and patches result in changes to systems. Hackers can compare a system before and after an update to discover what changed, and possibly where previously unannounced vulnerabilities existed in systems. Hackers use this information to create weapons to exploit those who are too slow to deploy patches.

In May 2014 Symantec, the makers of Norton Antivirus noted that sophisticated attacks will compromise a computer even with antivirus products installed. Symantec quantified the problem, noting that antivirus today detects at most 45% of all malware.[2] This low percentage results from trying to solve an impossible problem, inability to analyze and quickly integrate the deluge of new malware the antivirus vendors receive into their signature libraries, and time delay in the retrospective analysis cycle.

Walls and Moats

Early hackers used the Internet's willingness to forward any message to search the Internet for computers with vulnerabilities. Hackers would send out millions of messages attempting to connect to any computer with vulnerabilities. This was like 'rattling the doors' of prospective victims until the hacker discovered an open door. When a computer responded to the knock the hacker would connect to the computer and execute their attack.

The security community looked to history for inspiration and built digital walls around computers, reminiscent of castle walls and moats. The idea was to prevent hackers and malware from getting access to computers rather than play catch-up with malware. Government agencies and commercial companies

The Guardians

created *firewalls* that are security devices between two networks. Firewalls block anyone trying to create a connection to a network, preventing scanning attacks from the Internet from getting into (in some cases out of) a network. The firewall became the first line of defense blocking traffic that has no legitimate reason to enter a network.

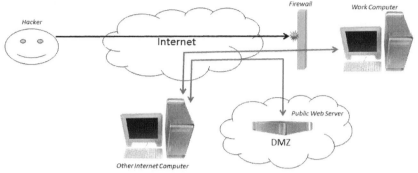

Figure 3 - Firewalls blocking illegitimate traffic from a network

Hackers had to find a new way to get access to victims and pursued devices outside the firewalls — the servers. Users have to request web pages and send email to get legitimate work done. The computers serving web pages are in front of firewalls to permit those outside a corporate firewall to initiate connections to the webserver. The web and email servers were outside the firewall in what guardians call the *demilitarized zone*, or DMZ.[3]

Hackers targeted the servers and routing devices residing in the DMZ since there was little protection in front of them, and if cyber defenders did not maintain the servers in the DMZ they were easy pickings. Hackers simply scanned the Internet looking for machines outside firewalls until they found a vulnerable one, and pounced on it, performing what they call *pharming*.

Another means to defeating firewalls is to exploit the legitimate traffic crossing a firewall and the retrospective analysis cycle. Hackers can create a minor variant of known malware and email the malware to a legitimate user behind a firewall. The variant slips past defenses and infects a machine when a user opens the file. Now the malware is behind the firewall and has two significant advantages. The firewall will allow the infected machine to initiate a connection to the hacker residing outside the firewall and slip past defenses. Second, the infected machine is behind the firewall and often most of the other outward facing security controls, and may attack other machines behind the firewall without being noticed. The firewall doesn't defend attacks from within.

Hackers may also penetrate a web server, not to infect the server with malware as this would only infect one machine, but to load their malware on the server. When legitimate users communicate with the server they download the hacker's malware to their host that then infects their machine. This is referred to as *drive-by attacks* — since a computer gets infected just by visiting the website.

Building a Castle on Quicksand

Not all vulnerabilities are the same. Think of cyberspace as a stack of blocks. On the bottom is the communications network. On top of the network are the hardware blocks representing each computing device. On top of the hardware is the operating system running the hardware and acting as the intermediary for applications. This level also contains other software, such

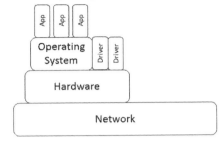

Figure 4 - The Stack

as the drivers that instruct devices like printers how to operate. On top of this layer are the applications.

If a hacker can compromise a lower layer, they may affect all the blocks on top of it. Most security controls are just applications running on an operating system. So, if a hacker can compromise a computer's operating system they can disable the security controls on the computer.

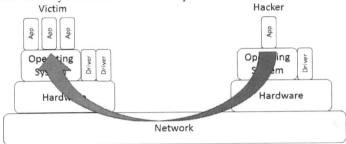

Figure 5 - Compromising the Stack

Homogeneity

Having armies use uniform weapon systems on a battlefield increases their effectiveness and efficiencies by introducing common manufacturing, transportation, training and maintenance. Soldiers can be more effective by using similar weapons and ammunition, and to cannibalize parts from similar systems to get damaged systems back into operations faster. But uniformity isn't without risks. Should an adversary discover a weakness in uniform systems, called a *common cause failure*, they may exploit the vulnerability across an entire army with devastating results.

Organizations also benefit from uniformity in cyberspace. Organizations can benefit from purchasing discounts, training users and administrators, and interoperability of systems, applications, and data formats. Likewise, uniformity enables an enterprise to install new vendor patches, updates, and security controls rapidly across an enterprise to eliminate vulnerabilities before hackers can exploit them. However, a uniform architecture may allow a single malware to "infect" the entire infrastructure, much like a disease infects a common population in a pandemic.

The Guardians

Guardians may use different versions of antivirus software throughout an environment to increase the chance of detecting malicious code since theoretically these different brands contain different libraries of virus signatures. Organizations may segment their networks and apply security appliances from different vendors in these segments. An organization with multiple connections to the Internet may apply firewalls from different vendors on the connections. These steps may allow guardians to reap the benefits of different technologies and signatures to monitor their assets, but may require increased costs and labor to install, monitor, and maintain these different technologies.

Defense in Depth

Guardians combine numerous security tools such as firewalls, intrusion detection systems, antivirus programs, automated patching tools, spyware detectors and non-technical processes such as vetting employees. The guardian community adopted the phrase "Defense in Depth" to refer to layering tools and techniques to prevent, detect, and respond to cyberattacks.[4]

However, don't confuse the military concept of Defense in Depth with the cyber security concept.

In the past generals organized their armies into long lines opposing an enemy. The two armies would approach each other and meet in a battle of attrition. However, a smart general might focus their army at a single point in their opponent's defense. Once an army drove through the initial lines of enemy soldiers, there might be little stopping them from destroying the opponent's supplies and continuing on to their objective.

Defense in depth is a military strategy that changes this paradigm by exploiting a military principle, "every attack loses impetus as it progresses."[5]

The goal of a defense in depth is to not stretch a defending force across a battlefield and cover the entire front but to create an *elastic defense* to conserve combat strength as an enemy advances. The defender establishes a series of layered defensive positions to slow an enemy and increase the attacker's casualties over time and space. As the attacker approaches, the defender resists the enemy, then breaks contact and moves to another position to delay and attrite the advancing enemy army. The attacker is bloodied as they move deeper into enemy territory, and their supplies are stretched throughout the defender's territory where they are susceptible to attack. The attacker is forced to react to numerous defenders and counter attacks, thinning their advancing forces. Eventually the attacker may lose momentum as they drive deeper into the more heavily defended territory. At this point the defender attacks and defeats the now weakened attackers.

The cyberspace version of Defense in Depth refers to layering numerous cyber defense technologies including perimeter firewalls, intrusion detection systems, and antivirus scanners in the hope one of these detects and/or prevents a specific attack. Effective defense requires more than different tools—but tools using different techniques. However nearly all defensive tools use retrospective analysis and are therefore unable to detect or protect against new attacks.

As hackers inundate public and private organizations with cyberattacks the concept of defense in depth has taken on a life of its own. Guardians place more security tools within their networks, which bring with them the implicit need to install, maintain, operate, respond, and audit the security tools. If an organization does not staff and train their people to meet the needs of these controls, these controls may overwhelm the staff and prevent them from maintaining their systems or ignore users' needs. Trying to maintain this complexity may transform security into a "checklist" mentality, where controls are installed, but not properly configured, managed, or maintained, and the added security decreases an organization's ability to defend a network effectively.

The National Institute of Technology Risk Management Framework lists hundreds of security controls the U.S. Government recommends defenders implement. The framework doesn't provide justification for individual tools, nor explains the effectiveness of these controls on attackers, nor how implementing these controls may impact operations or other defenses. The Gramm-Leach-Bliley Act (financial institutions) and Health Insurance Portability and Accounting Act (medical institutions), and Payment Card Industry (PCI) Data Security Standard (credit card industry) also require public and private organizations to implement lists of security tools. The security community is putting tremendous effort and funds into promoting defense in depth by making security bigger and more complex, but there is little evidence that the security is more effective.[6]

A 2013 study found that layering security controls did not significantly improve defense effectiveness. The researchers compared 37 security products from 24 different vendors to detect and defeat 1,711 real world attacks. The researchers found "none of the 37 security products detected all exploits, and only 3% of 606 unique combinations of two security products managed to detect all [attacks]. Further, [they discovered that] there is a large diversity in the security performance between individual security products or combinations of security products."[7]

Adding security controls also increases the complexity of an organization's infrastructure. Guardians may become concerned that this complexity will impact an organization's ability to execute its mission. The guardians may respond by only partially or improperly implementing a security tool. A recent inspection of a military organization's security discovered a guardian had decided that utilizing all firewall features might impact a user's network experience, creating a backlash that he didn't want to deal with. He decided to install the device, but not install any rules on the device, effectively turning the firewall into an open door that permitted any traffic into and out of the military network. The organization received credit for the control being installed, but this only provided senior leaders with a false sense of security.

The Guardians

As security vendors deal with new and innovative attacks they add new functionality to their products that inevitably increases the complexity of the controls. In 2011 Peiter Zatko, known within the hacker community as Mudge and now a DARPA Program Manager, conducted a study called the *DARPA Cyber Analytic Framework*. Mudge discovered that over time the complexity of hacker's attacks had remained constant while security control complexity had grown exponentially. Mudge concluded that commercial security tools aren't significantly raising the bar to hackers. However the resulting increased complexity in security tools has introduced another challenge. Many security tools, such as antivirus products must operate with higher authorization and subsequent trust level to protect a system. These security tools are also susceptible to bugs and vulnerabilities in their code. Their increased potential for vulnerabilities, combined with operating at a higher trust level, results in the potential for an attacker to compromise an enterprise by attacking vulnerabilities in the very security tools deployed to protect the enterprise.

 The Problem: Not Convergent

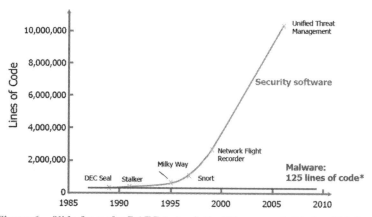

Figure 6 – Slide from the DARPA Analytical Framework Study of Malware[8]

Mudge found that one-third of all Department of Defense mandatory security updates involved security tools themselves, meaning **the tools meant to protect military networks introduced vulnerabilities into the network and represented a serious threat to the Department of Defense.**[9]

Others have discovered that vulnerabilities in a network that run at a higher authorization create a very tempting target. A 2014 study found 165 vulnerabilities in a four-year period in antivirus products, and concluded, "[It] is clear that antivirus software can be targeted just like other components or services of computer systems."[10] Similarly the 2014 Heartbleed exploit used a vulnerability in Secure Socket Layer tools designed to allow secure information sharing on the Internet.[11] Intrusion detection systems and firewalls have also had serious vulnerabilities, and in some cases been targeted and exploited by hackers.[12]

Guardians don't have a set of tools that work either effectively or efficiently. The need for so many tools demonstrates their lack of effectiveness. Due to the Retrospective Analysis Cycle these tools must be maintained to be useful, so guardians must constantly install patches and updates so they don't become vulnerable. The tools are often not integrated together so they run simultaneously and slow computers, decreasing performance and preventing users from getting their work done effectively. Sometimes increasing security tools frustrate users, who then deactivate the tools. When security and user convenience collide, convenience always wins.

Bounty

If vulnerabilities allow hackers to penetrate a system, then a good solution may be to remove vulnerabilities before hackers can exploit them. This leads to another tactic in the security community known as *vulnerability bounties* where security vendors create a marketplace to purchase information about vulnerabilities from hackers. The theory is that paying bounties buys vendors time to create patches and updates to their systems and guardians to install these patches and updates that remove the vulnerabilities.

Large vendors have been successful using this strategy to purchase potentially damaging vulnerabilities. Small vendors may not be able to afford to pay bounties. This situation may also create a *perverse effect*, where an environment evolves into a situation contrary to the original action's intent. An example is the 'cobra effect' that occurred in British India when a British bounty for killing cobras created a perverse incentive for people to breed cobras for the income. Paying for cyber vulnerabilities may create a similar perverse incentive for software developers to place vulnerabilities into systems, then act like a hacker and get paid a bounty for information related to a vulnerability they created.

Criminals and nation states will not sell their vulnerabilities if they believe they can receive greater gains by exploiting them. Likewise governments may purchase vulnerabilities if they believe they can use them to access their adversary's networks. This creates a conflict of interest between governments using vulnerabilities to access nations that pose a threat to their national security, and sharing the vulnerability with a vendor who will then use the information to protect their networks and potentially make everyone's networks more secure.

Stupid Users

Today the most common way to compromise a network is to send a legitimate user an email or a social network message with embedded malicious code, or a link to a site that contains malicious code. The user is tricked into opening the attachment or clicking on a link and malware compromises the victim's computer and often defeats the guardian's elaborate defenses. Guardians profess, "*Users are the weakest link in the security chain*," and blame the users for their "*stupid behavior that places the network at risk.*"

The security professionals point out that if a hacker can trick a user they can get a foothold on a network that they may expand to the entire enterprise. Management responds by requiring users to complete boring and repetitive security training to teach them about the threats of email and social networks.

We need to stop and think about this situation. Guardians have created elaborate defenses and may have years of formal education, college degrees, certifications, and training but they can't protect the user or the enterprise. Their activities have revealed that average people, those individuals with the least knowledge about computer security, are responsible for protecting the enterprise. Managers should ask themselves, "If despite all the defenses and training one person can make one mistake that places the corporate, government, or personal information and systems at risk, then perhaps it's time to rethink if an enterprise should expose all their information and systems to hackers?"

Response

Eventually, after a hacker begins exploiting computers, a guardian is going to discover the incident. But they may not discover that the compromised machine is on their network. A study found that two out of three successful breaches took a month or more to discover, and seventy percent of victims discovered they were compromised only after a third party notified them of the compromise.[13] To paraphrase — a guardian will most likely discover their security failed, and a hacker has compromised their systems, when they receive a phone call or email from another guardian, not when a security tool alerts them.

Guardians have responded by creating public and secret information sharing forums. Groups such as the Forum of Incident Response and Security Teams (FIRST) provide an environment for guardians to share information about attacks, hackers, and malware. If a guardian detects a computer attacking their systems they may contact the guardians responsible for the attacking computer to ask them to take action. After guardians discover how they've been victimized they may share what they've learned with others, and together they'll clean the perpetrators out of networks.

When a guardian discovers a hacker has compromised a machine they typically want to clean the hacker out of their network, and prevent future penetrations from the hacker. They often will unplug infected machines from the network to prevent the hacker from stealing any more information or from damaging machines to cover up their tracks. The process to cleanup after a hacker can be time consuming and costly. Guardians will investigate how hackers obtained access and any resulting impact from the attack, erase everything on the infected computers to eliminate any hacker-installed malware and backdoors, then reload the machine from clean media so users can return to work. They also may change passwords and verify every account to ensure the hackers haven't installed accounts.

Cleaning hackers out of infected systems may not eliminate the hacker from the network. Guardians often have to wait until a vendor or developer of a vulnerable system creates and deploys a patch before they can rebuild a system from scratch, install the system and place it back into operations. Otherwise a hacker could walk right back in using the previous exploit.

Professor Sal Stolfo at Columbia University has been demonstrating for years that other devices on a network may provide a hacker a place to plant his flag.[14] He noted that networked printers are really computers with complex, extensive, and extendable software that is easily exploited by hackers and often overlooked and not maintained by guardians. A hacker may establish a connection to a printer and take control of the device. The hacker could have the printer send copies of every printout to the hacker, or use it to infect or reinfect machines after guardians have cleaned hackers out of infected computers. Peripherals like printers, smart televisions, and smart phones may provide a hacker with the means to maintain persistence on a victim's network even if the guardians erase infected computers.

As guardians unplug infected machines the hackers will lose communications with the systems, and may suspect that guardians have detected them. Hackers will suspect guardians are in their retrospective analysis cycle and the window of opportunity for the technique they use is quickly closing, and will need to change their tactics and technologies to become invisible again.

Guardians may contact law enforcement and government intelligence organizations that may be less inclined to alert hackers. These organizations may want to leave infected systems online to monitor the hacker's activities. This will allow these organizations to learn more about the hackers, and perhaps prosecute them in court. Prosecuting hackers may prevent these hackers from conducting future attacks, and public prosecution may deter others from becoming hackers. At least that's the theory. We will see later that an inability to identify hackers, hackers working for foreign nation's governments, and hackers operating in other nation's sovereign territory severely reduces the threat of prosecution.

Conclusion

The speed, geography, and small cost to develop and maintain digital weapons permit hackers to develop and send multiple attacks to victims. Unlike the kinetic battlefield attackers are not constrained by a desire for uniformity, rather they use diverse attacks until they achieve success.

Security may increase the difficulty to penetrate a network to the point that some hackers are not successful. Security may increase the hacker's fear of being physically apprehended and punished to the point that it may deter malicious behavior. Security may buy guardians time to respond if deterrence fails. But security doesn't protect a network from hackers.

A guardian's security investment may raise the skills or resources necessary for sophisticated hackers to be successful. A resourced and sophisticated hacker may decide a significant reward justifies a significant investment to defeat a guardian's defenses. A nation state hacker may spend considerably more to find a single way into a network than the guardians spend to protect all paths into their network. Thus, defenses may give a guardian a false sense of security since the most sophisticated hackers are much more stealthy and persistent than the lessor hackers they have detected.

Managers must understand not only what defenses can do, but their limitations, and how more security controls affect the system's usefulness and performance. The added security may also increase complexity, expense, and exposure, as well as increase burden to acquire, operate, and maintain.[15]

Managers must also understand that regardless of their security team or how much they spend on security tools, they may not keep out motivated and resourced hackers who believe their systems or information is valuable.

The largest risks to public and private organizations don't come from buggy computer code, 'stupid' users, or malicious insiders. **The largest risks to public and private organizations are the commercial vendors, government leaders, and "security experts" that have misled leaders into exposing their sensitive information and systems online and to protect them with ineffective defenses.** The result is an over confidence in the tools used to protect information and systems. The greatest danger arises when people with sensitive information, lulled by a false sense of security, expose their information in cyberspace. And cyberspace is teeming with individuals motivated to cause mischief and who understand they probably won't be punished.

Chapter 5. The Antagonists

"History teaches us that the character of each individual war is always different and most certainly will change, but the enduring nature of war as a human endeavor will remain largely unchanged."
- General James N. Mattis (1950-)
26th Secretary of Defense, and Retired from the U.S. Marine Corps

"If you think technology can solve your security problems,
then you don't understand the problems,
and you don't understand technology."
- Bruce Schneier (1963-)

Don't Hack Me Dude!

There are diverse groups and individuals that use various tactics, techniques and tools to create mischief in cyberspace. Regardless of this variety hackers only have three goals: gather information, exploit systems, and disrupt activities.[1]

Gathering information involves accessing systems to obtain or read the information on the systems that the hacker has no legitimate reason to access. Criminals compromise personal, corporate, or government systems to make money. A criminal may steal credit card information and use the information to make purchases, or compromise personal and corporate bank information and transfer ill-gotten funds electronically. Employees may access company information systems to embezzle funds, learn corporate secrets or peer's personal issues. National intelligence services compromise foreign information systems and use the information to protect national security and further national goals. Regardless of the label we give these activities, the goal of these acts is to gather and use information in ways the perpetrator is not authorized by the information owner. The techniques may range from clandestine penetration and stealthy exfiltration of personal, corporate, or government information, to a wholesale smash-and-grab of everything the attacker can find on a system. And our interpretation of these actions is clouded by where we sit within those groups.

Exploiting systems refers to hackers accessing and using system resources for their benefit. How often have you wished you had a more powerful computer, faster Internet connection, or more storage space? Cyberspace can give a hacker all these. Hackers may break into a computer to use the computer's hard drive to store stolen files. They may break into a computer to make the victim's computer do the hacker's work such as sending out spam email or searching for the key that unlocks secret computer encryption codes. Or a hacker may connect to a neighbor's wireless access point to use their faster Internet connection.

Hackers also exploit people directly. Prior to the 2003 invasion of Iraq the U.S. military compromised the Iraqi "private and secure" military network and used the network to send emails to Iraqi generals. The emails told the generals the U.S. did not have an issue with Iraq and the Iraqis, but with Saddam Hussein and his two sons. The emails told generals to park their vehicles, go home, and the military would be reconstituted after the regime change. Many Iraqi generals believed these emails and complied.[2]

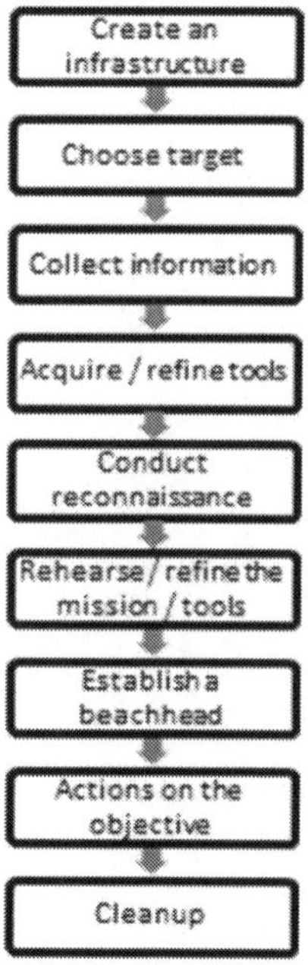

Gathering information and exploiting systems may not deliberately damage a computer. While the

result of both can and many times are damaging to individuals and organizations, the activities may not produce obvious indications they occurred or damaged the systems involved. *Disrupting activities* refers to hackers deliberately degrading or damaging systems or the information on systems to reduce a victim's ability to achieve their goals. For example, a hacker could send a command to turn off a computer or application, or cause an application to go into an error state and die or *crash*.

Many organizations have developed models to explain the process hackers use to achieve their goals. But hacker's processes vary depending on the hacker's skills, knowledge, resources, access, and motivations, sometimes known as SKRAM.[3] The steps hackers use also depend on the hacker's goals, their target's goals, the perceived threat from defenses they may encounter, and time available for the mission.

Preparations

When an amateur hacker wakes up one morning and decides to attack a victim that day, it often ends badly for the hacker. Success in nearly any endeavor requires preparation. Long before a professional hacker launches an attack they invest time and resources **creating infrastructures** to support their operations. This may consist of obtaining computers and software, collecting vast online storage and launch sites, and building massive support systems.

The next step is to **choose an individual or organization to exploit**. If a hacker's objectives are particular individuals or groups in a *targeted attack,* then

Figure 7 - Generic Hacker Attack Process

they may need to have a specific attack to compromise the target's technology or processes. If a hacker selects *targets of opportunity,* then the hacker uses a generic attack to compromise many targets.

A targeted attack may require the hacker to gather specific information about the target, where a target of opportunity may not require any specific intelligence about a target. Most of the malware we hear about in the news media is against targets of opportunity that scan the Internet hoping to catch anyone susceptible to a specific vulnerability. Spying on a specific government system is a targeted attack and may require custom tools and techniques.

After a hacker has identified a target they need to **collect information about an individual or group and their information systems**. A hacker could use a search engine, commercial vendors, and other information sources.

If a hacker is geographically close to their target they may also search through discarded personal and organization materials to discover sensitive information. This *dumpster diving* may reward a hacker with personal and sensitive information including account information and personnel names. A particular rich treasure trove are computers storage media like hard drives, tape backups, and USB drives that may contain residual data on them when thrown out, given to others, sold, or stolen.

Many people, including Bill Gates, Oliver North, and Bill Clinton learned email and other information may not stay hidden even after they've deleted it. Most computers don't erase data when a user deletes files. Deleting tells the computer to ignore and write over the information if the computer needs the space. The data remains on the computer until the computer needs the space and writes over the "deleted" data. It's trivially easy to "undelete" data and access the information before the computer writes over it. The U.S. Government learned this in the early 1990s when the Department of Justice auctioned computers containing information from the Federal Witness Protection Program. The exposure of witness locations and identities forced U.S. Marshals to relocate witnesses.

After a hacker knows their target they may need to **acquire and refine tools** needed to accomplish their goals.

Like most people, hackers want to spend minimal effort accomplishing a task. Sometimes a hacker may know of a vulnerability in a system they can use to access the system. To exploit this vulnerability the hacker may only need to send a message to the software running on a remote computer to interact with it.

In other cases the hacker may need to create a *variant* of a previously developed attack. Changing an existing attack is easier than searching for a new vulnerability. Additionally a variant of a previously identified attack may not standout as unique, further hiding its significance to investigators, whereas a new vulnerability may convince guardians the hacker was sophisticated and worthy of more interest.[4]

Sophisticated attacks may involve developing or acquiring customized cyber weapons for their particular target. Hackers may accidentally discover new vulnerabilities, however this often requires specialized skills and tools, and time. Hacker may manually search through software their targets use to discover a vulnerability or use applications to discover vulnerabilities such as *fuzzers*. Fuzzers repeatedly throw random data at applications, and eventually the application may not deal with an input and "crashes" — computer verbiage for dying. The crash may indicate a bug in the application that the hacker may use to break into or out of the system. Next the hacker restarts the application and tries to reproduce the crash to determine what caused the crash and if the hacker can use the newly discovered bug to break into a computer or network.[5]

If new vulnerabilities become public knowledge the vendors and security companies will publish updates to eliminate the hacker's ability to use the vulnerabilities to gain access to their targets. Hackers carefully guard knowledge about zero-day vulnerabilities due to all the work required to discover new vulnerabilities, the potential for unlimited access to victim computers, and short life cycle once publicized.

A hacker will often automate the steps to exploit a target to eliminate a redundant chore and reduce the chance the hacker makes a mistake. Converting vulnerabilities into useful tools is called *weaponization*, and the resulting applications are called *malware*, or malicious software. The simplest malware is a list of instructions for a computer to perform, called a *script*.

The hacker's skills, creativity and resources are the limiting factors in malware creation. A hacker can create applications that automatically harvest user's logon names and passwords from a victim's machine, give the hacker interactive access and control of the victim's machine, or damage the computer or data on the computer to prevent its use.

Once a hacker begins **reconnaissance** of their intended target, they transition from benign information collection to actively touching a victim's systems. In the past hackers would probe an intended target network by sending packets to the victim's machine to see what systems and applications the target was running. This may produce a lot of obvious hacker traffic a guardian could see if they are looking.

After gathering information about their intended victim hackers may **rehearse and refine their mission and tools**. Rehearsals may involve thinking through all the steps the hacker will take, what may or may not occur, how the hacker would identify success or failure at each step, and how to respond to these indicators. A well-resourced hacker, such as a government agency, may use the information discovered about their target to reproduce their victim's infrastructure. The hacker can use this reproduction to **refine their tools** for the intended infrastructure they are attacking. The hackers may buy identical computers and software as their intended victim, search for vulnerabilities on this technology, customize cyber tools to use the vulnerabilities to access the real target, and then test and refine attacks prior to launching actual attacks. These testbeds greatly improve a hacker's probability of success.

Once the hacker starts the attack they will **establish a beachhead** as the initial intrusion into an infrastructure. In a military amphibious landing the initial landing and occupation of an enemy beach is the most perilous stage because the invader is committing their forces and placing them in harm's way. Similarly, in a cyber operation a hacker launches malicious actions to gain an initial foothold in the victim's infrastructure. The method to deliver malware or commands to a target is called the *Attack Vector*.

Hackers don't limit themselves to technical attacks against buggy operating systems and applications. Some hackers manipulate people to gain a foothold on a network. In these attacks a hacker is a *confidence person*. These hackers use *social engineering* to create social interactions and exploit human weaknesses and entice victims to do something the victim shouldn't. For example, a hacker may make a phone call masquerading as a help desk and ask a victim for a password.

Today the most common way to make a beachhead is to contact an individual already inside, such as an employee, and trick them into running malicious code. In a phishing attack (pronounced "fishing") a hacker emails victim's malware or a link to a '*drive-by*' webpage that contains malware. Originally hackers would send numerous legitimate-looking emails hoping a victim would read the email and either click on a link or open a malware attachment. In some instances hackers created legitimate looking websites that appear to be a trustworthy organization's site hoping to acquire legitimate user's login names, passwords, credit card information, or access to their computer. Phishing is like throwing out a net to catch something. Hackers have been successful by making email look like popular subjects including:

- Help desk or email account deactivation scams claiming an account will be deactivated if the recipient doesn't visit the website and enter their account information
- Banking or inheritance scams claiming a victim will receive or lose a large amount of money if they don't contact the sender and provide banking information
- Advance fee fraud scams or money mule scams that claim to have millions of dollars they will give victims if they provide "a small down payment"
- Fake pharmaceuticals and mortgage deals that are too good to be ignored
- Adult photos and videos containing malware to take control of a victim's computer.

A variant of this technique is called *spear phishing*. Hackers research social network sites, and company and personal web sites to gain information about a target, their interests, and people they know. Then the hacker builds a custom subject and message that appears legitimate to come from the victim's acquaintance. Often people fall for these schemes, clicking on attachments or website links that contain malware or ask for sensitive information. To the hacker it's like 'spearing' a particularly juicy fish.

Whaling refers to a hacker going after a very important person such as a politician or business executive. Spear phishing and whaling may require a hacker perform significantly more research and work than traditional phishing, but this effort may be offset by the potential payoff from compromising and exploiting a powerful or wealthy individual or organization

Since guardians watch and warn important people about hackers, a hacker may attack a less watched support person such as a secretary, human resources, or purchasing agent who often must open email attachments or visit websites to perform their jobs. These people often believe they are not important in the big picture and therefore have nothing to offer a hacker. However compromising the support person's computers establishes the 'beachhead' in the target environment and creates the initial means for conducting follow-on actions. Once on this system, the attacker can use their access to expand the attack and compromise other machines inside the victim's perimeter.

In December 2009 security researcher Thomas Ryan wanted to research simple social engineering techniques. Ryan created several fake social network accounts on sites such as Facebook, LinkedIn, and Twitter for fictitious woman *Robyn Sage*. Allegedly Ryan named Sage after the U.S. Special Forces Qualification Course exercise called Robin Sage, and obtained her provocative pictures from a pornography-related website "to attract more attention." He posted that Sage was a 25-year-old "cyber threat analyst" at the Naval Network Warfare Command in Norfolk, Virginia. She graduated from MIT and had ten years of work experience (making her fifteen when she graduated from MIT). He then used the social network sites to contact nearly 300 security, military, and intelligence government and defense contractor personnel.

Despite the fabricated profile and the obvious information discrepancies on the social network pages numerous military and intelligence employees, and defense and commercial companies offered Sage consulting work, gifts, government and corporate jobs, options to speak at a variety of security conferences, and dinner invitations. Some even asked if Sage would review security papers.

Ryan points out that Sage's profile did not fool everyone. By the second day several potential marks tried to verify Sage's identity through the phone number Ryan posted, checked email addresses outside the social networking sites, or verify her through the MIT alumni network. Others suspected Sage's fake identity based on her improbable profiles. No one announced their suspicions, and people continued to contact Sage throughout the experiment. In the 28-day experiment Ryan learned about the ease in exploiting individuals' using gender, occupation, education, credentials, and friends and their connections.[6]

And... Action

Eventually a hacker wants to achieve the goal that was the impetus for the attack. This phase is referred to as ***conducting actions on the objective.*** With the rare exception of a thrill seeker simply trying to see how far they can access a target, hackers have specific objectives to gather information, exploit systems, or disrupt activities.

On many corporate and government systems the users are given *user access* to restrict their computer to only running authorized applications and creating and saving their personal files. A system administrator typically has *administrator access* to permit them to do anything on a computer including creating new accounts, installing new programs or reading and erasing other people's files. A hacker wants administrator access so they can run any code on the victim's computers and erase evidence of their dastardly deeds. Administrator access is like obtaining the apartment manager's master key that allows the hacker to pass into any apartment in the building.[7] So one of the first steps a hacker or malware performs once it has gained access to a computer is to *elevate privileges*. This usually involves stealing logon and password credentials, accessing more important computers, file systems, and compromising administrator computers and accounts.

A hacker might install keystroke loggers, or *keyloggers*, such as an application that records everything typed on a computer keyboard. If a hacker has physical access to a computer, they could plug a keylogger device into the keyboard in a public computer in a cyber café, public library, school, hotel or office. Some keyloggers can be configured to send the collected information to an email account, or the perpetrator might return later and download the information unsuspecting users typed into the computer including passwords and credit card information. This information may help a hacker elevate their privileges.

Once a hacker has elevated their privileges, they may have complete access to machines and systems. Now the hacker may use a system's built-in commands that legitimate employees use to do their jobs to search the infrastructure for files, internal networks and resources. Hackers may use their privileged access to move to other parts of the environment to search for important information. At this point the hacker's activities look like a legitimate user's activities. The hacker has created a symbiotic relationship, not only using the owner's systems and capabilities against themselves, but also negating most of the defensive tools looking for malicious behavior. Once the hacker has achieved this situation, it may be very difficult for guardians to detect and track a hacker's activities.

An organization may not have sufficient resources to monitor and protect all their online resources. A typical and rational strategy for guardians is to determine their most important resources such as its super-secret recipes or customer contact list and protect those resources. However, it's important to remember that a hacker isn't necessarily looking for resources the victim believes is the most important, but rather the hacker is looking for the information and systems the hacker believes is most important. A hacker may want computers to control so they can launch attacks against another target. Here the hacker may bypass a corporation's security protecting their most important resources, and compromise and use their "least important" resources.

Once a hacker has invested so much effort into obtaining access to a target's infrastructure they want to maintain their access. A hacker may use their privileged access to install *backdoors* that allow the hacker to reconnect to the victim. Hacker may create rogue accounts that allow the hacker to log back into the victim's infrastructure or install software on a victim's computer allowing the hacker to bypass security and reconnect to the victim in the future. They may install *beacons* that call out from the compromised computer to a computer controlled by the hacker, which allows the hacker to bypass security and reenter the victim's computer at any time. A hacker may install numerous backdoors and beacons to ensure if a guardian discovers and removes one backdoor or beacon the others remain and allow the attacker to maintain *persistence* on the defender's infrastructure.

At this point the hacker will execute actions to achieve their initial objectives, such as harvesting information, installing software or damaging victim's systems, and are discussed later.

After an attack the hacker may want to eliminate any evidence of their activities by *sanitizing* their victim's system. A hacker may erase computer logs and their malware to hide evidence the hacker had been there. If the hacker believed guardians have detected them, they could erase or damage the victim's entire systems to cover their tracks and delay investigations.

Attackers are free to combine the processes and effects in any order against multiple victims to obtain their objectives. For example, an attacker could compromise a machine, harvest useful information from it, then use the compromised machine as a hop-off point to compromise other machines. When the attacker believes they are detected they can "burn" the infrastructure to hinder investigations by erasing victim's computers.

Today sophisticated hackers have developed automated suites to perform many tasks. These suites may generate infrastructures and run attacks at the lightning speed of the computer. One advantage of this automation is it allows the attacker to monitor their infrastructure. When the hacker suspects a victim has discovered their activities the hacker's system automatically closes up shop and moves everything to other sites, foiling their victim's investigations.

SKRAM

A perpetrator's ability and willingness to perform an operation is based on their knowledge, resources, access, and motives. These enable and constrain the actions a hacker can perform. In the case of national survival, a nation may be willing and able to bring tremendous resources to bear on a problem. The

[8] A hacker that doesn't have these resources may have to change the means to achieve the goal, change the end goal, or outsource the project.

The easiest way to outsource a hack may be to buy hacker abilities. Government presentations often label threats based on a group's perceived abilities. These government presentations often label nations as 'sophisticated' and terrorist groups as 'not possessing the sophistication to conduct cyber operations.' These presentations fail to note that terrorist groups may buy or coerce sophisticated hackers to get cyber capabilities, and use third-person *cutouts* and anonymous communications to dupe hackers from realizing who is really sponsoring their activities.

Less sophisticated *crackers* or *script kiddies* make up for their lack of technical knowledge by collecting and reusing resources developed by sophisticated hackers. Thomas Wadlow uses the metaphor of wasps to generalize about cracker's behavior. Wadlow notes that crackers look for an easy way into a system. They are difficult and expensive to remove once in. Since crackers may have time on their hands, attacking them can be foolish and dangerous, and ignoring them may prevent legitimate users from using legitimate resources.[9] These crackers also perform a useful service for sophisticated hackers. Cracker's activities are often obvious and allow sophisticated attackers to hide in the cracker's noise.

There are numerous *hacker undergrounds* where hackers and crackers give away, trade, and sell knowledge of vulnerabilities, malware and other useful applications like fuzzers, and malware development suites. A simple Google search will provide sites where hackers openly share and sell malware, vulnerabilities, tools and techniques. Access to these activities and tools is often free to those interested. However, not all hackers are so magnanimous and carelessly searching through hacker sites may get the curious infected. Also, carelessly searching through hacker sites may cause the curious to come to the interest of law enforcement or intelligence agencies. These agencies lurk on hacker sites looking for evidence of nefarious undertakings, the latest attack tools or vulnerabilities, and targets or victims that the hackers may be discussing.

While understanding technology goes a long way in understanding hacker's methods, hackers also study people.

Advanced Persistent Threats

Many guardians do an admirable job defending their networks. These guardians operate security programs that are effective protecting against the vast majority of hackers and malware. However, these same programs may provide a false sense of security against sophisticated and resourced criminals, nation states, or amateurs. These hackers may find, purchase, or create new or slightly modified attacks that guardians have not previously detected and incorporated into their existing defenses. A 2010 Verizon/US Secret Service report found that 54% of the malware used in successful intrusions were either modified or custom-built malware.[10] These new attacks defeat the Retrospective Analysis Cycle and the vast majority of security controls that rely on this cycle. Once hackers use these attacks and have a foothold on their victim's networks they often can stay undetected for weeks, months, or years harvesting information from the networks.

The security community created the term *Advanced Persistent Threat*, or APT for sophisticated hackers that establish a stealthy and continuous presence on a victim's network, and to differentiate these attackers from "common" hackers.

The Antagonists

The APT label caught on with the news media, which began labeling hackers targeting public and private organizations for political or economic motives.

Spending more money or hiring more guardians will not prevent every APT attack. General Keith Alexander, then Director of the NSA and responsible for the defense of the U.S. military networks, repeatedly stated he could not prevent hackers from penetrating and harvesting information off government networks even with all the resources of the NSA.[11] And he should know about the abilities of APTs — as the Director of the NSA he managed America's APTs against other nations, transnational criminals, and terrorists.[12,13]

The National Institute of Science and Technology, a U.S. government think-tank responsible for advancing the nation's measurement sciences, standards, and technology has stated that APT's "require a major change in strategic thinking to understand that this class of threat cannot always be kept outside of the defensive perimeter of an organization. Rather, this is a threat that is all likelihood, has achieved a foothold within the organization."[14]

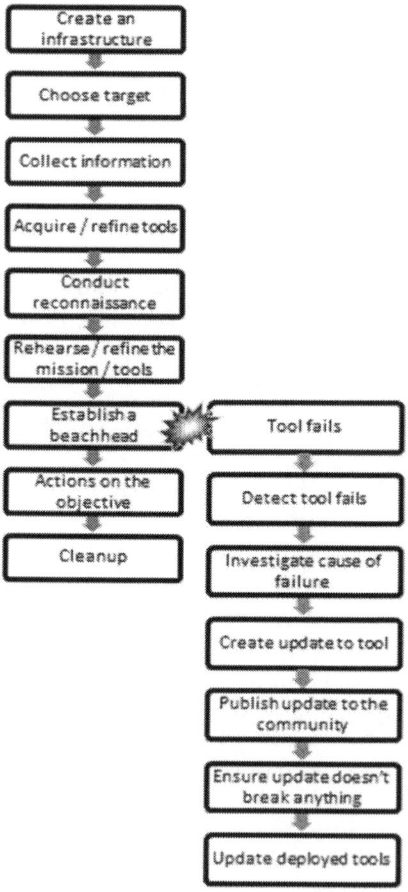

APTs have been very successful at penetrating sensitive government and corporate networks. However, Professor Dan Guido of NYU

Figure 8 - Comparison of a Hacker's and a Guardian's Processes

Polytechnic School of Engineering found that the vast majority of APTs use exploits developed by guardians and researchers and not nation states. As a security researcher who has developed exploits, his research concluded that an undergraduate computer science student with 40 hours of training could create most exploits used by APT hackers. To paraphrase Professor Guido, exploiting today's systems and the security controls protecting them requires a slight modification to existing methods that undergraduate computer students possess.[15]

This should not be construed as saying that APT hackers are not capable of possessing and using sophisticated hacking tools and techniques. The tools a hacker uses don't differentiate APT hackers from other hackers. Their *tradecraft*, or the techniques and activities to employ the tools, differentiates APT hackers.

They desire to maintain a hidden presence on their victim's network. An APT hacker will only use the sophistication necessary to accomplish the task they desire, and may try increasingly sophisticated tools until they are successful. If they use sophisticated tools to gain access to their victim's networks, they may ratchet back and use less sophisticated tools on their victim's networks. The bottom line is that guardians may not determine from the analysis of a tool if they are dealing with an amateur hacker, or a nation-state APT hacker.

Conclusion

When we compare the hacker's process against the guardian's process we see how the guardians are forced to react to hackers. Hackers are free to research and develop their systems and processes and then attack at the time and place of their choosing. Using only technical cyber analysis guardians must accept the first attacks and then develop defenses to protect themselves and others from this attack, while repairing any damage and continuing to operate in the face of certain future attacks.

For a guardian to get ahead of the hackers they need to move up the Hacker Attack Process (Figure 8) and attack the hacker's processes and infrastructure. This transforms the problem from a technical challenge to a counter-intelligence, intelligence, and law-enforcement challenge. We will see later how this creates technical, policy, and legal issues.

Now we have a basic understanding. Let's look at some more challenges and tactics in cyber conflict.

The Antagonists

Chapter 6. Battle in the Shadows

"A fool thinks himself to be wise,
but a wise man knows himself to be a fool."

- William Shakespeare

Looking Glass

In 2012 a government spy invited me to a presentation in one of the many *Intelligence Community* (IC) facilities located around the Washington DC beltway. When I arrived I took my seat at the back of the room. For the next hour an animated intelligence analyst explained to the audience how it had taken eighteen months, but they had finally identified foreign perpetrators responsible for penetrating hundreds of computers on Department of Defense networks. It was a source of pride.

He explained how numerous agencies within the IC had cooperated to identify this culprit located in a foreign country. The IC had kept Department of Defense guardians in the dark about the perpetrator's activities so they didn't react and inadvertently alert the culprit that they had been detected. Should this occur the perpetrator might shut down their operations, change their methods and tools to prevent future detection, and move on to other targets. This would have shut down the intelligence analyst's ability to watch and track the hacker back to his den. The intelligence sleuth explained that they had learned how the hacker operated and the tools he used. And they had discovered the name of the hacker. They even showed photographs of the hacker's girlfriend collected from the hacker's social websites.

I raised my hand.

"Now what?" I said.

There was stunned silence as heads swiveled around to stare at me.

I pointed out that we had left government networks open for eighteen months to track the adversary while sacrificing more of our data to the hacker, and spending manpower and resources to identify a perpetrator who likely had already abandoned his perch in an Internet café and moved on. Even if we could identify him the IC wasn't about to provide the hacker's government with the evidence they had just shown me so his countrymen could arrest him. Providing this intelligence to the hacker's country would be giving away our surveillance techniques. Due the government classification of the briefing most

Battle in the Shadows

U.S. government employees wouldn't be allowed to know the information the spook had just shared. And based on the hacker's success against the Department of Defense, if his native country didn't employ the perpetrators before the incident they would certainly provide him with a job if we tipped our hand. The perpetrator was in effect, protected by their country and ours.

The analyst fumbled with an answer, stating he didn't get to decide what others did with the information he had just shared with the audience.

The result was another report to the White House, awards for those who had participated, and the continued sacrifice of our information and the warfighters who rely on this information. The perpetrator was never apprehended and continues practicing his craft.

Chasing Ghosts and Tracking Shadows

The ability to hide a perpetrator's activities and identity is both a blessing and a curse of cyberspace. Hackers rarely perform *overt* actions where the victim can detect the activity and identify the perpetrators. Many hackers desire *clandestine* operations that hide their activities and by default the identity of the perpetrators. However, nearly all malicious activities are eventually detected. Thus hackers most often perform *covert* operations where the victim may eventually identify the activity but not identify the perpetrators.

Prosecuting attackers requires knowing who to hold responsible, a concept known as *attribution*. When a computer is hacked, guardians try to unmask the identity of the person responsible, and track them online to find where they are located. When hackers release a new worm or botnet the authorities try to identify those responsible for creating and releasing them into cyberspace.

The government has used tremendous human and financial resources to develop strategies and tools to find and track people online. Senior government leaders believe having the ability to identify those responsible for malicious acts and holding them accountable will deter others from taking part in these "nefarious" activities.

But it doesn't always work that way.

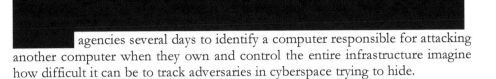

agencies several days to identify a computer responsible for attacking another computer when they own and control the entire infrastructure imagine how difficult it can be to track adversaries in cyberspace trying to hide.

Being Your Worst Enemy

Movies and television shows depict a police detective, hacker, or spy finding a computer's IP address and then knowing definitively the name and location of the person at the address. However, every computer does not have its own unique IP address, and knowing an IP address does not identify a computer's user. These two facts result from choices we made in building our networks.

The original DARPA ARPANet research assumed every researcher could trust every other researcher on the network. The resulting protocols permit anyone to use any IP address, email address, or content in a message. People can place false source addresses in messages to fool victims into misunderstanding the source of one or a billion messages. From these early beginnings the ability to identify and track individuals responsible for actions in cyberspace only got more complicated.

Many networks unintentionally complicate attribution by using technology such as network address translation (NAT). NAT is a management tool that changes a message's sender and receiver IP address as traffic leaves and returns to a network. Most home networks use NAT, assigning one public IP address to the home and other addresses to each machine connected to the network. Messages from the computers appear to someone outside the network to come from the single IP address associated with that home. Since all the traffic leaving the network has the NAT router's IP address it's difficult for someone outside a NAT network to determine which machine originated an attack — mom's iPad, dad's desktop, the kid's game console, or a neighbor that connected into the home wireless network.

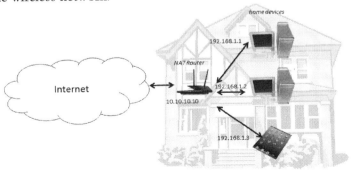

Figure 9 - Network Address Translation

Battle in the Shadows

Dynamic Host Configuration Protocol (DHCP) is another tool administrators use to assign IP addresses to devices as they connect to a network. Without DHCP every time someone wanted to connect a computer or device (like a printer) to a network they would need to assign an IP address manually to their computer. With DHCP a computer broadcasts a message asking for an IP address. The DHCP server searches for an available IP addresses from its pool of addresses and returns an IP to the requesting device, which then configures itself to become part of the network. When a device leaves the network the device's discarded IP address is added back to the pool of available IP addresses. Most service providers, broadband home networks, cyber cafes, and large public and private networks use this technique because it makes life easier by automating the management of networks. However since these technologies hide and change IP addresses they unintentionally make tracking and identifying activities in cyberspace difficult and unreliable.

Remember that two-thirds of all attacks are detected by third parties weeks to months after the hacker began their attack. By that time the hacker may have disconnected from their network and returned the IP address to the pool of available addresses and reassigned it to others. Many home and organization networks are not configured to maintain logs of IP address assignments, don't log sufficient information to identify a hacker, or delete the logs after a very short period.

This leads to a fundamental paradox of cyber conflict. The technology we use to make life easier also enables attackers to hide in cyberspace.

I See You

In 1999 the French mathematician and engineer Cyril Houri, created InfoSplit to find the geographic location of IP addresses. *Geolocation* services combine the information a client's computer provides with information from the client's Internet service provider, public network information sources, and their databases to estimate the physical location of a machine. This location is usually a latitude and longitude that can be plotted on a map. Today companies like Quova, that purchased InfoSplit in 2004, provide geolocation to a variety of customers.

In 2000, the French government brought criminal charges against the Internet search engine Yahoo for allowing the sale of Nazi memorabilia on its online auction. This case introduced geolocation as a means to filter content based on the estimated physical location of the requestor to comply with local laws, regulations, and customs.

In the United States banks and credit card companies use geolocation to comply with the Internet Gambling Enforcement Act of 2006 that restricts the use of payment systems for gambling. Vendors use Geolocation to deny online access to live sports events for IP addresses in the home cities of sports teams to increase game attendance by those living near the stadium.

Retailers use geolocation to customize a client's online experience by providing custom advertisements based on the customer's location. A person in

Virginia who requests football scores may receive National Football League scores while a person in London may receive Union of European Football Associations scores. Geolocation can make life easier by delivering advice based on the projected local weather or save lives by providing timely warnings of impending storms or natural disasters.

Vendors and financial institutions use geolocation technology to prevent Internet crime. A vendor or financial institution can calculate the distance from the shipping address to the IP address of the computer requesting a transaction. If the distance exceeds a company threshold, then the institution can require additional information before approving the sale. Vendors can also reduce losses by restricting sales to IP addresses in locations having historically sponsored cybercrime such as regions of Nigeria and Romania.

Organizations can use geolocation to deny access to online accounts and subscriptions. Libraries can use geolocation to deny access to library resources from outside a tax-paying county. Retailers can enforce Digital Rights Management (DRM) by restricting online sales of movies and ebooks based on the requestor's location. Let's say a publisher allows bookstores to sell a new book beginning at midnight locally. Online booksellers could have a rolling sale that started in Kiribati, better known as Christmas Island in the South Pacific, and rolling west to permit buyers to purchase the book as their region strikes midnight.

Geolocation companies claim their technology maintains privacy since they can only get within 20-50 miles of a client's real location based on the client's Internet address. Finding someone who is trying to hide is another story.

Hiding in Plain Sight

Geolocation has been around for years, and so has means to defeat the technology. Geolocation works by making informed guesses about an IP address. The obvious way to avoid being tracked is to come from another computer.

The plethora of open and insecure wireless access points is a good place to start. Many public homes, offices, cafes, restaurants, schools, libraries, and airports offer free and anonymous access to the Internet. These locations are mini service providers that don't require real identity information to use them nor maintain logs of their customer's activities. These offer the perfect place to begin an operation.

Hackers may further obfuscate their location and identity through *proxy servers* — computers that act like mirrors to bounce messages and responses. A user (or hacker) sends a message to a destination through a computer running proxy software. The *proxy* strips off and records the sender's address and forwards the message to the destination using the proxy's return address. From the destination's perspective the message came from the proxy, not the source, and responds to the proxy. The proxy takes this response, strips off its address, and forwards the message to the original requestor.

Battle in the Shadows

There are hundreds of free proxies around the world that hackers can use to fool recipients into providing geographically restricted content. Proxy servers are also useful for employees to bypass employer's online web-surfing restriction, dissidents to bypass government monitoring or blocks, and to hinder investigations.

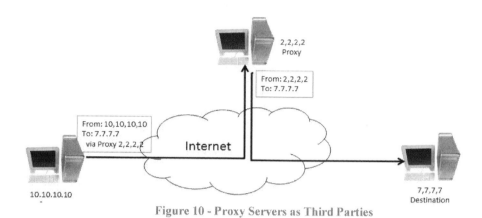

Figure 10 - Proxy Servers as Third Parties

Proxies are not foolproof. Often proxy servers do not conceal the content of messages, allowing people to read the messages that traverse a proxy. Also, hackers may not know who operates the proxy server, or if a government or ISP is monitoring the proxy server and recording the proxy's activities and can link the source and destination communications.

Also helping hackers are the hundreds (if not thousands) of companies around the world that provide Internet access, web hosting, email hosting, cloud hosting, social networking, and other services. Most of these services offer virtual anonymity by allowing people to establish email addresses, websites, social networking accounts, and chat accounts without validating their identity. These companies carry with them unique philosophies about participation in anonymity within the Internet. Additionally they may also carry similar cultural beliefs and attitudes shared with the central government of the country in which they reside. Because of their beliefs they may aggressively combat efforts to determine the identity of their customers, thus inadvertently providing hackers with an ally against law enforcement and guardians. Others may, through patriotism or coercion, actively assist governments to identify and track their customer's activities.

Other services deliberately help individuals anonymously traverse the Internet. A prime example is *The Onion Router* or *TOR*. TOR uses the U.S. Navy patented onion routing protocol and a large group of volunteer machines across the world to enable anonymous communications across the Internet. TOR hides the origin and destination addresses of traffic that traverses it, allowing its users to visit websites, post information about repressive regimes, and share music files. Hackers also leverage tools like TOR to hide their activities from detection and backtracking.

TOR eliminates a problem with proxy servers. If a hacker repeatedly sends messages using the same proxy then investigators could record all the messages arriving and departing the proxy to identify the hacker. TOR consists of thousands of computers worldwide. When a hacker sends traffic into the TOR system, TOR repeatedly wraps the message and the source and destination addresses in layers of encryption, where each layer of encryption is like the layers of an onion. A TOR machine sends a encrypted message to another random TOR machine around the world. That machine strips off a single layer of encryption and forwards the message to another TOR machine. Eventually as the message is repeatedly stripped of encryption layers and forwarded to seemingly random machines across the world the last layer of encryption is taken off and the unencrypted message is sent out of the TOR network to its destination. Thus when a hacker sends multiple messages using TOR each exits the TOR network from different machines greatly complicating tracking the sender.

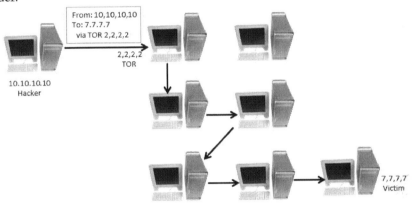

Figure 11 - The Onion Routing

Hacker can also compromise computers around the globe and use these as intermediary "hop off" points to attack other systems, or "drop off" point to store the attack tools and information they harvest from other's computers. These "cutouts" act as intermediaries between the hackers and their victims.

Hackers create cutouts by compromising and installing software on machines that provide the hacker with control over the machine. The hacker's software may turn off security and monitoring tools on the compromised machine, configure the computer to listen for and execute instructions from the hacker, and cause it to act as the hacker's digital slave or zombie. Today hackers sell access to these compromised computers to other hackers, creating a black market of unwitting and on-demand slave computers.

Similar to a proxy, a hacker sends traffic from the hacker's machine to the cutout where the hacker's software strips off the hacker's address and attaches the cutouts address. The cutout then forwards the traffic to the victim with the cutout's return address. The victim only sees the address of the cutout not the

Battle in the Shadows

hacker. Similarly, any response from a victim will go to the cutout and have the cutout's address, not the final destination of the hacker.

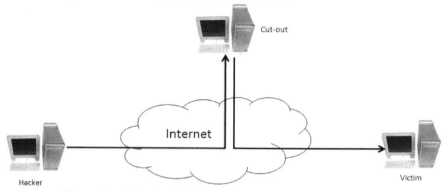

Figure 12 - A Hacker Using a Cutout to Attack a Victim

Cutouts provide a hacker with greater anonymity in their attacks since most organizations can only trace a hacker back to the last machine before their system. A victim could ask the owner of the cutout to investigate an incident, or hack into the cutout itself to determine those responsible for an attack. A victim could ask the cutout's Internet Service Provider to provide information on whom a particular machine is communicating, which they most likely will not consider without a warrant from a law enforcement agency. However, if the victim uses NAT the cutouts traffic may be lost in the noise of the other machines in the network.

The more sophisticated the hacker, the more likely they are to use multiple hop-points when conducting malicious activity. Multiple hop-points allow hackers to achieve a high level of anonymity, since the attacker can layer multiple anonymity and deception services. The apparent Chinese government sponsored attacks on international public and private organizations are noted to use numerous cutouts to bypass guardians looking for Chinese activities.

Enemy of my Enemy...

Hackers have learned to exploit the presence and absence of legal agreements between nations for their benefit. Tracing the source of an attack may require investigators to ask the owner or the owner's government for information from machines taking part in a cyber incident. These systems fall under the local legal framework that may be non-cooperative or hostile to U.S. goals, and may openly deny assistance to U.S. investigations into an attack.

Likewise U.S. law enforcement agencies such as the United States Secret Service and the Federal Bureau of Investigation are more likely to receive requests for assistance from countries such as Canada and the United Kingdom than Iran or Venezuela. Hackers can leverage this international tension and use hostile nations as hop-points to help establish and maintain their anonymity.

Equally frustrating to guardians are indifferent nations that either lack the resources or choose not to apply resources to aid in cyber-attack investigations.

This indifference may result from the lack of effective laws that adequately identify cyber activities as crime, the lack of the requisite skills or capacity, or the lack of desire to investigate compromised systems that may only a hop-point of an attack. Today we often see this indifference in third world and developing countries.

Let's be honest. An information-based society may be more interested in helping others with cyber investigations if there is a possibility of reciprocating when they find themselves the victim. A developing nation may be less inclined to dedicate limited resources to help industrial or information-based nations investigate cybercrimes that do not affect them directly.

Everyone, including hackers, must send their traffic through an ISP, and many ISPs inadvertently contribute to the malicious activity occurring in cyberspace. ISPs get paid for providing a connection between a customer's computer and the Internet. Some ISPs filter malicious traffic heading to their customers from the Internet because this incoming malicious traffic may impact their customers.

A hacker's malicious traffic has to leave the hacker's computer and cross an ISP on its way to the Internet. An ISP doesn't benefit from using its limited resources to monitor and remove potential malicious traffic *leaving* their network, known as *egress filtering*. When ISPs filter traffic leaving their networks they risk accidentally filtering legitimate traffic and impacting their customers. This potential for negative impacts with no direct benefits explains why most ISPs don't remove suspicious traffic leaving a customer's network.

Hackers use numerous techniques to exploit this decision. The first is by attaching false information in their messages, called *spoofing*, to lie about the source of messages and to further confuse attribution. A recipient of a spoofed message will see the hacker's traffic coming from the false address the hacker places in the traffic.

Researchers refer to a situation where individuals each make choices that make themselves better, but worst for everyone a *Tragedy of the Commons*. An ISP may not believe it rational to consume resources filtering outgoing malicious traffic that doesn't improve their customer's experience, but reduces malicious activities to others. However, cyberspace would be a little better for everyone if every ISP filtered malicious traffic *leaving* their network.

Scurrying out of the Light

Hackers know guardians may eventually discover their activities, and smart hackers plan for the day when they are discovered.

Malware developers obscure how malware functions to hide the perpetrator's identity from prosecution, hide the vulnerability that the malware uses, prevent the victims from understanding the goals of the malware, and maintain the perpetrator's access to the victim's networks.

A hacker can further aid in hiding the source of an attack by deliberately planting false information within malware. Analysts speak of planting false information to manipulate a perpetrator's identity as *false flags operations*. Since cyberspace is composed of digital information, hackers can deliberately embed false information in malware, tools, commands, and other evidence investigators will find.

Typically a system user will configure their browsers to their native language. Since browsers share this information with servers, guardians see the language their visitors prefer. Hackers can browse victim's sites with their browsers set to another language than their native language to deceive analysts as to the hacker's native language, and their nationality. Likewise hackers can embed phrases and foreign language in malware to throw off investigations, such as phrases from the Qur'an, or Chinese language commands in attack tools. Smart analysts know they can rarely trust the information they discover in investigations.

In 2010 the Iranian government reported malware had infected the control systems of their uranium enrichment centrifuges. These centrifuges rapidly spin as they separate and refine uranium. Apparently malware that later became known as Stuxnet caused the centrifuges to spin apart while reporting everything was running normally. The result was to damage and delay Iranian nuclear research efforts for years.

The news media quickly reported Stuxnet was a joint U.S.-Israeli campaign. Cyber investigators claimed the malware was very sophisticated and "that only a nation state could have developed this code."[1] One investigator found an obscure Hebrew word buried deep within Stuxnet that they claim is a biblical reference, and a date that pertained to Persia.[2] The researcher claimed the reference was proof the Israeli government was involved in developing Stuxnet and targeting Iran.

The news media and cyber experts followed these clues to the natural conclusion: (1) Stuxnet was sophisticated; (2) The U.S. and Israel have sophisticated cyber warfare programs; (3) The U.S. and Israel had an incentive to damage the Iranian nuclear weapons program; (4) Therefore the U.S. and Israel must have collaborated on building and deploying Stuxnet. Perhaps people saw what they wanted, and not reality?

According to these analysts sophisticated nations developed Stuxnet, but forgot guardians eventually discover and analyze cyber weapons. According to these analysts, these sophisticated hackers deliberately placed code within their weapon to implicate them.

Despite numerous reports that alleged the U.S. or Israel built the Stuxnet worm to target Iranian uranium enrichment facilities, the worm contained no evidence of either the developer or actual target. The news media used supposition and insinuation with little supporting evidence. In fact, the media had no evidence that the worm ever infected the Iranian facility. The only facts Stuxnet damaged the Iranian facility were official statements from Iran, whose leadership is legendary for their secrecy, rhetoric and deception and are often discounted by the West.[3] Yet we believe Iranian government statements when they speak about an attack against one of their most sensitive and secret research programs that they believe is critical to their survival?

An alternative theory is that Iran fabricated the entire Stuxnet incident. Iranians may have created Stuxnet as a ruse to cause the international community to see them as a victim. Stuxnet could also be an attempt to deceive the West into believing the malware damaged and delayed the Iranian nuclear research program when in reality the program continues unimpeded.

Soon after announcements of Stuxnet the U.S. government blamed Iranian sponsored hackers for several cyberattacks against U.S. financial institutions. Experts said these attacks were in retaliation for Stuxnet. Perhaps Tehran fabricated Stuxnet to deceive the West as to their nuclear weapons research and justify cyberattacks against the west? Perhaps none of these theories are true, and a third party is manipulating both Iran and the U.S. for their own goals?

A theory is that China is responsible for Stuxnet. China has stated that they want to prevent their third largest supplier of oil from obtaining nuclear weapons.[4] However China doesn't want to impede the flow of petroleum. Since China designed the Iranian facility and built much of the facilities' technology, poisoning the Iranian systems was trivial for Beijing. China may have infected the Iranian facility and left evidence in the worm to implicate Israel and the U.S. for the attack.

The news media and analysts may not have the entire story wrong. The point is that there was no real evidence it occurred or the U.S. or Israel were responsibly. The evidence was based on malware analysis, anonymous reports, opinions, and speculation. And everything in cyberspace can be fabricated.

Tool for the Defense

Faced with the difficulty in tracking and identifying hackers our guardians, law enforcement agencies, and intelligence agencies also use deception. Guardians create fake data or systems, called *honeypots,* which appear as legitimate data or systems to bait hackers and learn about their tools and techniques. Similarly, guardian can configure computers to respond differently to apparent hacker probes to confuse and delay attackers.

Guardians can also embed *beacons* into files that call home when a hacker copies and accesses the files. A beacon collects and reports information about the perpetrator who opened the file, including their location.

Guardians may embed *watermarks* in documents, which are unique sets of characters or images hidden in sensitive files. Guardians then establish digital sentries on networks that examine the traffic leaving the guardian's networks. The sentries alert guardians to possible mischief when they observe the unique watermark leaving the network.

Guardians may also place "tripwires" on sensitive data. These tripwires automatically alert when anyone tries to access this data. The Internal Revenue Service (IRS) uses a version of tripwires on high profile citizen tax accounts, such as politicians and celebrities. The tripwires alert IRS officials if an IRS employee, or a hacker, accesses any of the "flagged" accounts.

Battle in the Shadows

Guardians can place taps on devices and networks that enable them to record everything that occurs on a network creating a network version of a data flight recorder. While a skilled hacker can delete system logs to hide their activities these data recorders register all network traffic without hackers seeing the information is being recorded, and captures the hacker's tools and techniques for analysis.

Often bureaucrats talk of attribution as a single concept. However, there are many forms of attribution, and the type needed depends on what the analyst intends to do with the results and the potential consequences if they get the identity of the perpetrator wrong.

A guardian may only care that some hacker penetrated their system so they know to clean the perpetrator out of the system. A U.S. intelligence agency may initially only want to know if a hacker is outside the continental United States so they can apply many other intelligence resources to the attribution problem, since they may be forbidden from investigating domestic issues. An analyst may want to gain a long-term understanding of a hacker to determine their intent and to prevent future compromises. The White House may want to know the government responsible and the long-term goal of a foreign cyber campaign.

When an incident occurs leaders are quick to demand investigators identify those responsible and their intent. However, an investigation to identify those responsible for a series of incidents may require many steps, which include:

1. Identify that a suspicious event occurred
2. Determine the suspicious event was a malicious attack
3. Identify the location of the last hop in an attack
4. Identify the tools and techniques used in an attack
5. Determine the capability of the tool and technique
6. Determine what the hacker or malware performed
7. Determine the source of the attack
8. Identify the individual who launched the attack
9. Identify the responsible party that developed the hacker's tools
10. Identify the impact of a campaign of attacks
11. Identify the individual responsible or sponsor of a campaign
12. Identify the intended strategic goals of a campaign

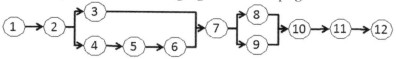

Figure 13 - An Example of a Successful Attribution Graph

As an analyst discovers more information about an attack, they may combine the information into an Attribution Graph (Figure 13). Identifying those responsible for a series of incidents and their intended goals occurs at the end of the attribution graph, if at all. Sophisticated hackers will leave no evidence as to their identity. Furthermore, a mistake at any place in the attribution graph, either through error, false assumption, or a hacker's deception may cause all future conclusions in the graph to be false.

When a cyber incident occurs the victim may want to know what the perpetrator was intending to accomplish. Since hacker's tools and techniques are very common, it may be impossible to determine if the intent was criminal, curiosity, intelligence collection, or preparation for a destructive attack. Determining intent may require identifying the perpetrator, and skilled perpetrators are rarely identified. This undoubtedly leads to speculation, such as occurred in Solar Sunrise, Stuxnet, and the 2014 Sony hacking incident.

Loose Lips Sink (Digital) Ships

Officials often identify hackers in the same way they identify criminals and spies: through a hacker's arrogance, ignorance, laziness, and bureaucracies. Many hackers appear self-absorbed in technology, yet intellectually arrogant in their trade. They often forget there may be someone (or a team of investigators) who is just a little better skilled or resourced then themselves.

The perpetrators of many high-profile incidents, from the 1988 Morris worm, Solar Sunrise, and 2010 WikiLeaks incident were only caught because they launched attacks from homes or schools, or bragged to friends. This arrogance and ignorance has led to the downfall of many amateurs.

When a hacker gets lazy, like attacking repeatedly from their home, they shouldn't be surprised when law enforcement officials visit them. Or when they hack from a wireless network and then check email from the same computer not realizing the activity was recorded and aided in identifying the hacker. Or a hacker keeps the computer used to perform a criminal act, only to have law enforcement analysts recover all the data they thought they erased.

Public and private bureaucracies create trails that analysts and investigators can follow. Discussions regarding cyber operations, government contracts and email provide terrific sources of intelligence. In January 2015 the U.S. government reported that U.S. intelligence agencies collected internal communications between North Korea government leaders that convinced U.S. government leaders of North Korea's guilt in the 2014 Sony Entertainment hack.

Conclusion

Analysts work towards attributing hacker's activities while hackers work to evade the analysts. Automated tools that aid investigators search and analyze evidence have improved in the past ten years. However hackers also have automation on their side to hinder investigations. The result is that investigators often must search for evidence of hackers in a digital cat-and-mouse chase. Hiding the source of an attack, erasing logs, deploying self-erasing programs, obfuscating how malware operates, and using encryption to encode their programs and communications delays detection and hinders investigations, helping hackers protect their identity and increase the probability of achieving their objective. IP addresses and digital information in attacks is so easily manipulated as to be meaningless. The quantity of attacks we see today, sophistication of the attacks, and the size of storage media that analysts must examine results in cyberattacks occurring within milliseconds, but attribution taking weeks and months often without ever reaching a definitive conclusion.

Attribution is a battle of wits between the hackers and the guardians. Attribution may be trivial against average individuals in cyberspace, but impossible against informed and careful hackers. Many high-profile investigations have gone decades without definitive attribution and most will never be attributed. There's a saying in the hacker community, "Everyone knows the good hackers but no one knows the great ones."

Even the Director of National Intelligence admits that cyberattacks can be "deniable and unattributable."[5] Nations may spend their time identifying hackers that lack the ability to engage in cyber warfare using techniques that don't work against skilled adversaries. This lack of attribution has stimulated malicious cyber activities and cybercrime.

Chapter 7. Geeks in the Wire

"By discovering the enemy's dispositions and remaining invisible ourselves, we can keep our forces concentrated, while the enemy's must be divided."
- Sun Tzu
The Art of War

"The price of freedom is eternal vigilance."
- Thomas Jefferson (1743 - 1826)
3rd President of the United States

"We can read anything – we can't read everything."
- Unofficial Mantra of the National Security Agency

The Digital Gold Rush

During the bloody First World War the Germans became experts at intercepting their opponent's messages and deciphering their important military and government secrets. In the after-war years the German government knew they needed to find a better way to keep their own messages secret. In 1926 the German military adopted the Enigma machine to do just that, and by the outbreak of the Second World War the German government was using *Enigma* to protect their secrets. The Enigma machine looked like a typewriter with a set of letter keys and a set of lettered lights above the keyboard. An operator would set wired wheels called rotors to a daily setting known only by himself and the intended receiver. Pressing a letter key would cause a bulb under another letter to light and display the secret encoding of the pressed key. After a key is pressed one or more rotors would turn changing the code and causing repeated letters to have different coded results. The Enigma enabled an operator to convert a message into what appeared to be a meaningless list of random characters that they could transmit to its destination without eavesdroppers understanding the content of the message. The receiver would set their Enigma device rotors to the same initial settings and type the apparent random letters they received into their machine and read the original message.

German leaders believed breaking an Enigma encoded message without knowing the correct code would require trying nearly all the 150,000,000,000, 000,000,000 possible combinations the Enigma could produce and breaking only one message would take the Allies four million years if the Allies applied

100,000 people trying a different combination every second without sleeping or eating. The Germans believed messages encoded by Enigma were unbreakable and trusted transmitting their most secret messages using the Enigma encoding.

But some within the German government were not happy with political events transpiring in Germany and in the late 1930s a disenchanted employee of the German Army Cipher Bureau sold the French a copy of the Enigma operating manual. Using information in the operating manual the French tried unsuccessfully to break the secrets of the Enigma. The French shared a copy of the manual with the Poles, and in 1932 the Poles discovered that Enigma messages were not random and from this discovery broke some coded messages by hand.

At start of the Second World War the British code breakers at the Government Code and Cyber School at Bletchley Park, the predecessors of the United Kingdom signals intelligence agency known as the Government Communications Headquarters (GCHQ) were also trying to break Enigma messages.[1] Using the Pole's results a British mathematician named Alan Turing conceived of a special purpose electronic computer called the bombe that could mechanically break Enigma encoded messages in hours.[2] GCHQ built numerous bombe computers that allowed the Allies to read up to 3,000 German military and diplomatic messages daily.[3]

Historians credit the Allied breaking of the German codes as one of the single most important contributions to defeating the Germans and ending World War II. Breaking Enigma-encoded messages allowed the Allies to learn German secrets during the Battle of Britain and confirm the German's were not prepared for the Allied invasion of Europe. The most significant contribution may have been intercepting the German U-boat submarine communications that allowed the Allies to move their convoys away from the German U-boats and to direct warships and aircraft to intercept and sink the U-boats that had the potential to starve the besieged British.

While highly successful the bombe was a special purpose computer that could only break the Enigma code. This special-purpose machine automated a mechanical step-by-step problem and greatly decreased the time it took the Allies to break Enigma messages. But Turing longed to build a general-purpose computer that could solve many problems. In 1943 engineer Tommy Flowers and Max Newman improved on the bombe and built a 1,500 vacuum tube code-breaking machine called *Colossus* — the world's first programmable digital computer. It's ironic the first digital programmable computer was built to enable spying.

Intelligence involves activities to collect, analyze, and disseminate information so decision makers can grasp what is occurring or about to occur and make informed decisions. The Chinese General Sun Tzu understood the power of intelligence when he wrote, "The Art of War" in the sixth century BC. Sun Tzu noted that collecting information on friends and enemies enables a leader to understand their opponent's capabilities and intentions, protect themselves, and exploit their opponent's weaknesses.[4,5]

Many organizations conduct intelligence operations under a variety of names; spies perform espionage, militaries perform reconnaissance, law enforcement officials and private investigators conduct investigations and surveillance, and businesses perform business intelligence or corporate espionage. And cyberspace has transformed intelligence operations for all.

Open Source Information

The simplest intelligence operation is analyzing readily available, public information, referred to as open source intelligence, or OSINT (pronounced "oh-sint"). Compiling information before cyberspace required researchers to search phone books, mortgage records, personal and medical histories, and purchase records. Much information, such as compiled purchase histories, didn't exist or had to be amassed manually. This was time consuming and often required individuals to obtain and search through books. In repressive regimes the information may not have been accessible, or was available at personal risk.

Thanks to cyberspace, vast repositories of public information are available today. Whether researching family trees, finding old friends, or looking for the perfect house in the perfect community access to information has changed how people live. This information has also aided intelligence operations. Today nearly anyone can access, compile, and analyze individuals and groups if they know where to look.

Only a few years ago credit card companies and banks used a person's mother's maiden name as a security question to validate a customer's identity over the phone. Today genealogy websites and online newspaper obituaries provide this information to anyone and only the most unwitting business would use this information in a security question to identify a customer.[6] Similarly, some people are careful to use unlisted phone numbers or cell phones to hide their home address. Meanwhile local or state governments post their home purchases, real-estate taxes, and mortgages on the Internet, which provide their names, home price and addresses. Total anonymity has become a myth for the average person.

The U.S. discovered in the 1980's that government contracts and budgets provided the Soviet Union with a wealth of useful information about the U.S. government and its priorities.[7] In the past discovering details of U.S. government contracts required visiting government or contractor offices or requesting information through the mail. The proliferation of cyberspace has resulted in the government revealing much more information to the public to assure the American people that the government is using public funds appropriately.[8] The federal budgets, solicitations, contracts, and program fact sheets provide competitors, the curious, and foreign intelligence agencies with tremendous information regarding government interests, research, and work on weapon systems, deployments, and information systems. Government contracts for maintenance, janitorial, and security services provide information on the inner workings of government operations, to include the location of facilities where work is performed, personnel involved, and technical details of programs. Contractor and personal web sites, blog sites, and social networks, press releases, published papers and presentations given at workshops and conferences provide more information on government interests, missions, and their inner workings.

During previous wars soldiers, sailors, and citizens were warned about careless talk regarding military missions and convoys. The phrase "Loose Lips Sink Ships" reminded Americans of the danger of careless information sharing. Today's service members send email to friends and families, post videos of operations on youtube.com and blog on planned and completed missions. Likewise, guardians responsible for managing and defending government information networks post questions on technical blogs that inadvertently reveal details about their networks and their defenses, which helps hackers break into these networks.

Connecting the Dots

A smart and resourced analyst can combine and connect information from many information sources such as email addresses, government property documents, genealogy websites, and personal websites to compile useful information about an individual or group. The analyst may build graphs to determine who talks to whom, their relationships, goals, and intent. Similarly, analysts can build graphs of topics by combining people, organizations, and terms referenced in documents to connect to other related documents.[9] People are only limited by their imagination in the use of information. And this information has fundamentally changed what we discover about people and organizations.

Online obituaries provide criminals with an automated method to search for local funerals, and the home address of the deceased and their family members. Criminals link this information with genealogy websites and government real estate and tax information to determine when family members will be at funerals, leaving their homes unattended for the criminals to raid.

South African Eric Matta mapped the Central Intelligence Agency unclassified networks and identified the names of CIA employees without touching the CIA network. He performed his work using only Internet search engines and network lookup tools.[10]

By combining restricted and commercial information – such as credit reports, medical data, police reports, tax records, flight and travel records, credit reports, credit charges and purchase histories an analyst can determine even more information on the lives, interests, and future plans of individuals and groups. And this research is making people money.

Jeff Jonas created a data mining technology called NORA, or Non-Obvious Relationships Awareness. His company Systems Research and Development (SRD), funded by the CIA and purchased by IBM in 2005, created software for casino security. NORA searches through data and combines data with other sources to find deep relationships — such as a casino employee who once shared a phone number with a casino customer winning excessively. Sharing a telephone number years ago doesn't prove there is collusion today, but it may provide interesting coincidences that may merit further investigation.[11] Jonas demonstrated that all the 9/11 terrorists could be found in three degrees of separation using this technique.

The Defense Advanced Research Projects Agency (DARPA), the Pentagon's research and development arm had a much more aggressive effort called the Total Information Awareness program, or TIA. The TIA program proposed to combine open source and classified information with advanced data mining programs to provide the government with advanced notice of possible terrorist attacks. The program was apparently cancelled after a public outcry that the government had enabled 'big brother' to spy on U.S. citizens.[12]

In 2013 Edward Snowden released information regarding NSA harvesting telephone conversation data from domestic telecommunication companies.[13] Usually we think that a phone conversation is the important component of a phone call. However, phone calls also have data about the calls, called *metadata*. A call's metadata may include the phone number of the caller and recipient; the unique serial numbers of the phones involved, the time, date, and duration of the call; and the location of the participants during the phone call. The NSA used the phone metadata to build a visual map of social groups, sometimes called their *community of interest*, in a process they named "call chaining."[14]

Government spokesman are quick to point out that the NSA was forbidden from obtaining the content of the phone calls or the name or address of the telephone customers. However, anyone can find the registered name and mailing address of a phone number using the numerous reverse phone lookups websites. The government has argued that the telecommunications records did not contain personal information and therefore there was no need to show probable cause or obtain a court warrant. However, collecting communications records allows retroactive surveillance[15] — meaning if the NSA determined someone was a "person of interest" the NSA could examine historic records to determine whom they talked in the past. In 2015 a federal appeals court declared that the NSA telephone metadata collection was illegal under the Patriot Act.

The vast majority of information is available for the asking. When individuals and organization restrict access to information, they inadvertently signal the importance of the information to others. These restricted information sources then become targets.

Sensitive Information

Historically obtaining sensitive information about governments and the private sector required careful, time consuming and expensive preparation of intelligence sources and methods. In the recent past governments locked military technology blueprints in filing cabinets, and cryptologic systems that keep communications secret in safes. Obtaining sensitive information required

Geeks in the Wire

"collectors" to burglarize facilities to steal data or technology, manipulate or "turn human assets" at considerable personal risk, or develop sophisticated collection technologies such as covert acoustic sensors ("bugs"), radio interception technology, satellites, and high altitude surveillance aircraft like the U-2 and SR-71 spy planes.

As information technology became popular researchers, developers, and operators converted their plans and technology to electronic images and computer programs stored in computers. Today the organizations that design and use these devices have connected these computers to networks shared with the adversaries these systems were designed to defeat.

The defense contractors funded by the Government to develop the F-35 Joint Strike Fighter placed the aircraft's engineering plans on computers connected to the Internet. Apparently these engineering plans provided sufficient technical information to enable foreign countries to degrade or defeat the aircraft.[16] Evidently the contractors didn't believe placing the F-35 information on a network connected to adversaries who could exploit these plans to defeat the aircraft was a bad idea. To paraphrase:

1. The Department of Defense funded the research and development of the F-35 to present a threat to adversaries; then
2. The U.S. government and their contractors advertised to the world how sophisticated the F-35 would be, and how it would represent a threat to foreign nation's security; then
3. Defense contractors allegedly placed the engineering plans on a worldwide network, providing foreign nations with indirect access to the devices storing these plans; then
4. Foreign intelligence services or their proxies penetrated these networks and took copies of the F-35 plans; then
5. U.S. Government leaders and contractors expound on how we should punish the foreign nations for trying to protect their national security by stealing the plans.

Adversaries have been harvesting information off U.S. government and defense corporation networks from thousands of miles away with little real cost or risk for three decades. In 2010 Deputy Secretary of Defense Lynn noted that over 100 foreign intelligence organizations were trying to break into U.S. and others countries' systems.[17]

According to the U.S. Air Force the Chinese alone exfiltrated 10-20 terabytes of information from U.S. government and defense industry unclassified information systems from 2002 to 2006.[18] This is equivalent in size to half of the printed Library of Congress being taken, or thirteen compact disks of information stolen every day for five years. General Cartwright, at the time the Vice-Chairman of the Joint Chiefs of Staff, noted that the information could help a foreign power identify weak points in networks, understand how U.S. leadership thinks, discover U.S. communication patterns, and prepare for attacking valuable information systems.

There is rarely a smoking gun that identifies these activities as Chinese sponsored. One assessment determined the information doesn't have direct value to criminals and based on scale and required resources "it makes sense" that this activity is state-sponsored. Even if non-state perpetrators are obtaining and selling the information to China, the state is creating the demand if not sponsoring the perpetrators, making this a state sponsored threat.[19]

Intelligence is about finding information and cyberspace is both a concentrator and conductor of information. The result has been a digital version of the gold rush for international and domestic, public and private intelligence services. However, the U.S. is not only a victim — they are a perpetrator.

No Such Agency

The NSA is the U.S. government's high-tech intelligence agency responsible for collecting *SIGINT*, or *signals intelligence*, a government euphemism for the interception of electronic messages.[20] NSA employees and contractors spend their days monitoring the radio, microwave, and cable traffic of foreign nations. Often the information is encrypted with codes, so the NSA also creates U.S. government codes and breaks foreign adversary's codes.[21]

The government established the NSA by a secret presidential memorandum in 1952. In its infancy the existence of the NSA was a secret with people in the know referring to the NSA as "No Such Agency."

The NSA maintains its secrecy because of concerns with what psychologists call the *Hawthorne Effect*, referring to a person's tendency to change their behavior if they believe they are being watched. The NSA must collect information from targets without them knowing or suspecting. If someone believes an intelligence organization might listen to their conversations, they might change how they communicate causing those listening to go deaf. Worse, if someone believes they are being overheard they could place false information into communications to manipulate the listeners.

The existence of the NSA became public in the 1970s when the Church Committee investigated intelligence abuses and the Watergate scandal and found the NSA guilty of intelligence abuses. On August 17, 1975 Senator Frank Church stated on NBC's Meet the Press:[22]

> *"In the need to develop a capacity to know what potential enemies are doing, the United States government has perfected a technological capability that enables us to monitor the messages that go through the air.... Now, that is necessary and important to the United States as we look abroad at enemies or potential enemies. We must know, at the same time, that capability at any time could be turned around on the American people, and no American would have any privacy left such is the capability to monitor everything—telephone conversations, telegrams, it doesn't matter. There would be no place to hide.*
>
> *If this government ever became a tyrant, if a dictator ever took charge in this country, the technological capacity that the Intelligence Community has given the government could enable it to impose total tyranny, and there would be no way to fight back because the most careful effort to combine together in resistance to the government, no matter how*

privately it was done, is within the reach of the government to know. Such is the capability of this technology.

I don't want to see this country ever go across the bridge. I know the capacity that is there to make tyranny total in America, and we must see to it that this agency and all agencies that possess this technology operate within the law and under proper supervision so that we never cross over that abyss. That is the abyss from which there is no return."

Without mentioning the agency Senator Church had disclosed that the U.S. had a significant message interception and listening capability, and the threat this capability could pose to the American people if it was not controlled.

The NSA uses a vast array of advanced technology to collect communication signals. These collections target broadband telecommunications used by international carriers down to individual's smart phones and home wireless access points. The NSA's army of satellites vacuum the radio waves targeting communications over hostile territory. At sea they use naval vessels and U.S. Navy EP-3 ARIES aircraft to intercept messages off foreign coasts. The intercepted signals are often transmitted to the NSA headquarters at Fort Meade, Maryland where they are processed, and reported back to customers.

Sometimes they work with allies to increase their ability to eavesdrop internationally. The pop culture and media use the term *Echelon* to refer to the SIGINT collection capabilities of the United States, Canada, United Kingdom, Australia, and New Zealand; five English speaking countries collectively referred to as *5-Eyes*.[23] The 5-Eyes cooperate to install and operate large land-based "terrestrial" interception stations that listen across borders, and analyze and interpret the resulting intelligence. Echelon is alleged to have monitored military and diplomatic traffic of the Soviet Union and Soviet Pact countries, and now to support modern concerns such as terrorism, drug trafficking, and diplomatic intelligence. Others nations have expressed concern over the 5-Eyes conducting industrial and economic espionage and invasion of privacy. In 1990 British and New Zealand journalists alleged that the United States was exploiting Echelon for industrial espionage, rather than military and diplomatic espionage.[24] In 1995 the Baltimore Sun alleged that Echelon vacuumed "all the faxes and phone-calls between Airbus, the Saudi national airline and the Saudi Government" resulting in the NSA reporting that officials at the European aerospace company Airbus had been bribing Saudi officials to secure a $6 billion contract. The European Parliament has recommended the citizens of its member states use encryption to protect their private communications from Echelon.[25]

In June 2014 Edward Snowden released information showing that the NSA spied on German Chancellor Angela Merkel's mobile phone communications. Germans were outraged, the Chancellor ousted ████████████████ in Berlin, and the German Federal Prosecutor Herald Range announced launching formal investigations of the allegations. While Chancellor Merkel repeatedly stated, "Spying among friends is not at all acceptable," the Germany federal intelligence service BND (Bundesnachrichtendienst) also spies on its allies including fellow

NATO members.[26] Most if not all nations keep tabs on their friends and enemies.

We need to remember the government isn't limited to collecting intelligence against foreign nations. In 1994 President Clinton signed into law the Communications Assistance for Law Enforcement Act that requires telecommunications companies and manufacturers of telecommunications equipment, internet voice-over IP digital phone systems, and broadband Internet technology to modify their equipment to ensure law enforcement agencies can conduct domestic electronic surveillance.[27]

Computer Network Exploitation

Previously the NSA had to develop and deploy *assets* to collect intelligence. Today worldwide Internet connectivity and the vulnerable devices and telecommunications systems that reside there present an unparalleled opportunity.[28] This computer espionage, or *Computer Network Exploitation*, as it's called within the U.S. government enables the NSA to "live on our adversary's networks" and harvest their information. The information is transmitted to NSA facilities where they break codes, read messages, process the resulting intelligence, and write reports for the White House, Pentagon, other government agencies, and our allies.[29] NSA senior leaders refer to themselves as the "Chief of Station of the Internet" playing on the U.S. government name for the chief intelligence official in a foreign embassy that controls all intelligence operations in that country.

Cyberspace has changed intelligence and made Sun Tzu's observations important today in ways he could never have imagined due to the potential gains and negligible risks. ███████████████████████████████████ ██████████████████████████████[30] Today intelligence organizations are challenged to sift, filter, and aggregate all the information and provide "credible, validated, and actionable intelligence" in a timely manner to decision makers.

Conservation of Data

Cyber espionage is so commonplace due to a fundamental principle of cyberspace. In the physical world, when you take something you possess it and someone else doesn't, what physicists call the conservation of mass. In cyberspace there is no conservation of information. A perpetrator can make an exact copy of data or programs and leave the original, often without leaving obvious evidence they made a copy.

When a computer sends a file, the source makes a copy of the file and sends the copy to the requestor, and the original remains in its location. The sender and receiver can make unlimited copies. Someone could also make a copy of the file along the transmission routes – from wiretaps on the fiber optic lines, interceptions on wireless access points and cell towers, and satellite uplinks/downlinks stations.

But you say, "I encrypt my files, and a hacker would have to find the sensitive files and decrypt them to make any sense of the information." Encrypting important files to keep the message's contents private unintentionally makes it easy to identify the important files. Encryption tools attempt to convert documents from their original format into what appears as random data. The more random a document appears the harder it may be for a hacker to analyze and defeat its encryption and discover its secrets. Analysts use techniques such as *entropy analysis* to measures a document's randomness. Using *entropy analysis* an analyst can search through millions of files and identify the most likely encrypted and therefore important documents and then focus on breaking them.

The Enigma story shows that governments have been using computers to break encryption since the 1940's. Mathematicians will say that modern encryption techniques are so strong they can't be broken in your lifetime. However, like all programs, encryption techniques contain vulnerabilities in the computer code that enable hackers.

Intelligence

A good cyber intelligence campaign can create tremendous paybacks. Embarrassing photos or stories can be used to blackmail or damage one's reputation such as when the hacker group Anonymous compromised the computer security firm HBGary Federal. In this incident hackers stole tens of thousands of sensitive emails and files from HBGary Federal and posted the corporate information online, severely damaged their reputation and business as a security firm.

Medical information has been used to identify the health and habits of government leaders. [31] Today this information may be accessible from the computer of the politician's doctor.

Financial information can be used for fraud, embezzlement, or identity theft. Proprietary trade secrets may provide a business advantage, and allow a competitor to duplicate or defeat a technology, from the latest Formula-1 racing automobile to a military weapon system.

A compromise of government information may damage a nation's security. A compromise of a government's intelligence information may cause the loss of their intelligence sources and methods that prevents them from understanding what is occurring in international events. Information could enable a foreign power to misrepresent the true situation and set them up for a deception campaign. Sun Tzu notes that in warfare a smart leader will use espionage activities as a precursor to an attack, to detect and identify weakness in the defenses, and to sabotage them when necessary to guarantee a successful attack. In cyberspace, once a digital spy has obtained access to a network they can sabotage information systems and plant logic bombs to degrade, disable, or destroy information and information systems on command.

Cyber spies are not restricted to reacting in cyberspace to intercepted information. Collecting information in cyberspace that allows a nation to understand the design of systems will assist an adversary to defeat the system outside of cyberspace. Whether a building design, an airport security plan or a military weapon system, downloading and understanding the design may help discover a weakness that an adversary can exploit to sabotage a facility or aircraft. Similarly, reading a target's email or travel itinerary may allow a perpetrator to discover a weakness in their plans and enable the attacker to kidnap or assassinate an individual or group.

International Espionage

Espionage is in a nether area in international legality. Nations take a more liberal definition if they are performing the espionage versus the victim of espionage. Nation's justify their espionage activities as means to verify their security rather than take the word of other nations at face value. However when they are the victims they object, often on the grounds that the perpetrators violating treaties concerning human rights and privacy and non-interference with another nation's internal affairs. Likewise, a person conducting traditional spycraft for their parent nation may be seen as a hero within their nation, but a criminal in the nation they are spying, punishable by prison, torture, or death.

The Hague Land Warfare Regulation of 1907 declared nations have a legal right to conduct espionage against other nations. Article 24 states "... measures necessary for obtaining information about the enemy and the country are considered permissible."[32]

Nations also have differenced regarding their use of intelligence. U.S. law states the Intelligence Community supports the government, not the private sector. If the Intelligence Community finds intelligence where the U.S. is at an unfair disadvantage through bribes, kickbacks, or intelligence to private companies they may advise the Department of State, Department of Commerce, or FBI so they can address the issue. Other countries, such as France, Israel, and China routinely provide intelligence collected by their national intelligence organizations to businesses.

Most nations today have national and/or regional laws regarding cybercrime, however, these differ when crossing national borders. Some nations provide a haven for cybercriminal activities. Others, such as China, prosecute domestic cybercrime as a capital offense, while being empathetic or quietly supporting international cyber conflict.

In the U.S. the Computer Fraud and Abuse Act of 1986 declared it illegal to "Knowingly accessing a computer without authorization in order to obtain national security data," and "Intentionally accessing a computer without authorization to obtain [protected information]." Protected information includes information in a financial record of a financial institution or consumer reporting agency, "Information from any department or agency of the United

States, information from any protected computer if the conduct involves an interstate or foreign communication." It also outlawed "Intentionally accessing without authorization a government computer and affecting the use of the government's operation of the computer, and knowingly accessing a protected computer with the intent to defraud and there by obtaining anything of value." The Economic Espionage Act of 1996 Title 6 outlaws exposing corporate trade secrets to benefit a foreign power or harm a domestic corporation. The National Information Infrastructure Protection Act of 1996 amends the Computer Fraud and Abuse Act. Clearly, anyone in the U.S. performing these actions is violating U.S. laws and can be prosecuted if identified and apprehended.

According to The Hague Regulation Article 29, a spy must be within the state they're collecting. Thus, an individual sitting in a neighboring country or in international airspace or waters listening to radio signals emanating from the target country is not a spy or violating international law under The Hague Regulation. However, if the radio interception is not sanctioned by the nation where it's being collected then the perpetrators may be prosecuted by that nation.

This leads to a legal paradox; conducting cyber espionage against another nation from thousands of miles away may be legal under international law and within the country where the spy lives, but may violate the victim's local laws.

This begs, what constitutes international espionage in the cyber age? Who constitutes an agent of a state in cyber espionage? An employee of an intelligence organization is clearly a spy. Is a member of the armed forces conducting information collection as part of their official duties if they are inside the target country and in uniform considered military personnel? What if they are off duty? Is a student in a communist state owned and operated college a spy or just a curious student? How about a professor teaching cyber espionage activities to their students? The international legal community has not addressed these questions, so we must wait for international law to catch up to technology.

On May 19, 2014 the Western District in Pennsylvania indicted five Chinese military hackers on charges of computer hacking, economic espionage, and other offenses directed against six American companies in the U.S. nuclear power, metals, and solar products industries. These charges allege the hackers conducted industrial espionage — calling their actions theft. This marked the first time criminal charges have been filed against known state actors for hacking. FBI Executive Assistant Director Robert Anderson emphasized, "If you are going to attack Americans—whether for criminal or national security purposes—we are going to hold you accountable. No matter what country you live in."[33]

U.S. authorities have decided they will arrest and prosecute hackers for conducting espionage. However, these five Chinese military personnel live in China when they penetrate U.S. public and private computers on behalf of their nation. The U.S. can approach the Chinese government and demand they turn over the five Chinese government employees allegedly conducting espionage against the US, but there is no reason for the Chinese to comply with this demand. The U.S. government can and has prosecuted individuals once they are within the U.S. border for aiding hackers in the theft of sensitive information.[34] The U.S. can perform *extraordinary rendition* and kidnap the suspects and forcefully extradite them to the U.S. to face prosecution under U.S. laws. In 1989 the United States invaded Panama and captured the military leader Manuel Noriega. The U.S. government transported Noriega to the U.S. as a military prisoner, tried under criminal charges, found guilty, and sentenced to prison.

[35]

It's more likely the public indictments and press releases were a political act of desperation. The Chinese government won't hand over their military personnel for actions they most likely authorized and are not against international law. However, the U.S. government has told the rest of the world it's admissible to arrest and prosecute intelligence operators. Edward Snowden's revelation the NSA was spying on other nations may place U.S. cyber intelligence hackers at risk. What happens when an employee of the NSA travels to Asia on vacation, and Chinese agents kidnap and forcefully *rendition* the employee to China, where the Chinese government charges them with espionage against the state?

Conclusion

The rise of worldwide, interconnected communication networks where people store information on insecure computers provides a terrific opportunity for national intelligence organizations. However, spies, law enforcement agents, criminals, and voyeurs may use the same tactics, technologies, and procedures to collect information from their unwitting victims. The perpetrators and victims hide its nature by calling it electronic exploitation, digital surveillance, signals intelligence, cyber espionage, system monitoring, hacking, or enabling operations.

Geeks in the Wire

Chapter 8. Equities

"Battle not with monsters, lest ye become a monster,
and if you gaze into the abyss, the abyss gazes also into you."
- Friedrich Nietzsche (1844 - 1900)

"Money plays the largest part in determining the course of history."
- Karl Marx (1818 – 1883)
Communist Manifesto

Churchill's Paradox

On November 14, 1940 British Prime Minister Winston Churchill faced a quandary. For over two months Germany had conducted massive, nightly aerial raids on British cities, and now British intelligence had learned German bombers were about to conduct a major aerial bombing on the city of Coventry. There is conflicting evidence if the intelligence was from the British interception and decryption of German radio traffic,[1] or interception of the directional radio beams that guided German bombers to targets.[2] Whatever the case, Churchill suspected if he evacuated Coventry then German agents would report the evacuation immediately preceding a German bombing. This would raise suspicion in the German High Command that the British had compromised a key German technology. Churchill was concerned the German's might respond to this suspicion by modifying Enigma and eliminate a critical source of British intelligence. It's alleged Churchill 'sacrificed' the city of Coventry to protect British intelligence capabilities. That evening the German Luftwaffe dropped over 500 tons of bombs on the population of Coventry, killing over 500 citizens.

An intelligence operation that provides one side of a conflict with its adversary's plans, capabilities, or weaknesses has the potential to produce tremendous advantages. However, possessing intelligence creates a paradox. Using or sharing intelligence may reveal to adversaries the *sources* of the intelligence, or the *methods* used to obtain the intelligence. Adversaries may then react to eliminate the sources and methods to prevent future intelligence collection. The *Coventry Argument* has become synonymous for deliberately sacrificing a likely victim to an enemy to protect an intelligence resource.[3]

On April 14, 1986 President Ronald Reagan announced on national television that earlier that day U.S. military aircraft had bombed targets in Libya. The aerial raid was in response to Libya's April 5, terrorist bombing of a West Berlin discotheque frequented by U.S. servicemen that left one soldier dead and 230 people wounded. Reagan explained that the U.S. government had recorded evidence between the Libyan government and its Peoples Bureau operating in Berlin. The evidence was "... direct, precise, and irrefutable..." and included communications prior to the attack from the Libyan government directing a terrorist attack against Americans to "... cause maximum and indiscriminate casualties." The evidence included conversations the day prior to the bombing that the bombing would be carried out the following day, and the day following the bombing reporting "... the great success of the [bombing] mission."[4]

President Reagan all but said his intelligence came from the interception of Libyan communications. This revelation undoubtedly informed the Libyans their communications were insecure and caused the Libyan government to change how they communicated. Reagan felt he had to order a military strike against the sponsors of the terrorist attack. However, he needed to justify his decision to the American people and the international community and potentially lose the ability to secretly collect future Libyan communications.

Intelligence is not an end to itself; intelligence operations only have value if it provides benefits. In each story events forced the heads of state to prioritize conflicting government goals. These leaders needed to act on their intelligence without compromising the sources and methods used to collect that information. If this wasn't possible, then the leader had to decide if protecting intelligence resources was more important than acting on the intelligence and losing the resources. It shouldn't be a surprise that this contention now includes the conflicting goals associated with cyber conflict.

Turf War

Today governments conduct international cyber espionage, cyberattacks, domestic and international law enforcement surveillance, and defense. Many see the challenges associated with cyberconflict as a lack of resources. The IC needs more to collect intelligence on foreign threats and transnational terrorists. The Pentagon needs more to deter foreign aggression and damage or destroy foreign threats in cyberspace. Law enforcement agencies need more to monitor and track criminals and foreign intelligence services. And everyone needs to secure their information and systems from hackers. The public and private actors involved in cyberconflict have goals and priorities simultaneously competing for the limited pool of skilled and qualified personnel and funding. The result is an inevitable turf war within Washington DC over control of the nation's cyber missions, resources and technologies.

The problem isn't that the U.S. Government isn't spending enough money on the challenges. The problem is competing goals as each organization pursues its particular *equities* with single-minded determination.[5] In many situations when one organization achieves its goals it prevents another from achieving their goals. If the U.S. government had a bottomless pit of money, the problems could not be solved. The conflicting and mutually exclusive priorities and goals, limited funds, and increased senior government interest in cyberconflict have become the chess pieces in a vast political war.

And the winner is…

As noted earlier nation state sponsored cyber spies use the same technology as other hackers, and their government, military and commercial victims use the same vulnerable commercial operating systems and security systems on their networks. The NSA recognized that if it alerted U.S. agencies about newly discovered vulnerabilities in their systems these agencies would demand their vendors publish updates to eliminate these vulnerabilities. The NSA's targets would also get these vendor updates and use them to eliminate the doors the NSA uses to enter networks, preventing the NSA from conducting further espionage.

This leads to the *Hardening Paradox*. When government networks created from commercial systems become more secure, their adversaries' networks become more secure.

The paradox soon became apparent in classified Pentagon meetings.

Senior leaders soon recognized the conflict. On February 8th 2007 General James Cartwright, Commander of the U.S. Strategic Command gave an impassioned speech at the Air Warfare Symposium in Orlando, Florida. Speaking on the military approach to manage cyberspace General Cartwright noted, "Current U.S. cyber warfare strategy is dysfunctional." He went on, "The offensive, defensive and reconnaissance efforts among U.S. cyber forces are incompatible and don't communicate with one another, resulting in a disjointed effort."[6]

To protect the NSA's equities it needed to gain control of the cyber conflict missions, authorities, and budget. In 2008, the NSA began a quiet but aggressive effort to pursue all aspects of cyber conflict. Stepping into an apparent leadership void it began wrestling control of cyber missions from other government agencies and moving them under the NSA's umbrella.

The NSA effort began subtly by offering employees from its work force, called detailees, to work in other agencies. Detailees assist these agencies, provide insider information back to the Fort, and represent the NSA's interests in meetings within the agencies. Detailees provide the NSA with a front seat and voice at every meeting regarding cyberspace.

Spreading its Wings

In 2008, in response to publicized attacks into public and private information systems President George W. Bush established the Comprehensive National Cybersecurity Initiative (CNCI) to strengthen the nation's cyber security environment. The White House placed CNCI under the Office of the Director of National Intelligence. Since the Government considers intelligence budgets classified national security information, this decision ensured the CNCI program and its multibillion annual budget were kept out of the public eye.

The decision to make the CNCI a classified program was a strategic mistake for the White House. The news media continually reported of compromises to public and private information systems and the wholesale vacuuming of sensitive personal, corporate and government information. General Alexander, Director of the NSA, noted the loses of industrial information and intellectual property through cyber espionage constituted the "greatest transfer of wealth in history." He stated that U.S. companies lose $250 billion per year through intellectual property theft and another $114 billion due to cybercrime, and when the cost of down time is taken into consideration, the total is $338 billion per year.[7] Our nation's response was to create a massive classified program that didn't address critical issues and due to its restricted nature couldn't reassure the American people its government was addressing the issues. However, the program secrecy prevented public scrutiny and government oversight.

A 2010 GAO report noted, "While certain aspects and details of CNCI must necessarily remain classified, the lack of transparency regarding CNCI projects hinders accountability to Congress and the public. In addition, current classification may make it difficult for some agencies, as well as the private sector, to interact and contribute to the success of CNCI projects."[8]

CNCI became a funding pool for the pet projects of government agencies and defense contractors — a source of billions of dollars that gradually had little to do with cyber security. Within the U.S. Government CNCI became known as "welfare for government projects" as there was little oversight by either the White House or Congress, accountability for completion of planned projects, or evaluations of their effectiveness.

A typical example is CNCI-7, started to "Increase the security of classified networks." Government leaders had been adamant regarding the lack of security of the government's classified systems. The goal of this initiative was to harden and protect the networks containing the nation's most sensitive and perishable government information.[9] After Congress approved CNCI funds the government working group associated with the initiative changed the name of the project to "Increase the security of National Security Systems (NSSs)." 'Classified networks' are networks containing information and systems that have been formally labeled as classified information. NSSs are a much broader collection of networks that includes classified networks, and networks involving the command and control of military forces, weapon or weapons systems, or "critical to the direct fulfillment of military or intelligence missions."[10]

The working group, led by NSA detailees, believed changing the name permitted them to shift funds from classified information systems to the much larger and expensive unclassified government systems where the committee members felt they needed funds. While some of the funds were used on unclassified projects, the funds themselves were retained within the classified initiative. Congressional watchdogs didn't notice the subtle change.

Edward Snowden's harvest and theft of classified documents over several days demonstrated that despite public announcements the classified government information systems remained unprotected.

From its beginning leaders knew CNCI was in trouble. A November 2009 GAO briefing to the House Armed Services subcommittee on Terrorism, Unconventional Threats and Capabilities noted that "CNCI is unlikely to fully achieve its goal of reducing potential vulnerabilities, protecting against intrusion attempts, and anticipating future threats to federal information systems unless roles and responsibilities for cybersecurity activities across the federal government are more clearly defined and coordinated."[11] The people are the problem.

Hostile Takeover

In 2010, I spent a day at the Pentagon sitting through a number of briefings to congressional staffers. The briefings were typical cyber skull sessions, full of cyber slang, acronyms, and circular assumptions. Each of the presentations involved Secretary of Defense civilians briefing their vision for a new organization that would change our nation's defense and control of cyberspace. They argued the Pentagon should move all of its vast cyber defense and attack missions, personnel, and budgets to Fort Meade under the control and oversight of the NSA. They argued that only the NSA had the technical understanding and personnel to manage such a complex warfighting domain.

When the briefings ended I reviewed the list of individuals who had spoken on behalf of the Secretary of Defense. All the briefers who had identified themselves as employees of Office of the Secretary of Defense were NSA *detailees* temporarily assigned to the Secretary of Defense office.

Equities

As a result of these briefings, the Pentagon ordered all the military cyber responsibilities moved to Fort Meade and Congress concurred.

In 2010, the Director of the NSA was given command of U.S. Cyber Command, a new Department of Defense organization responsible for the defense of the military networks and attacking foreign networks. Through an intense marketing campaign and the careful placement of detailees the NSA had convinced the Pentagon and Congress to place all cyber intelligence, attack, and defense operations under the director of a military intelligence agency. However, by consolidating so much authority and power in one organization the Pentagon had created a monster.

In 2015 U.S. Cyber Command stood up the Joint Forces Headquarters – DoD Information Networks (JFHQ-DoDIN). U.S. Cyber Command organized this new command under DISA, the Pentagon's communication's organization, and gave DISA responsibility for defending networks and to allow Cyber Command to "focus on strategic operations." So after taking control of all cyber missions by advocating for a single command, Cyber Command spun off the defense mission because they discovered it was too difficult and time consuming, and allowed Cyber Command to focus on their offensive mission.

Another beltway strategy for obtaining project funds is to fill government presentations with technobabble, codewords, and metaphors.

Speakers claim problems are "highly technical," only they can understand the problems "critical to our national security," and they can't share the details "due to sensitivities."[15] With BlueSash the NSA used the phrase "attack sensing and warning" or ASW. ASW is synonymous with commercial "intrusion detection," and often uses common commercial technology to detect cyberattacks.[16] By confusing Congress and the Pentagon the NSA has obtained funds and installed their intrusion detection technology into the Department of Defense and then controlled information regarding attacks on military networks.

This isn't about technology or national security; it's about controlling the mission, budget, and information — it's about the power to control the equities.

The NSA didn't halt with the military in its efforts to consolidate control over cybersecurity. The NSA used CNCI to fund the development of a system called *Einstein* to monitor and detect perpetrators breaking into U.S. civilian government networks. Just as the NSA monitors all communications within the Department of Defense, it's also pursued the civilian government and dragged them into the Fort through Einstein and a "cooperative agreement" with the Department of Homeland Security.[17]

Einstein was allegedly established by CNCI-2 to detect perpetrators breaking into Executive Branch networks. The original Einstein, called E1 began in 2003.[18] The technology was nearly a decade old, and was essentially the military *Centaur* program, developed by the Department of Defense and a commercial communication company to track network usage for billing.[19] The proposed Einstein called E3, is a multi-billion-dollar system modeled after the NSA Blue Sash intrusion detection system that didn't prevent adversaries from penetrating the military networks.

During Congressional testimony following the 2015 Office of Personnel Management breach that resulted in the greatest loss of sensitive information, government leaders noted "the trick with Einstein is, as it currently is built, it has to know about a threat before it can detect or block it."[20] Einstein is a high-speed signature-based intrusion detection system; a signature-based, retrospective analysis system that comes with a total price tag of $3 billion, $479.8 million for 2016 alone.

DHS has extended the Einstein technology into networks operated by the private sector. Greg Schaffer, Assistant Secretary for Cyber Security and Communications at DHS, said in a 2010 interview that the department is evaluating whether Einstein "makes sense for expansion to critical infrastructure spaces".

The NSA claims it is the only one with the technical skills to run cyber operations for the entire government. At first glance the argument makes sense, after all the NSA is said to be the most technically advanced organization in the US, and some say the world. However, the NSA must still operate within the principles of cyberspace. The result is that the government doesn't have a magic security tool that protects its networks and we can assume the systems they would deploy to protect public systems would be less sophisticated than those protecting the military networks.

If I Told You...

A third strategy to protect agency equities is to tie everything to classified programs. The NSA has tied common cyber technologies such as intrusion detection to their highly classified cryptographic and signals intelligence programs. This tactic ensures the systems cannot be openly criticized, since any discussion of their capabilities and weaknesses announces weaknesses in classified programs, and the government has decided that a vulnerability in a classified system is itself classified information. Any technical discussions or criticisms of specific systems in the open would represent a security breach that could get the speaker criminally prosecuted.

This tactic also ensures oversight agencies such as Congress are not aware of the shortcomings of the systems. By tying unclassified government systems to classified programs the government also prevents other government agencies discussing cybersecurity. The result is multi-billion-dollar systems that have nothing to do with cryptography and signals intelligence, that fail repeatedly to protect systems and are not being critically evaluated for effectiveness.

Many within the government have been vocal that the NSA deliberately impedes their ability to defend their networks, referring to the NSA as "Never Say Anything," "Never Share Anything," and "Never Secure Anything." This perception is that a tremendous quantity of intelligence goes into the Fort, but a lack of useful intelligence coming out of the Fort to help guardians defend their networks.

Rod Beckstrom, the Director of the Department of Homeland Security National Cyber Security Center, and responsible for defending the U.S. civilian government networks, quit in March 2009 over concerns that the NSA's was dominating national cyber security efforts. He noted that the NSA effectively controlled the DHS cyber efforts through NSA detailees inside the DHS, their technology insertions (Einstein), and the NSA's attempts to move DHS organizations to Fort Meade. Similarly, Amit Yoran, the first director of the DHS National Cyber Security Division quit DHS after only one year over the bureaucracy, inefficiency, leadership failure, and frustration, noting, "handing the cyber mission to National Security Agency would still be ill-advised."

In Chapter 6 we discussed the challenges in cyber attribution, and how identifying a culprit and their intent occurs very late in an investigation. However, this identity is exactly the information senior leaders tell investigators they must discover immediately after an incident occurs.

This demand from senior leaders forces analysts to monitor hacker's activities and determine if an activity is espionage, criminal, preparation for a destructive attack, or some other goal. During this time an investigator is concerned if they notify guardians of the activity the guardian will react and inadvertently alert the hacker who would change their behavior, possible eliminating the analyst's ability to monitor them.

In the meantime, the hacker continues to access the victim's network to collect information from the victim and to bury themselves deeper into the victim's systems. Today intelligence agencies use the Coventry Argument to justify sacrificing personal, corporate, or government information and information networks to protect cyber intelligence sources and methods. The Intelligence Community is aiding foreign intelligence collection for the sake of their intelligence collection. Or to paraphrase – the Intelligence Community sacrifices the victim's goals for the sake of their intelligence goals.

Coventry Revisited

During the Second World War Prime Minister Winston Churchill was the leader of the British government and the executive branch. He sacrificed the city of Coventry calculating the losses at Coventry were outweighed by the lives saved through exploiting his intelligence sources and accelerating the end the war. Churchill noted "[War should be] directed by heads of government who have the knowledge which enables them to comprehend not only military but political and economic forces at work and who have the power to focus them all upon the goal." Churchill, as the senior civilian leader was responsible for the protection of the people and his actions at a macro-scale resulted in greater good.

Today, we have a defense intelligence agency that has always operated in complete secrecy in charge of our nation's cyber missions. It's important to realize that the men and women at the NSA are great Americans sacrificing lucrative commercial incomes for the sake of our national security. The problem isn't these hard-working and dedicated individuals. The problem isn't in the NSA technical capabilities. The problem is in the fundamental conflict of interest the Pentagon created when it merged all cyber missions under the NSA.

An intelligence organization can't defend our networks, because intelligence is just one component of cyber conflict. And advocating for intelligence equities over all others, or more to the point, having an intelligence organization determine whose equities will be protected, hinders other organizations from achieving their goals. And sometimes other equities are more important for the nation.

When the Intelligence Community uses the Coventry Argument they fail to recognize that unlike the Second World War, cyber conflict is a perpetual conflict with a vast set of persistent and adaptive adversaries. No one can 'win' — so what are the true costs and benefits of sacrificing information and systems?

Equities

Chapter 9. Insiders

"An ambassador has no need of spies; his character is always sacred."
- George Washington
First President of the United States

Cyber Insider

When a member of a group violates the group's norms, rules, or laws by discussing their private activities to people outside the group they become an *insider*. An insider may have a negative or positive connotation depending on your perspective, demonstrated by terms for insiders such as whistle blowers, spies, snitches, informants, undercover officers or operatives.

In the past the damage an insider could create was limited by the quality and quantity of documents they could clandestinely acquire, pilfer away from the group, and supply to outsiders.[1] Transitioning from paper documents to telecommunications systems, mobile devices, and massive storage media has enabled insiders to carry small devices into an organization, download a tremendous quantity of documents to the device, and walk the information out the front door. Alternatively, and insider may remotely siphon off an organization's sensitive documents using the organizations online presence and their desire to permit telework. Cyberspace has also expanded the pool of potential insiders with access to a group's sensitive information to vendors and outsourced business functions.

The majority of cyber defenses protect organizations from outside attacks. An insider may know the organization's capabilities, vulnerabilities, and security and have passwords and network accounts that provide access to the organization's resources and the ability to bypass the organization's security controls. Insiders may have skills and training to attack their organization's systems, and experience on the equipment they target to achieve their goals. While the community is inundated with reports of hackers breaking into public and private systems, one in seven major data breaches involve a trusted insider.[2]

Private Bradley Manning was a military insider that the Pentagon claimed caused extensive damage to U.S. intelligence organizations and international reputation. Manning's leaders provided him access to classified military computer networks where he searched for and copied three-quarters of a million classified or unclassified but sensitive military and diplomatic documents to compact disks. Manning then sent the sensitive information to Australian Julian Assange and WikiLeaks – a website dedicated to providing insiders a place to expose secrets anonymously. Friends of Manning claim he performed *civil disobedience*. The U.S. government saw Manning's exposure of classified information as espionage and in August 2013 sentenced him to 35 years' imprisonment.

Insiders are not limited to damaging government information. Swiss national Rudolf Elmer's former bank employer alleged Elmer was disgruntled and frustrated, and provided Swiss bank data to Julian Assange and WikiLeaks. Elmer was alleged to have wanted to denounce the illegal banking and tax evasion of an estimated 2,000 personal bank customers. His actions violated the strict Swiss bank secrecy laws.

In 2015 the German newspaper Süddeutsche Zeitung (SZ) announced it had a secret stash of private files from the Panamanian law firm Mossack Fonseca. These files were on offshore holding companies, which are often legal, but in many cases appeared to being used for illegal purposes. Over the next year reporters would search through the eleven million documents covering more than 200,000 companies, foundations and trusts, in what would be called the "Panama Papers." The reporters discovered sensitive financial and attorney-client documents that revealed the hidden financial dealings of the world's wealthiest, as well as current and former politicians and public officials, drug dealers, organized crime members, and tax evaders. The light shined on corruption from the Pentagon Papers would cause the collapse of several political leaders, and tarnishing of many others. The whistleblower responsible for the leak of 2.6 terabytes of sensitive data has not been identified, but claims he did it to reveal financial inequities and corruption that exists.[3]

Some call insiders who take information off government and corporate computers and post it on WikiLeaks whistle blowers who report the illegal and immoral activities of private corporations and governments. Others say that those that take information from restricted networks and place our spies, corporations, and nation at risk are themselves criminals and spies. Whichever view, WikiLeaks has changed the world by hosting secrets that cause catastrophic damage to reputations.

It's been argued that a factor contributing to the 2011 *Muslim Spring* and the collapse of numerous Middle Eastern nations including Egypt, Tunisia, and Libya was the political corruption discussed in U.S. diplomatic cables disclosed by Manning and published by WikiLeaks. Cyberspace is now a powerful weapon if nations will collapse based on the release of information into cyberspace.

Outsourcing Your Insiders

Contracted services, or *outsourcing*, can provide an organization with cost savings, access to talent, and ability to focus on the organization's core business. The outside accountant, cleaning service, mail handler, information technology support, customer service, or offsite storage company can also represent a threat to the security of an organization. The proliferation of software development, web content, mail services, "cloud services" and online data storage services has extended the "inside" perimeter of an organization into these outsource companies. Sometimes these third parties may not be malicious, but may be unwitting victims. A hacker could compromise a less-defended contractor and use them as a hop-off point into the real target.

Individuals might be leery of sending email with personal information directly to someone they don't know, but what about to the organization that processes all their email? When an organization's sensitive information is stored or processed on remote applications, the organization running that application has access to the information. There are few guarantees that every email you send or receive, and every document you store isn't being accessed by others, shared with employees, law enforcement or intelligence agencies, competitors, or criminals.

Individuals and organizations also use Internet tools and websites without thinking about the information the owners of those websites and their advertisers and sponsors may collect on them. Since the 1990's organizations have been collecting search, purchase, and geographic location information. Search engines, online shopping sites, and sponsoring online marketers can deduce information about browser's interests and deduce sensitive information.

Commercial cyber companies that operate search engines can also record, analyze, and share a user's interests and habits with governments or government contractors. It is probably very interesting to see the queries the employees at the National Security Agency, the Central Intelligence Agency, and the White House submit as searches to the Google search engine.

In limited cases a solution may be to create a separate, isolated network that restricts who can access information, protects networks from outside attacks, and limits employees to approved tools.

Intelligence Meets Groundhog Day

The purpose of secrecy is to prevent information sharing. The purpose of cyberspace is to enable information sharing. This creates a natural dichotomy. The government solution is to create *isolated*, or stand-alone information networks to share sensitive information between authorized individuals.

An isolated network is a set of computers connected over a network that isn't connected to a larger network, in effect an island in cyberspace. Isolated networks reduce the chances of hackers defeating critical systems or accessing important information. Only vetted users that have been checked for their trust and loyalty can access the information and systems in the isolated network. An isolated network may be in one building, or dispersed worldwide. If the network is dispersed the communications between remote pieces are protected to prevent adversaries from eavesdropping.

The challenge with isolated networks is getting real work done. In many cases users of these networks need to move information from other networks, such as the Internet, to the stand-alone network, and back. A common technique referred to as *sneaker-netting*, moves data between the networks using "removable media" such as thumbdrives, compact disks, tapes, or entire computers. This doesn't come without risks. An adversary could plant malicious programs on the media, or malware could infect a machine, and copy itself onto the media.

In 2008 a foreign intelligence service compromised U.S. classified networks in Operation Buckshot Yankee. According to Deputy Secretary of Defense William J. Lynn III, a user installed a thumbdrive with a malicious program into a computer on a classified military network. This malware searched for and copied "operational plans" from the classified network onto the thumbdrive. When an individual removed the thumbdrive from the classified computer and placed it in an Internet-connected computer, the malware sent the stolen data across the Internet to a foreign country. Neither the users of these computers, nor the government's extensive security programs detected the malware. The Intelligence Community detected the transfer of sensitive information to a foreign computer. The government reacted by restricting the use of removable media on government computers.

A lesson learned from the 9/11 terrorist attacks was that the U.S. intelligence, military, and government agencies could not share intelligence because each ran their own isolated network. In response they connected their classified networks together so anyone with the correct "access" and "need" could find intelligence. Budget cuts and the further consolidation of networks and systems further consolidated information. The result was Edward Snowden.

In 2013, Edward Snowden, an alleged former employee of the Central Intelligence Agency and National Security Agency and now a defense contractor became an insider. During the Spring of 2013 Snowden harvested countless highly classified documents from NSA computer systems. He then began a bizarre trek first to Hong Kong, and eventually to Moscow. During this adventure Snowden announced he was responsible for providing numerous classified intelligence documents to reporters.

Snowden had been a system administrator responsible for managing some of the NSA's most sensitive systems. He claims he was disenchanted with NSA's domestic surveillance and became a whistleblower. Intelligence officials reported that Snowden created an automated bot that searched classified networks for sensitive subjects and took approximately1.7 million files.[4] The most damaging documents, referred to as the "Keys to the Kingdom," show the capabilities and shortcomings of the U.S. intelligence programs.

The documents released by Snowden have exposed domestic and international NSA surveillance programs, and some claim shows the U.S. government violates its citizen's civil liberties in the name of protecting national security.[5] Snowden reported that the NSA monitors foreign nationals and collects "metadata" on all domestic phone calls. Although Congressman feigned shock and outrage, they must have fully known of the effort since the Congress approves the NSA budgets and programs. If Congress wasn't aware of these monitoring programs, then Congress would have announced criminal prosecutions for government funding improprieties and massive intelligence budget cuts. Instead there were a few public hearings and minor changes to appease constituents. From his new home in Moscow Snowden continues to dribble classified information to the media to keep his name in the limelight.

Snowden alleged information technology companies routinely provide the U.S. government with a tremendous amount of personal information. Bloomburg reported "thousands of technology, finance and manufacturing companies working closely with U.S. national security agencies, providing sensitive information and in return receiving benefits that include access to classified intelligence.[6] This may cause executives (in particular executives in foreign enterprises) to reconsider if using U.S. companies and technologies such as corporate clouds makes sense, costing U.S. technology companies revenue.

Other nations are no better off. Only days after the French President François Hollande demanded the United States stop spying on its allies, a French newspaper announced that the French General Directorate of External Security (DGSE) collects nearly all telephone calls, email, and social media that enters or leaves France.[7] Similar intelligence collection is also alleged to occur in Canada[8], and Brazil. The news media jumped on the realization that the U.S. Postal Service photographs every piece of mail as it traverses their offices — these photographs and resulting information may not be shared with anyone, but it certainly adds to the conspiracy hype.[9]

Many people believe Snowden and the government information he has released. The information appears credible and government officials often inadvertently confirm the information's authenticity soon after Snowden makes it public, further adding to Snowden's credibility. However, there is nothing preventing Snowden from creating fake documents and making them appear like the previous releases to further his own agenda. Indeed, the opposite was considered. When hackers compromised and published HBGary Federal corporate information in 2011, researchers discovered that HBGary Federal was alleged to have offered to publish fabricated information for the government to harm WikiLeaks's reputation.

The most significant long-term damage from Snowden is the potential loss of intelligence sources and methods. This involves not only direct intelligence sources that Snowden reveals but also future intelligence sources. Snowden demonstrated the U.S. government couldn't protect its most sensitive information. Those who shared information willingly (such as allies), through coercion (from FISA National Security Letters), or unknowingly (through the U.S. spy apparatus) saw their information exposed to the world. This may harm our ability to collaborate with industry and other nations, and those willing to conduct espionage on our nation's behalf.[10]

Placing information on an isolated network doesn't make it secure, but does create a target. The White House recognized the security shortcomings of our classified networks, "Classified networks house the Federal Government's most sensitive information and enable crucial war-fighting, diplomatic, counterterrorism, law enforcement, intelligence, and homeland security operations. Successful penetration or disruption of these networks could cause exceptionally grave damage to our national security."[11] In March 2013, the Director of National Intelligence James Clapper noted, "Most detected activity has targeted unclassified networks connected to the Internet, but foreign cyber actors are also targeting classified networks."[12] Relying on isolation is similar to placing the family jewels in a bank safe, where the bank lacks cameras, sensors, alarms, or a security response capability. The safe will delay a crook, but once they're in or an insider is turned, the treasures are gone. The U.S. government has learned this numerous times, including with Robert Hanssen, Operation Buckshot Yankee, Manning and now Snowden.

Snowden allegedly used common tools to vacuum the highest sensitive information from government networks, demonstrating the lack of security in the most sensitive Government information systems.[13] This occurred after the billion dollars spent on the White House Comprehensive National Cybersecurity Initiative and it's Initiative-7 to "Increase the security of our classified network."[14] This occurred after the 2010 realization that Private Manning ran rampant through government classified networks and the government's reaction to secure networks after that embarrassment. This occurred after the President's 2011 Executive Order 13587 — *Structural Reforms to Improve the Security of Classified Networks and the Responsible Sharing and Safeguarding of Classified Information* that specified in Section 2.1(b) "Implement an insider threat detection and prevention program."[15] And it occurred after the President's November 2012 Memorandum *Minimal Standard for Executive Branch Insider Threat Programs* requiring Agency heads to "…monitor user activity on all classified networks in order to detect activity indicative of insider threat behavior," within 180 days of the effective date of the policy."[16]

What is truly frightening is that officials discovered the perpetrators in the majority of classified information incidents only after they started providing the information to news media. After all the funds the government has spent to secure these networks, policies they have created, physical security placed around these facilities, oversight from organizations to ensure standards and policies are met, certifications that networks are secure before operations, and working groups and committees created after every incident **our best intrusion detection system for the classified networks is the news media.** If we aren't preventing or detecting malicious behavior, then the real question is how many times have insiders taken information from these networks and shared it with foreign intelligence services and never been detected?

Isolated networks don't make the information or systems residing there secure, but they do provide a false sense of security. Once a hacker is into any part of the network, they are an insider and may have unfettered access to the entire network. This digital civil disobedience represents a new paradigm for national leaders to consider. It will happen again.

Chapter 10. Shadow Boxing

Si vis pacem, para bellum
"If you wish for peace, prepare for war."

*"In the near future many conflicts will not take place on the open field of
battle, but rather on the Internet, fought with the aid of information solders,
that is hackers. This means that a small force of hackers is stronger than the
multi-thousand force of the current armed forces."*
- Nikolai Kuryanovich (1966-)
Russia State Duma Director and member of the Security Committee Deputy

In August 2008, war broke out between the nations of Georgia, Russia, and the
separatist governments of South Ossetia and Abkhazia. The Georgian military
rolled into South Ossetia, followed by the Russian military storming into the
nation of Georgia. Georgia claimed it was responding to attacks on its
peacekeepers and villages in South Ossetia, and Russia was moving non-
peacekeeping military forces into their country. The Russian government
claimed it was protecting Russians in South Ossetia. During the subsequent five
days the Georgian military indiscriminately shelled regions of their country to
force out the invaders, while Russian military jets dropped bombs on military
and civilian targets. Hundreds died and thousands were injured.

Before, during, and after the conflict hackers also conducted attacks against
the Georgian government and civilian infrastructures. Georgian officials alleged
that weeks before the Russian invasion the Russian government released
malware that *infected* hundreds of thousands of computers around the world.
Russian hackers sent commands to these zombie computers directing them to
flood Georgian government and news media with millions of useless messages,
and redirecting legitimate request for information to bogus Internet sites outside
Georgia. While no one was killed or injured as a result of these cyberattacks
'experts' noted the 'cyberattacks' complemented the physical invasion of the
Russian Army by creating psychological effects against the civilian population,
causing Georgian's to doubt the validity of information that got through, and
preventing those inside and outside of Georgia from understanding what was
occurring within the Georgia borders. The Georgian government (creatively)

remarked that the flood created "consequences similar in effect to a full-scale missile strike" and that this represented a "new phase in the history of warfare, being the first case in which a land invasion was coordinated with an online cyber offensive."[1] In the end, cyber experts proclaimed the Russian government supported the cyber operation, while the 'evidence' they presented could have been easily forged to deceive investigators.

On War

If digital systems store, process, and transport information, then destructive acts in cyberspace can place individuals, corporations, and nations at risk. Malicious hackers can erase personal information, credit card and financial information, corporate intellectual property, or national security information. Individuals may change information in databases, creating false orders for supplies or changing, misdelivering or canceling orders. Attacks against information systems can degrade, disable, or destroy systems and the information contained within them. Attacks may also cause physical effects by attacking the electronic control systems that operate river locks, open flood gates or sewage systems, disable radar systems, or deactivate power control systems. And all the above activities have already occurred.

In many ways cyberattacks are just a new twist to age-old struggles. Experts place traditional labels on those struggles such as vandalism, sabotage, and warfare depending on the perspective of the observer and their agenda. Cyberspace may enable nations, bullies, and criminals a street or a continent away to cause chaos with little or no physical risk to themselves, and if done correctly without leaving evidence that points to the perpetrators. And while information systems may make these activities easier, faster, less risky, or less expensive, the struggles are the same activities that plagued humankind over the millennium.

Information Dominance

The U.S. military defines cyberwarfare as one capability in its *effects-based operations* that were spawned out of the U.S. Air Force's success in the Persian Gulf War.[2] The goal of effects-based operations is to "cause the adversary to act in accordance with U.S. national interests by the application of superior technology against selected targets, to cause an effect." These effects are accomplished by combining military and non-military methods to attack secondary targets which may impact primary targets, but that limit collateral damage and risk to friendly forces.[3] Military strategists use effects-based operations to focus on an end state — the effect — rather than the meat-grinder approach of traditional attrition warfare.

Offensive cyber operations, what the government refers to as *Computer Network Attack* (CNA), is one weapon in the military arsenal for generating effects. **The goal of a cyberattack is not the actual attack, but to create an effect beneficial to the attacker.** If the Air Force has the goal of disabling a highly defended radar installation in the middle of a city, they could risk their aircraft and crew to drop bombs on the radar installation and risk striking innocent bystanders, or they could use a cyberattack to disable the power systems that feed electric power to the radar installation and obtain the same effect without risking their aircraft and crew or creating the political and human damage.

The news media tends to label everything "cyberattacks," but there are two different types of attacks: degrading attacks and destructive attacks.[4]

Open the Floodgates

Hackers can use Internet capabilities to degrade systems, or direct third parties to perform their dastardly deeds. For example, since anyone can send numerous Internet messages to anyone else, there is little stopping someone from sending billions of emails to someone. This flood of email messages would eventually fill the recipient's email storage. The victim may discover their mailbox full of junk email from random named individuals. As the victim begins deleting the emails new email messages arrive preventing legitimate email from being accepted. These *denial of*

Figure 14 - Denial of Service: A Simple Flood

service (DoS) attacks are like filling a mailbox with trash faster than the owner can take things out of the mailbox, and simultaneously preventing a mailman from putting any useful mail in the mailbox because it's full when they try.

If a hacker collects many compromised computers under their control, they may create a *botnet*—short for robot network. Hackers have built botnets with tens to hundreds of thousands of compromised computers across the globe. The hacker who is the master or controller of a botnet can send commands to the compromised *zombies* and order them to send out *spam* email for commercial profit or send millions of "junk" messages to a single address every second to overwhelm the receiver to prevent legitimate messages from getting through to the victim.

This *distributed denial of service* (DDoS) attack is the hacker version of crowdsourcing an attack to many machines that contribute to generate the force necessary to create a large effect.

The computer that receives this digital tsunami of messages doesn't know messages are useless until it uses its computing power and resources to process and reject each useless messages, which degrades its ability to respond to legitimate messages. Most "attacks" you hear about, such as the 2008 computer offensive against the Georgian government systems, and the 2013 attacks against U.S. banks were DDoS attacks.

Shadow Boxing

An alternative DDoS attack is the *mirror attack* or bounce attack. In a mirror attack a hacker uses unwitting third parties to flood a victim. A hacker can send thousands of bogus emails to illegitimate email addresses with the intended flood victim in the 'from' address. When the destination receives the emails they will reject the messages because of the illegitimate destination address and send a rejection message to the sender in the *'from'* address. Here the hacker has duped all the destinations into sending rejection notices to one address to flood the victim, reflecting the attacks off the destination address and onto the victim.

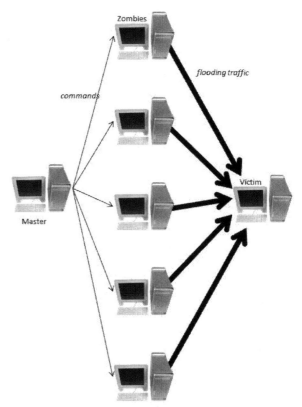

Figure 15 - DDoS - A Master with Zombies

While degrading attacks may reduce the victim's ability to do their job, hackers have not penetrated the victim's computer nor stolen information, and the flood has not damaged a computer. When the attacker stops sending messages, or guardians block the messages, the attack is over. During the attack the victim may not receive or process legitimate messages that were sent to the victim, but in many cases the victim of a DOS may operate normally shortly after the attack stops with little or no detrimental effect on the system.

The zombies and mirror sites are unwitting third parties hop-points between the hacker and the victim that hinders investigations and attribution. The traffic arriving at their victim comes from the hop-points and not the hacker. When the victim investigates the attack, they will see messages from unwitting victims and not the hacker responsible for the attack. To investigate who is responsible requires an investigator to either get access to the third party and see whom the zombie is communicating with, or collect intelligence from the third party to determine who is communicating with them.

Hackers use flooding attacks as smoke screens or diversions to prevent victims from noticing other operations. In the summer of 2014 flooding attacks against U.S. financial companies prevented the financial companies from processing legitimate online financial transactions. Meanwhile hackers sent emails to Internet users posing as banks or electronic payments

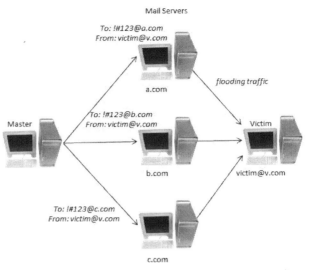

Figure 16 - A Master bouncing flood traffic off legitimate mail servers

organizations stating, "your direct deposit failed." Many people mistakenly believed these emails were legitimate due to the media reports on the cyber flooding of financial institutions. These users clicked on the email attachments and hyperlinks that caused their computers to download malware that harvested their information and sent it to hackers.

Hackers have become entrepreneurs, having developed and commercialized botnet systems. In 2011 Russian hacker websites began selling Dirt Jumper, professional quality software that provides all the services for botnet creation and management. Today the makers of Dirt Jumper, and its many variants and versions offer complete, easy to use solutions, while their website offers prices, discounts, technical support, and promotions. These tools put world-class cyber weapons into the hands of the average person at reasonable prices.

Militaries are also considering using flooding attacks against other nations. In May 2008, a U.S. military lawyer espoused the virtues of flooding attacks. He proposed the U.S. military develop its own denial of service capability he referred to as cyber carpet-bombing.[5] Carpet-bombing refers to aerial bombing that impact every part of a target area. The proposed concept missed many obvious issues. Most notably he recommended the U.S. military use its vast, worldwide military network infrastructure as the zombies to generate a distributed source of messages to flood an adversaries network. He overlooked that these U.S. government machines would generate massive amounts of traffic that would cross the military network, leave the military networks and enter the Internet backbone run by commercial companies, cross numerous sovereign nation's networks, before converging on its target.

All of this traffic would flood their own military networks, numerous government and commercial Internet service providers, and possibly many other countries creating a massive trail of temporary *collateral damage*. The military may violate their service agreements with their commercial Internet service providers that could cause the service provider to disconnect the military from the Internet. Any ISP permitting these activities might be liable for the resulting damage, or be found guilty of taking part in illegal activities by the direct or indirect victims of these floods. Perhaps the most alarming is that this paper noted the military significance of this activity. A foreign power could view the ISPs as providing a military capability and under international law the victim could attack the ISP's infrastructure and employees as legitimate military targets either in cyberspace or conventional kinetic attacks.

Destructive Attacks

Damaging a system refers to penetrating a system and changing the system or the information stored on the system. Unlike disruptive attacks, most destructive attacks require a vulnerability to access a system. Once the hacker or their malware enters systems they can change the information on the systems or the code that runs the system.

It may take hours to weeks to discover that hackers changed important information or systems. These changes could devastate financial, business, and military processes that rely on accurate, real-time and just-in-time information. A victim's recovery may range from having to erase a corrupted file or changing the value or settings in a file, to replacing files from previous backups (if available) to rebuilding machines by erasing the machines and reloading everything from scratch. The damage could be even worse if a person or organization doesn't have an up-to-date *backup* copy of the lost or changed information, preventing them from recovering.

In some cases a hacker can damage the physical components of a computer, preventing them from operating, or requiring guardians to replace physical components. Hackers refer to this as *bricking a machine* since the machine now more closely resembles a brick then a useful piece of technology.

Physical Attack

Most destructive cyber weapons only damage information such as erasing files. Victims can often rapidly recover from these attacks by rebuilding computers from their original software. Real damage occurs when hackers target electronic control systems that turn off electric power, open doors, manipulate heat and air condition, deactivate radar, open floodgates, and manipulate remote-controlled vehicles. These effects are visible, lasting, and more useful in warfare.

Cyber experts often say the 2010 Stuxnet attack that damaged the Iranian uranium enrichment infrastructure was the first intentional act of cyber war. However, in 1995, reporters alleged that the CIA had clandestine programs install Trojans into foreign computer chips and computer systems, called *chipping*.[6] Apparently the CIA conducted *supply chain attacks* by compromising systems during the manufacturing process. But this wasn't the earliest known use of cyber weapons. The U.S. took the opening shots over a decade earlier.

In July 1981, French President Francois Mitterrand took President Ronald Reagan aside at the Chateau Montebello in Quebec Canada and announced that French counterintelligence had recruited Soviet KGB counterintelligence officer Colonel Vladimir Vetrov. Vetrov, who the French had code named *Farewell* to hide his identity, had approached and offered the French a treasure trove of intelligence information showing how the KGB operated, and the names and locations of KGB's deeply buried secret agents.[7]

Over the next year Vetrov provided the French with the identities of 422 former soviet agents, 250 soviet technology intelligence officers, 170 other soviet intelligence officers, and 57 foreign spies.[8] But what shook the intelligence world were the 4,000 secret and top-secret KGB documents Vetrov provided the French.[9] These documents became known as the *Farewell Dossier* and demonstrated how the Soviets were buying or stealing advanced technologies to keep pace with the Cold War U.S. military industrial complex. The dossier demonstrated the weaknesses in the U.S. military defenses and the means the U.S. used to protect their secrets. The documents showed the Soviets had learned of the U.S. missile defense technology, and how the U.S. government budget information provided a wealth of useful intelligence. The Soviets had acquired space shuttle information from Bombay; stolen satellite, and chemical and biological weapon information from France; and space and missile information from Germany. The Farewell Dossier pointed out that the U.S. couldn't dominate the Cold War because the Soviets were stealing U.S. technology nearly as quickly as the U.S. created it. And it pointed out that technology research was the Soviet's weakness. The U.S. could change this situation.

Rather than stop the Soviets, the U.S. National Security Council proposed CIA Director William Casey 'help' the Soviets continue to steal technologies, while the CIA would sabotage the Soviets technology programs from the inside. The CIA used Vetov's list of Soviet technology interests to provide flawed designs for stealth aircraft and space defenses that caused the Soviets to waste tremendous time and money. The ultimate surprise was allowing the Soviets to steal flawed technology that would control the trans-Siberian pipeline. The CIA coordinated with a Canadian pipeline company to place a Trojan horse program in stolen pipeline control software that caused the pumps, turbines, and valves to fail, and caused an estimated three-kiloton explosion in the Urengoi Siberian gas fields, the largest non-nuclear explosion and fire ever seen from space.[10] No deaths were reported in the explosion, but the Soviets realized that they had been duped.[11]

Soviet leaders realized they could not trust the information they had previously stolen and needed to spend time and money verifying all the stolen technology. The CIA operation caused massive damage to the Soviet's intelligence apparatus, and massive economic damage.

One night in 1982, the drunk Vetrov fought with his mistress and killed an auxiliary police officer who came to her aid. Soviet authorities apprehended Vetrov and sentenced him to twelve years in prison for murder. In an ironic twist an insider in another country provided the KGB with one of Vetrov's hand-written lists of Soviet agent's that he had turned over to the French. The KGB analyzed the list and the handwriting and realized they had a mole, and the mole was Vetrov. The KGB executed Vetrov in 1985 as a traitor and NATO rolled-up the Soviet agents.[12]

The Farewell Dossier provides many lessons. First, some nations have experience developing and deploying customized digital weapons. Second, cyber weapons can damage cyberspace but also damage the physical world. Third, cyber weapons can cause catastrophic physical damage and have the potential for loss of life. Fourth, intelligence has little value if the recipient cannot act on the intelligence, but acting poorly on intelligence is disastrous to the source of the intelligence. In the case of the Farewell Dossier, Vetrov paid the ultimate price due to a French decision to share intelligence with a friendly nation who themselves had an insider.

Advantages

The goal of warfare is to obtain political objectives through the threat or use of violence. Senior leaders like cyber warfare because they believe it has significant advantages over traditional forms of warfare. The most notable advantage is that cyber weapons may allow a government leader to achieve goals while minimizing bloodshed and destruction on both sides of a disagreement, thus making cyber warfare appear a viable alternative to traditional forms of warfare.

Warriors are told they can use this new form of warfare to launch weapons across the globe and create disproportionately large effects with little effort and risk. This *asymmetry* between the small effort and resulting consequence is one of cyberattack's biggest draws. With just a few keystrokes or mouse clicks a government may cause catastrophic damage.

Simultaneously it's trivial to disguise those responsible for creating and launching a weapon. The CIA is responsible for *covert operations* or running operations that may be observable but not attributable to the United States. They would see cyber weapons as an excellent weapon in their covert operations purview. Similarly the military may use a cyberattack as a precursor to a kinetic attack. The military may deactivate or degrade a nation's radar and defenses prior to committing their aircraft in combat and make the effect appear as a maintenance failure.

It is easy to transition from espionage to sabotage in cyberspace. Once a hacker has access and is collecting intelligence on a computer, they can execute commands to perform destructive attacks. If a hacker suspects a victim has detected them, they can issue a "kill operating system" command, similar to burning a house or business to the ground after a burglary to hide evidence of the thefts and the identity of the perpetrators. The effect of these commands could be a simple annoying reboot of the machine to corrupting the data and operating system making the victim's computer useless until the victim rebuilds the machine. This occurred in March 2009 when a bot master issued the kill operating system command on a 100,000-machine botnet.[13]

Under most circumstances cyberattacks produce temporary effects making restoration easier and less costly. Rather than dropping bombs on civilian infrastructures and later spending billions to rebuild the infrastructures, cyberspace offers the opportunity to hack into the power system and flip a switch, turning the power off for a short period or damaging a generator or transformer rather than destroying the entire facility with conventional weapons. The reduction in the loss of life may reduce future animosity towards the attacker.

Challenges

U.S. warfighters love the idea of using bloodless cyber weapons against our adversaries. However, many in Washington D.C. are frustrated warfighters don't use the billion dollar capabilities they have developed and have referred to CNA as Computers Never Attack. This lack of willingness is due to the technical challenges of using cyber weapons, including the possibility of collateral damage, violating national sovereignty, isolating networks, and weapon transfer.

Collateral damage is a sanitary way to refer to incidental damage due to an attack. Cyber weapons may be indiscriminate and damage other networks or those reliant on the attacked networks. Weapons may spread and start a digital pandemic, or cause people to respond to a weapon that creates the same effect.

During the Persian Gulf War, the National Security Agency wanted to disable Iraq's financial systems through a cyberattack to prevent Saddam Hussein from accessing Iraqi funds to buy weapons or influence foreign governments and industries. Cooler heads prevailed. If the NSA had crippled Iraq's finances the effects would have rippled, potentially catastrophically, throughout the world's financial system, causing the world to lose trust in the global financial system. Cooler heads cancelled the operation.

Guardians are often surprised to discover impacts to missions when accidents or attacks affect cyber technologies and services. In 2001 the Code Red worm ripped across the Internet infecting Microsoft servers and accidentally flooding the Pentagon's Internet access points with scans searching for more machines to infect. To prevent the scans from flooding the military internal network the Pentagon blocked all incoming web traffic. The Pentagon was surprised by the number and variety of systems affected, including their accidentally stopping traffic on the Mississippi River since the Army Corps of Engineers used the Internet to control the locks on the Mississippi River.[14] If guardians don't understand the impact hackers have on their infrastructures imagine how difficult it must be for conscientious government hackers to understand the impact they will have on their victims.

Senior military leaders often argue, "In cyberspace national boundaries don't exist, making moot the question of sovereignty."[15] They are saying cyberspace is a new domain, and they don't want the old rules applying to them. This is wishful thinking. Every machine that makes up cyberspace is a physical machine, with the vast majority within a sovereign nation. Cyberattacks deliberately violate the sovereignty of the victim and may violate the sovereignty of every nation an attack travels through.

Cyberattacks could cause a conflict to escalate. Disabling communications may *digitally decapitate* a nation by causing the leadership to lose the ability to communicate and maintain control of their military forces or their nation. This may prevent leaders from communicating with military forces to tell them to suspend hostilities or disable weapon systems. This failure to respond may be seen by observers, opponents or the populace as a sign of further aggression or unwillingness to capitulate resulting in a protracted war and possibly an escalation of conflict. Thus, cyber warfare could result in greater death and destruction, not less.

Nations may see cyber weapons as a means to disable an opponent's nuclear weapons arsenal. However nuclear-enabled countries will perceive a cyberattack as an attempt by other nations to prevent the control of their nuclear arsenal. This loss of control may cause a nation to believe that they can no longer deter foreign aggression and that their antagonist believes that with their nuclear arsenal out of the picture they can win a confrontation.[16] As a result the Russian government declared that cyber incidents against their national command and control or nuclear control systems are acts of war, and reserves the right of response to these cyber attacks with up to a nuclear response.

In times of international tensions, a third party could create a highly visible destructive attack and embed misleading information in the attack to convince the victim that the other party was responsible for the attack. In March 2013, the Director of National Intelligence hinted regarding this possibility, noting "Most hacktivists use short-term denial-of-service operations or expose personally identifiable information held by target companies, as forms of political protest... However, a more radical group might form to inflict more systemic impacts — such as disrupting financial networks — or accidentally trigger unintended consequences that could be misinterpreted as a state-sponsored attack."[17]

Picking up a weapon from the battlefield and using it on the original wielder of the weapon has been happening since antiquity. And so has attempts to prevent reusing weapons. The ancient Roman army designed the pilum javelin with an untempered shank that would bend or break off when it struck, preventing adversaries from collecting thrown javelins from the battlefield and throwing them back at the Romans.

As noted earlier there is no conservation of information in cyberspace. Anyone can capture and make unlimited copies of digital information. Since cyber weapons are just another form of digital information the victim of a cyberattack can easily capture an attacker's cyber weapons and turn the weapons back on the attacker. However, unlike the traditional battlefield the victim may not understand how a weapon functions. Malware developers take steps to delay analysts by *obfuscating code* – which is hiding how code operates. However, obfuscation does not prevent analysis, it only delays analysis. It's only a matter of time before a victim *reverse engineers* a digital weapon and determines how it functions and turns the weapon on the suspected sender or some other third party.

This apparently occurred with the 2011 Stuxnet cyberattack against the Iranian nuclear centrifuges. Analysts around the world have reverse-engineered Stuxnet and embedded its capabilities in later weapons.

Escalation

Both a hacker and a guardian may consider espionage a prelude for a destructive attack.

Once a hacker gains access to a victim machine they will typically elevate their access and install monitoring software deep within the victim's systems. These systems are large, complex, and dynamic software. When a hacker modifies them to install and hide their tools, and remove evidence of their activities, they may damage the system.

Eventually the victim may detect the hacker however it may be difficult if not impossible to determine the perpetrators' intent. Guardians know that once a hacker has gained access to a computer, they may be a command away from a destructive effect. Hackers hinder guardians making informed guesses by deliberately obscuring how their malware operates to protect their technique and to keep victims in the dark as to the perpetrator's identity and goals. Complicating the analysis is that hackers can send commands that alter the functionality of malware. This may convert malware from searching and harvesting information to changing information and damaging systems. Deception and manipulation are a component in every government tool kit, so existing evidence of a hacker's intent may not be trusted. Even if an analyst can determine how a weapon functions, this may not be directly related to the strategic effect the perpetrator is pursuing. It may be impossible for a guardian to analyze malware and activities to determine if someone is conducting espionage, cybercrime, or preparing for a major cyberattack.

On January 30, 1991 General Norman Schwarzkopf gave a news conference and referred to the driver of a vehicle as "The luckiest man in Iraq." The video showed a laser-guided bomb destroying a bridge seconds after the vehicle had driven over it. When the U.S. released the video showing the bridge being destroyed, people believed the coalition destroying the bridge to prevent the escape of retreating Iraqi military forces.

However, Vice Admiral William Studeman was the Director of the NSA during Desert Storm, and later the acting Director of the CIA. Studeman has stated that one of the coalition's goals during Desert Storm was to disable every information infrastructure in Iraq except those being exploited by coalition intelligence agencies. Studeman notes that the desired effect in the bridge attack was not to destroy the bridge, but to destroy the fiber optic cable that rode across the bridge. Losing this cable *shepherded* Iraqi leaders off their relatively secure fiber optic communications and onto U.S. monitored radio systems.[18]

Shadow Boxing

People look for and interpret information in ways that confirms preconceptions. Cognitive scientists refer to this as confirmation bias. If a guardian suspects sabotage they may look for evidence of sabotage, and interpret any event as preconditions to sabotage, leading to incorrect conclusions and responses.

Coventry Revisited

Perhaps the most challenging issue in a cyberattack isn't technical. Cyber weapons are frail, and any change to a computer, such as the victim updating their operating system or antivirus system, could eliminate a weapon's necessary viability. To execute a planned attack with high confidence requires the hacker to have clandestine access to compromised machines on their victim's network so the hacker can observe if the victim changes the network environment before the hacker launches cyber weapons or activates its payload. In this situation the hacker will have to conduct an *intelligence gain/loss assessment*, where they compare the potential benefits of the attack with the costs of launching the attack. The victim may capture the attacker's cyber weapons and turn the weapons on the attacker. The attack may cause international collateral damage, through logical, physical, or social effects. The attack may even harm the attacker even if the assault wasn't attributable to the attacker by damaging the perceived integrity of systems the hacker or their sponsor relies.[19]

Most importantly, a target may notice suspicious network activity and unplugging networks, and with it the hacker's current and future access to the victim's network and all the intelligence that lives there. The *Coventry Argument* is often invoked in cases like this, referring to Prime Minister Winston Churchill's apparent willingness to sacrifice a British city for the sake of his intelligence resources during the World War II Battle of Britain. Intelligence agencies are leery to launch degrading or destructive attacks once they have a foothold on opponent's systems and are collecting intelligence, since a victim would react, possibly causing the loss of future intelligence from the network.

And intelligence agencies dominate control of our national cyber arsenals.

Conclusion

Nineteenth-century military strategist Carl von Clausewitz noted that violence is a tool in the politician's toolbox to aid in achieving their political goals. The U.S. military fell in love with digital violence and began investing heavenly in 1990's as a low cost, low risk alternative to putting soldiers in harm's way.[20] Foreign militaries have also developed offensive cyber capabilities, and over 100 foreign intelligence services are actively trying to break into U.S. systems.[21] Nations are turning to cyberspace, believing a relatively small investment may enable them to exploit an opponent's reliance on cyberspace to achieve their political goals with little physical risk.

Cyber zealots often overestimate the impact of cyber weapons. While cyberattacks provide governments with additional capabilities in protecting their security and projecting power, they are of little real value unless supporting a physical attack. During the Gulf War U.S. precision-guided munitions knocked out Saddam's communications and power systems while targeting his information systems. While these efforts seriously degraded the Iraq military, his military didn't surrender when the power went out. The coalition forces defeated the Iraqi military when they destroyed much of his combat power, advanced, and threatened the Iraqi capital of Baghdad.

Likewise, the United States isn't going to surrender because some computers don't work, nor is cyber warfare a remedy for conflict. "People in Bosnia will kill each other with butter knives. Computer viruses aren't going to stop that kind of conflict," noted former soldier, author, and LA Times analyst William Arkin.[22] Cyber weapons will not replace traditional weapons.

National hackers may constrain their use of cyber weapons based on their perceived benefits and costs, including the potential consequences of releasing a new weapon on the world. In the U.S. the President authorizes the release of offensive cyber weapons and is responsible for the consequences. However, every nation has slightly different utility calculations. A nation unconstrained by the potential negative consequences of cyber weapons, or fighting for its survival may perceive destructive cyber weapons as a viable opportunity.

However, cyberspace offers these same capabilities to the average person. An unconstrained private hacker may use destructive weapons without understanding the potential consequences, or if the perceived benefits outweigh the costs. And a benefit may be to lay blame for a destructive attack on an innocent third party.

With all the potential doubt and deliberate misdirection there's a real chance of serious unintended consequences when acting as an antagonist in cyber conflict. In times of increased stress such as a major political crisis, the time when leaders need intelligence and intelligence organizations are likely to step-up intelligence operations, a victim may mistake an attempted espionage activity as a prelude to a destructive attack. Cyber events could escalate outside cyberspace due to misinterpretations, cultural differences, and nationalism with horrifying consequences.

Cyber weapons may offer a national leader opportunity to impact adversaries. However, these leaders must understand all the potential consequences of their use.

Shadow Boxing

Chapter 11. Strategies

"History teaches us that wars began when
governments believe the price of aggression is cheap."
- Ronald Reagan (1911 – 2004)
40th President of the United States
Speech given January 16, 1984

"Thus far the chief purpose of our military establishment has been to win wars.
From now on its chief purpose must be to avert them.
It can have almost no other useful purpose."
- Bernard Brodie (1910 – 1978)
The Absolute Weapon: Atomic Power and World Order

Following World War II the United States needed a national plan for the containment and use of nuclear weapons. In response, Bernard Brodie developed the U.S. nuclear deterrence strategy. Brodie argued using nuclear weapons in response to conventional threats would lead to nuclear escalation while deterring the use of nuclear weapons through a credible overwhelming second strike nuclear capability would lead to a more secure outcome for both sides.[1] The importance of nuclear weapons was not on their use but in the threat of their use.[2]

In the ensuing *cold war* both sides created massive conventional and nuclear forces, fought proxy wars around the world, and conducted tremendous intelligence campaigns until the 1991 collapse of the Soviet Union. Nevertheless, advocates of the policy argue the U.S. nuclear strategy called *Mutually Assured Destruction* or MAD deterred super powers from ever using their vast arsenals of nuclear weapons.[3] Surely we can apply lessons learned from nuclear strategies to deter digital aggression?

Coercion

The U.S. nuclear strategy is part of a larger group of strategies that rely on *coercion*. Coercive strategies use an implicit or explicit threat to manipulate an adversary into behaving involuntarily; coercion is the diplomacy of violence.[4] Two coercive strategies are deterrence and compellence.

Strategies

A method to compare alternative strategies is called utility theory. *Utility* is a perceived value an individual or organization receives from choosing a strategy calculated by the perceived benefits they receive reduced by their perceived costs.

$$Utility = Benefits_p - Costs_p$$

Utility theory hypothesizes a rational individual will compare alternative choices or strategies and pursue a choice where the perceived benefits outweigh the perceived costs. Utility theory isn't concerned with reality. It's concerned with an individual's perception of the costs and benefits, and the issues and values that influence these perceptions.

Deterrence involves an *actor demanding* a *target* not perform an *action*, a *punishment* if the action achieves a *trigger*, and then waiting. Deterrence is successful if the threat of punishment convinces the target to not perform the action. Deterrence fails if the target crosses the trigger whereby the demand turns into punishment. A rational target will not pursue an action if the perceived punishment outweighs the perceived benefits of taking the actions. Deterrence is defensive, passive, and seeks to maintain the status quo until a target performs an action, at which time the target is challenging the actor to respond.

Compellence is another coercive strategy. Compellence requires an actor to apply a punishment until the target changes their actions because the punishment imposed by the actor outweighs the benefits of their actions. In compellence the choice and consequences rests with both parties since the actor must apply punishment until the target stops an action. Compellence is an active strategy and requires the actor to use energy to punish, requires the target to stop some action, and has a timeline, suspense, or deadline.

Coercive strategies require actors clearly communicate to targets the triggers they must avoid or perform, and the punishment if they don't comply. When a target is not aware of these properties before a punishment is applied the strategy is not coercive, but retribution.[5]

Coercion requires the target believe the actor is capable and willing to impose the punishment. After the Second World War, the world knew the United States had detonated a nuclear bomb, and public demonstrations of ballistic missiles and strategic bombers proved the U.S. could deliver on the threat. President Eisenhower promised massive retaliation to any attack, and these public policy statements projected our willingness to use 'the bomb.' MAD appeared a credible strategy.

A means to observe the relationship must exist. In nuclear deterrence an aggressor detonating a thermonuclear bomb was a clearly visible indication of failing to deter. Likewise, detonating a thermonuclear bomb on the aggressor country was a clearly visible punishment.

A later deterrence strategy was Flexible Response. Proposed by Henry Kissinger, and enabled by advances in technology, Flexible Response proposed a stair step approach with gradual escalation, rather than an all-or-nothing nuclear response, providing the President with greater flexibility and more credibility. This approach allowed the President to escalate starting with conventional forces, then limited use of tactical battlefield nuclear weapons[6], then an all-out nuclear exchange.

A successful coercive strategy requires the target believe the actor will execute costly punishment as a consequence of defiance. With MAD the punishment for using a nuclear weapon was a massive, overwhelming second-strike capability that would not only destroy the remaining Soviet Union nuclear and conventional military arsenal, but also obliterate the Soviet society, and most likely reduce Earth to a smoldering and uninhabitable ruin.

Coercive strategies don't require the actor possess superior capabilities, only that the total perceived costs exceed the perceived benefits. Terrorists, guerilla forces, and criminals use coercive strategies successfully against larger, stronger targets. Using terror against the civilian population, and unconventional warfare against traditional military forces can convince civilian and military leaders to capitulate.

In 1990 President George H.W. Bush responded to Saddam Hussein's invasion of Kuwait when he "drew a line in the sand" stating that the goal of the massive U.S. and coalition military deployment to the Middle East was to defend Saudi Arabia. The White House plan was to use political pressure and economic sanctions to force Saddam's forces out of Kuwait. Bush's compellence strategy had little immediate impact on Saddam since Saddam wasn't after Saudi Arabia but rather the oil resources in Kuwait.

As the coalition grew and moved into the Saudi Arabian desert, Saddam responded by rounding up westerners in Iraq and Kuwait and used them as "human shields" to protect Iraqi military installations. The United Nations Security Council passed several resolutions condemning Iraq for holding foreign nationals as hostages. Coalition governments condemned Saddam for violating the 1949 Geneva Convention and promised to not back down.

Saddam couldn't sustain the growing political and economic costs imposed by Bush and his coalition, and on December 6, Saddam permitted westerners to leave. At the same time demands from the coalition, world events and domestic politics caused President Bush's line in the sand to shift. Bush used the threat of military force if Saddam didn't pull his forces out of Kuwait by January 15th. Saddam didn't believe the U.S. would invade his country and countered by threatening to destroy invading forces in a "mother of all battles." On January 17th the coalition forces attacked into Kuwait and Iraq. Bush failed to compel Saddam to pull his forces from Kuwait, and Saddam failed to deter a coalition invasion.

Now lets look at cyberspace.

Passive Denial Strategies

The most common guardian cyber strategy is to deny hackers from penetrating systems by constantly updating defensive technologies, policies, and processes. Maintaining systems and applying security patches doesn't make an organization secure — security buys time. Informed guardians know the reactive and retrospective nature of cyberspace will nearly guarantee a skilled or lucky hacker will eventually be successful if they are willing and able to make the investment. When a guardian detects that a hacker has penetrated they respond by cleaning the hackers out of their network and go on with their work.

When a hacker considers an operation their obvious benefits may include a financial gain from stealing economic or financial information, or increasing a nation's national security by stealing political, military, or economic information. However, benefits may also include intangibles such as increasing the ego and reputation of the individual or group performing an operation. Costs may include the time to prepare and execute an attack, use and loss of rare cyber tools, probability of attribution, the probability of being apprehended and punished, and any political repercussions of a cyberattack. Simple utility calculations show that the low cost to acquire and use attack tools, benefits when successful, and the lack of punishment will motivate hackers to continue.

We noted earlier that bank safes don't make banks secure. A thief will break into a building, cut through a safe, and take the contents if there is no possibility of being caught. A safe that is monitored may buy the owner time to detect an attack, alert authorities, and have them react. It's the potential fear of apprehension and punishment that concerns criminals, and transforms a passive defense strategy into a coercive strategy.

A cyber guardian may attempt to discourage hackers by portraying strong defenses that increase the hacker's costs. However, it's very difficult to portray defenses in cyberspace. A guardian would have to convey to hackers the difficulty by allowing reconnaissance of their network or purposefully leak defense information to hackers.

However, strong defenses may create an unintentional consequence. Since defenses cost time and money to install and maintain, guardians place their strongest defenses on their most important assets, which inadvertently announces a guardian is defending something of value. These defenses signal to a hacker that dedicating additional time, skills, and resources may achieve more benefit, unintentionally encouraging hackers.

Successfully penetrating a network guardians publicly announced as "highly secure" may provide a significantly boost to a hacker's ego and reputation within their community. This potential ego boost may change a hacker's utility calculations and encourage them to invest more resources so they can successfully penetrate "secure" networks.

Hackers know they are rarely punished and have become the cyber bullies that take the digital milk-money from guardian pacifists. Eventually guardians want to stick up for themselves.

Cyber Deterrence

Before we can say deterrence can be an effective national cyber strategy, we should point out challenges in applying this strategy. Cyber deterrence is not about defending a network and then punishing a hacker when they perform malicious actions. Applying punishment is an indication a deterrence strategy failed. Cyber deterrence is about averting an attack through the threat of punishment.

Deterrence requires a hacker believe a guardian can detect malicious behavior, then identify the individuals or group responsible for these actions, and then exert a punishment to the hacker that exceeds their perceived benefits.[7]

While the press reports of law enforcement agents arresting cyber "kiddy" hackers, and movies show the government tracking everything and everyone, reality is that the activities of sophisticated hackers are often detected months after their initial penetration. The victims of a cyberattack can rarely attribute sophisticated attacks unless a hacker deliberately takes credit for an attack.

Sensitive government programs may exist that can identify some hacker's and their activities. However, deterrence requires a visible threat of punishment. Punishing someone who has been detected, tracked, or identified using classified government programs may alert the hacker and possibly the world to the classified capability. Hackers would then change their technology or technique resulting in the government losing these tracking and identification sources and methods. So the government can't use these classified capabilities to support a deterrence role or they will go blind, and lose the ability to threaten.

The criminal justice system is at the heart of cyber deterrence. It represents actions that can, will, and have been taken against some past offenders. However, the ability for domestic and international legal systems to punish hackers who operates from or on behalf of a nation-state is severely limited since they are operating with their nation's blessings (See Chapter 8 – International Espionage).

A viable deterrence strategy requires hackers perceive their benefits outweigh the political and economic gains obtained through cyber espionage or attacks. The punishment under MAD was massive nation-ending (and perhaps world-ending) nuclear retaliation. Just as guardians often recover quickly from most cyberattacks, hackers may quickly recover from a punishing attack.

Coercion will only be successful if the target believes if they don't comply the situation will get worse. The MAD strategy was successful because both sides believed that could not survive a full-scale nuclear exchange. In cyberspace when an actor launches a cyberattack they are revealing a vulnerability to the victim and eliminating the possibility of using the attack repeatedly.[8] Thus if guardians launch a retaliatory cyber strike against a hacker they are telling the hacker they have a vulnerability, and providing their weapon to the hacker. The hacker can repair their system, remove the vulnerability used in their retaliatory attack and be confident the guardian cannot attack again using that vulnerability. And the hacker now has their weapon to use against others. The guardian's attack will prevent future attacks and arm the hacker, effectively neutralizing the deterrence effects.

Strategies

A guardian must have the will and the means to instill punishment that may appear as retribution in hindsight. Effects such as bricking Internet routers will deny Internet connectivity and communications for a short to mid-term. Bricking user's computers may cost the average home, businesses, and government users the loss of information and temporarily prevent them from communicating. Punishment could also include damage to the environment such as bursting pipelines or creating the loss of life or fear of future loss of life through train or plane crashes, elevator crashes, and damaging hydroelectric dams, water and sewage treatment plants, chemical refinery accidents and contamination of the water table or agriculture. But are the American people okay with a massive cyber (or kinetic) response to an unattributable cyberattack? More importantly do hackers believe the U.S. will execute these counterattacks to deter them from executing malicious activities?

The U.S. nuclear deterrence strategy revolved around a single antagonist, the Soviet Union. The U.S. believed it understood the Soviet Union, its values, and its utility calculations. Both nations had extensive espionage programs to confirm threats, costs, and the ability to deter the other from the first use of nuclear weapons. Espionage enabled the superpowers to understand the other and resulted in a more secure world.

In cyberspace there are numerous adversaries all playing the game at the same time. These players include not only numerous nations, but also thousands of individuals, groups, and agencies all with different agendas, skills, resources, and cost/pain thresholds. We often can't determine the identity of the persons performing an act in cyberspace or understand a hacker's goal from the observable evidence.

The U.S. government's philosophy is that the government doesn't need perfect attribution before taking actions, just a preponderance of evidence supporting the attribution. In 2014 the U.S. government claimed North Korea was responsible for the 2014 compromise of Sony Entertainment. The government provided a few supporting facts such as North Korean hackers use the same software discovered during the Sony investigation. However other hackers use the same software, and these hackers could have fabricated the circumstantial evidence provided by the U.S. government to lay blame at the North Korean's digital doorstep.

Using the "I've got a secret" defense severely damaged the U.S. government case, both in convincing the world of North Korean government participation in the attack, and in justifying the resulting U.S. economic sanctions on North Korea.

Are we willing to base national policy, such as our response to Sony to punish North Korea, or to counterattack and damage another nation, without attributing those responsible? Or worse, were we manipulated by a third party into taking action against North Korea? Or was President Obama frustrated with North Korea prior to the Sony incident, and the Sony incident provided a convenient and plausible excuse for the White House to apply economic sanctions the White House was considering prior to the attack?

Star Wars or Economic Destruction

In 1983 President Reagan destabilized the nuclear deterrence equilibrium when he introduced the Strategic Defense Initiative (SDI). This strategy, often referred to as Star Wars after the 1977 George Lucas film, was aimed at developing technology to defend against ballistic, strategic nuclear missiles. The theory was that the U.S. could develop advanced technology to identify, track, and destroy incoming intercontinental and submarine-launched ballistic missiles. Destroying the Soviet's missiles removed their offensive advantage, and eliminated the response component of the Soviet deterrence theory. SDI destabilized MAD and placed nuclear weapon dominance back in the U.S. hands.

Eliminating the Soviets ability to strike reduced the benefit of their offensive and response technologies, and the Soviet's strategic strength. At its most basic concepts SDI was a passive, defensive strategy based on one side possessing advanced technology. By focusing on defense the U.S. mitigated the Soviet offensive nuclear investment, while still possessing a viable offensive nuclear option. It's important to remember that SDI wasn't effective because it prevented delivery of nuclear weapons, but because the Soviet Union perceived it would be effective at preventing the delivery of nuclear weapons.

The mainstream media and many within the scientific community argued that SDI was unrealistic, unscientific, and destabilized MAD, forcing the two superpowers back into an arms race. Some supporters of Reagan and SDI countered that the goal wasn't to develop a defensive wall, but to force the economically insolvent Soviet Union to invest heavily in research and development, leading to their economic collapse and end of the Cold War.

Either deliberately, or accidentally, SDI became part of the U.S. strategy. The White House convinced Soviet leaders that the U.S. could mitigate Soviet nuclear first strike and response options. The Soviets believed they were losing the arms race and responded by investing heavily in research and development of their own SDI technology and conventional and nuclear weapons. This spending was detrimental to the overall Soviet economy and is credited with aiding in the collapse of the Soviet Union.

Blockades

Compellence is another strategy used in cyberspace. Blockades can be a compellence strategy that attempts to prevent something from crossing a self-defined line to force a reaction. Blockades that do not have a goal of forcing an action are not a compellence strategy, but a simple denial strategy.

Strategies

The Cuban Missile Crisis was a successful use of compellence. Russia made a secret deal with Cuba to place nuclear weapons on the Island of Cuba after the failed 1961 Bay of Pig invasion and the U.S. placing nuclear weapons in Europe. The U.S. response was to establish a naval blockade of Cuba in October 1962. The goal was not to prevent vessels from entering Cuba, but rather to force Russia to remove nuclear missiles from Cuba. Russia removed the nuclear missiles from Cuba, and the U.S. removed nuclear missiles from Turkey and Italy.

Blockades occur every day in cyberspace to degrade or disable communications. The goal of a digital blockade may be to deny specific messages from entering or leaving an area, a complete blockade that deactivates or physical damages routing infrastructures, or disrupting traffic to impact operations such as flooding attacks. Nations, corporations, and ISPs deny individuals and groups access to portions of the Internet and the resources and communications that exist there. These are denial strategies.

Totalitarian regimes such as Egypt, Burma, Iran, and China have self-imposed blockades to control social networks and text messages. During the winter 2011 Egypt protests, the Egyptian government directed their Internet service providers disable public access to stop protest coordinators from texting and creating flash mobs. The strategy unintentionally led to the people going to the streets in protest.

Every sailor knows a blockade is never 100% effective – something is going to get through. In Egypt people found alternative means to communicate including long-distance telephone calls to modems, then sending messages and text to people outside of Egypt. People leaving the country carried information, photos, video, and audio recordings in miniature thumbdrives. Protestors used physical messages and couriers to bypass the government's technical barriers. While the government blockade didn't significantly impact the protestors, it had a significant impact on commerce.

Many governments have been shaken by the Internet, their citizen's access to uncensored information, and the role it has played in political instability and regime changes.[9] Their natural reaction is to control cyberspace. Even the U.S. government has investigated this option, until cooler heads prevailed.

Since 2010 Congressional proposals for censoring sensitive information posted on the Internet, control of the Internet during emergencies, and a so-called Internet Kill Switch demonstrate a lack of understanding regarding the false sense of security and the economic consequences of flipping the switch in a global economy. Besides bringing our economy to a grinding halt (and irritating constituents) our government has transitioned so much of its own processes to the Internet that shutting the Internet down would bring our national government to its knees.

Unfortunately we did not realize that the Department of Defense hosted the Federal Voting Assistance Program. This website enables U.S. citizens to request information on absentee voting. With our block in place customers of the French ISP who tried to request an absentee voting application were denied access to the site during an election year.

U.S. citizens abroad, the news media, and conspiracy theorists had a field day. According to them the Pentagon was now "denying U.S. expatriates their constitutional right to vote" immediately before a presidential election. Our deliberate embargo of the French ISP led to numerous news articles, briefings to senior leaders and the White House, and Congressional inquiries and testimonies.[10]

We lifted the block in time for U.S. citizens to register to vote, and several of the French guardians became our cyberspace friends.

Retribution and Response Actions

Many armchair military strategists argue that offense is always the strongest form of warfare. They say the U.S. should focus on offensive cyber operations in response to hackers breaking into our systems.

This belief is probably a legacy of sixty years of the threat of thermonuclear war and the U.S. MAD strategy. However professional soldiers know that offense has an advantage over defense only if the attacker is assured they can deliver their weapon effects onto their targets and the weapon has a significant impact on the target. If these assertions prove false, then the defender may have the advantage.

During the First World War the heavy and bulky machinegun was unsuitable for the offense since soldiers needed to carry weapons across battlefields. However, the machinegun provided a two-man crew defending a position the firepower of tens of soldiers armed with rifles. In this situation the trenches, machineguns, artillery, and gas warfare technology of the time gave the defender the stronger form of combat and resulted in years of bloody attrition trench warfare. The tremendous improvements in mobility brought about by improvements with the internal combustion engine relegated trench warfare to the past.

Strategies

History shows that advantages between offense and defense are cyclic, brought about by changes in technology and the tactics and strategies to exploit the technology. It is not true that an attacker always has the advantage.

Today government agencies and contractors that promote cyber weapon consulting, training, and technology argue that victims should launch retaliatory counter-attacks in response to hackers.[11] Often those advocating retaliatory attacks don't consider the preconditions to deterrence such as announcing a trigger and projecting a credible threat of punishment. Under this situation the retaliatory attacks are not part of a deterrence strategy, but a retribution strategy.

In the United States, the authority to execute an attack against a foreign power is retained by the President. However, since 2005 the Pentagon has been asking for unilateral authority to conduct offensive cyber operations in response to cyberattacks against the United States. Military members (and their contractors) argue that they have the right to self-defense – just as a military force may defend itself from a surprise physical attack. They argue that moving at the speed of cyberspace requires the military have preapproval to counter-attack.

Under international law *jus ad bellum* or "when it is just to begin to fight" self-defense is a legal justification to use armed force and declare war. Paraphrasing United Nations Charter Article 2(4) Article 51 the only means to begin wars is an imminent threat in response to an armed attack, or with Security Council sanction.

But the crucial challenge of digital retribution is one of the strengths of cyberconflict — the inability to attribute the activities of sophisticated adversaries. Some argue that a guardian need not attribute an attack prior to counter-attacking. General Keith Alexander, at the time Director of the NSA and Commander U.S. Cyber Command noted, "We have the inherent right to defend first and then attribute."[12]

Businesses are frustrated over being continually cyber assaulted by hackers and are also discussing taking matters in their own hands. After repeated attacks on the financial industry banks are openly discussing hiring hackers to launch punishing cyberattacks against the hackers attacking their bank's systems.[13]

Cyber hawks comment that "soldiers don't care who's shooting at them — they return fire." This phrase greatly simplifies what professional soldiers do, and the challenges to responding in cyberspace. Advocates of retribution overlook the difference between a mob and a disciplined military unit, the role of military leaders to minimize violence and collateral damage, and the differences between a traditional kinetic battlefield and cyberspace.

A soldier can't return fire until they know that they are under fire, and in cyberspace a guardian may not distinguish an attack from a computer malfunction until they analyze the incident, and this analysis takes time. Additionally, unless the guardian is operating a nuclear power plant or works for a tyrant, a cyberattack doesn't threaten their survival, and an immediate response may not be necessary. Lastly, as we learned earlier, the defender needs to discover the source of an attack and whether the attack started from that location, hopped through that location, or was never in that location. A counter-attack against a neutral, previously compromised victim may inadvertently damage hospital, financial, communication, or public utility systems. And hackers may deliberately manipulate defenders to cause a retribution attack to damage an innocent, high-visibility target.

A destructive response to a cyber incident may also result in an escalation of conflict. The result is that a counter-attack may not be an appropriate effective or efficient strategy or use of resources.

In August 15, 2012 the temperature in Dhahran, Saudi Arabia was racing towards 110 degrees Fahrenheit. Employees of the Aramco oil company were at home preparing for one of Islam's holiest nights of the year; Lailat al Qadr, or the Night of Power celebrating Allah's revelation of the Koran to Muhammad.

At the same time an insider sat comfortable in an Aramco corporate office at one of their 40,000 computers and contemplated what they were about to do. Aramco is the Saudi Arabian national petroleum company based in Dhahran, Saudi Arabia that owns and operates the world's largest crude oil reserves. As the insider sat at the terminal they launched malware that would eventually be called Shamoon, into the Aramco corporate network. While the Aramco network was highly defended from an outside attack, the insider was already inside and bypassed all of this security. The worm raced through the network copying itself to every machine it could access. Within hours 30,000 computers on the company network, 75% of the company systems, were infected. Shamoon copied a small amount of information out of the network to a remote system. Then, after racing secretly through the network the worm slept. At 11:08am Shamoon ordered every infected computer to erase all information from the computers and placed an image of a burning American flag on the hard drive, making every system unreadable, and the computers unbootable.

The company petroleum control systems were isolated from this corporate network, however in an instant millions of emails, documents, spreadsheets, and data files on 30,000 computers were gone. While refining operations themselves were not directly damaged, the management systems the CEO used to run the company were gone, including the systems used to track every drop of oil pumped out of the oil fields from the pumps through refineries, pipelines, port and tankers. The Aramco CEO couldn't know how much oil was in the system, was being refined, or was being shipped to each customer. Their refinement infrastructure wasn't harmed but their ability to use data from their system to make business decisions was knocked into the sand. The company came to a stop.

Aramco took immediate action to shut down the corporate network and begin the cleanup. Guardians pulled the hard drives from all the company computers and stacked them in giant piles, and then searched for replacements. Within a week there wasn't a harddrive available anywhere in the Middle East, and Aramco was ordering tens of thousands to replace the ones infected. It took months for Aramco to rebuild systems and bring services back online. In the meantime, employees and managers couldn't effectively communicate, let alone accomplish work. Employees were forced to go "old school" and used couriers both locally and internationally to carry corporate and business messages. While the time and cost of replacing the harddrives were high, the real loss was the information lost on the hard drives and lost productivity.

Investigators believe the Aramco incident was a deliberate retribution attack by Iranian agents in response to Stuxnet. No hacker has been publicly identified.

Manipulation of Utility

A strategy can focus on the direct manipulation of the hacker's cost or benefit components of their utility calculations. If a hacker is interested in espionage, then their reward is the resultant stolen information. A guardian could manipulate the attacker's confidence in the information they obtain. If a hacker cannot be assured that the information is genuine, then their reward is lowered and their utility calculation may be manipulated in the guardian's favor. The U.S. used his strategy in their Farewell Dossier project (see Chapter 11 – Physical Attack).

In traditional deterrence theory the fear of punishment has focused on bodily harm, such as through military action, or the removal of privileges, such as being detained in jail or applying import/export trade restrictions. Likewise traditional deterrence theory focused on a threat of physical attacks from other nations with similar or at least significant in power and size. With the current state of affairs a single hacker might be as devastating as nation-states.

However, the hacker's source of power is the hacker's ability to reuse their tools, capabilities, access, and knowledge. Every time a hacker executes an operation they provide this information to their victims and risk transferring their power to their victims.

Guardians can remove the vulnerability that gave the hacker access or manipulate the information the adversary thinks they are exfiltrating. A guardian can "counter-attack" the adversary in informational terms by putting the hacker in a position where they must use more capabilities to obtain their goal resulting in a greater technological transfer from the hacker to the guardian. By sharing information about hacker's tools, IP addresses (both home and hop-points), and techniques guardians can reduce the pool of potential victims a hacker can exploit. This would force hackers to change their technologies and tactics constantly. This technique may increase a hacker's costs without requiring attribution attacks.

By raising the perceived cost above an adversary's cost threshold, a guardian may keep an adversary in a constant cycle of reconnaissance and exploit development. Some hackers may eventually decide the costs of cyber operations are greater than the benefits, and move on to other projects.

Nation state hackers will perceive significant benefits for information critical to their national survival. Impacting these hacker's utility calculations may be difficult. However, a nation is not limited to cyber effects to punish or deter hackers. The U.S. could use its political, military, and economic strength to punish other nations for cyber incidents. On the international stage we may use demarches, the international legal system, economic sanctions, and military actions. And these nations may not be willing to threaten their political, military, or economic health for the benefits of their malicious cyber programs.

One challenge is that we may become worse off if we punish nations that support malicious cyber activities. Other nations may follow our lead and punish the U.S. for the criminal and government cyber activities originating from within the U.S. borders. In this age of international economics and trade this could force the U.S. government to take a more active role in monitoring, tracking, and apprehending domestic cyber actors perceived as a threat by other nations.

Active Defense

In response to the 9/11 terrorist attacks President George W. Bush announced a new U.S. counter-terrorist strategy. He said, "We must take the battle to the enemy, disrupt his plans and confront the worst threats before they emerge. In the world we have entered, the only path to safety is the path of action. And this nation will act." The resulting *4-D Strategy,* short for Defeat, Deny, Diminish and Defend, involved collecting intelligence on terrorist cells and preemptively disrupting and destroying them before the terrorists could execute their plans. [14]

This strategy is called *Active Defense,* and is "the employment of limited offensive actions and counterattacks to deny a contested area or position to the enemy."[15] Active defense involves conducting surveillance on potential enemies. If a nation learns that an adversary is preparing to attack they use military forces to destroy, disable, or destabilize the imminent and impending attack, and then retreat to safety.

The goal of this preemptive, surprise *spoiling attack* is not to gain territory, but to protect their home. Preemptive strikes may minimize damage to one's own country and disrupt the adversary's offensive preparation, perhaps preventing an impending attack. The attack may also generate psychological and political shock and force the adversary to accept a beneficial solution.

Critics of active defense argue that a no-notice preemptive attack is breaking the peace before hostilities have occurred and may violate numerous treaties including the UN charter.[16]

Examples of preemptive attacks include the 1941 Japanese surprise attack against Pearl Harbor, Hawaii, the 1952 Chinese military support to North Korea due to General Douglas MacArthur's public threat to march north and invade China, and the 1962 Sino-India War over disputed land between India and China.

Strategies

In August 2010, Deputy Secretary of Defense William J. Lynn III mentioned active defense as a U.S. cyber strategy.[17] The U.S. military active defense cyber strategy involves guardians penetrating hacker's systems to discover their activities and interests and then attacking and counter-attacking to degrade adversaries in cyberspace. Proponents argue active defense is not retribution. They argue that "...unless we find a way to use offensive capabilities as part of deterrence or strategic deterrence ... we will be unable to defeat [opponents]."[18]

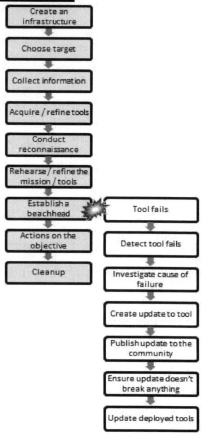

Active defense fundamentally changes the guardians mission from a purely technical cyber defense problem to a counter-intelligence or law enforcement problem. Under active defense guardians conduct surveillance on foreign threats, track hacker activities, and sometimes attack the hackers themselves.

As U.S. leaders become frustrated at being the victim of cyber espionage and want to use the U.S. offensive cyber arsenal to protect the U.S. interests in cyberspace. They argue that once someone decides to launch a cyberattack it's too late to defend. They contend that Cyber Command can "prowl for cyber trouble and ... with a few keystrokes or by activating secret codes long ago secreted in a prospective foe's computer system – thwart any attack."[19]

Let's look at two cases; when a guardian has no indication an adversary is preparing for an attack, and when a guardian has indications an adversary is preparing to attack.

In the first case, a guardian has no

Hacker's and Guardian's Processes

indications someone on a network will launch a future attack, so they will need to conduct cyber espionage to determine if the users of the network are conspiring. This requires the guardian penetrate the suspected networks to gather intelligence on their activities.

From the suspected network's perspective, this espionage is the very act that the U.S. claims is the justification to respond with destructive attacks. The victim of this espionage may detect the activity, not understand the intent of the espionage, and believe (correctly) that this activity is a precursor to a destructive attack. If this is the case, the victim may take a play from the U.S. playbook and attack whomever they believe is responsible for this espionage to prevent a future attack. Thus whether the suspected network is innocent or guilty of preparing to attack, the U.S. actions may instigate a potential cyber war.

The second case is when suspicious activity is coming from a network. If the adversary is not sophisticated, then the adversary may not represent a significant threat to our systems and we should not use sophisticated resources to monitor them. If a guardian uses sophisticated tools to penetrate the network then we have to assume the adversary will record these tools, and may use them against others or announce them to the world to prevent their future use.

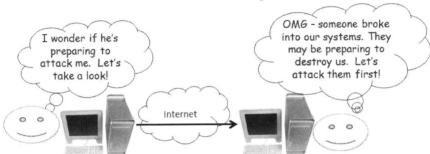

Figure 18 - Active Defense: A Self-Fulfilling Prophecy?

On the other hand, sophisticated adversaries may perform their research and planning offline and use vulnerable third party machines and free sites (i.e. libraries, cyber cafes) to launch operations and collect information.

We also have to assume a sophisticated adversary can break onto other networks since we are afraid they will attack and penetrate ours. But if we are afraid the adversary can get onto another network, then perhaps a third party penetrated these systems and is using this network as a hop-off point. If this is the case, then an active-defense strategy may target the hop-off point that is the source of malicious activity, not the responsible party.

Of course, if a hacker is operating domestically their activities become a law enforcement issue that requires probable cause and warrants to perform surveillance. Since the military and Intelligence Community are forbidden to operate domestically a military active-defense strategy won't deter activities originating from hackers or hop-off points inside the continental United States.

If the adversary is overseas, then guardians will need to determine if the target is within the border of an ally (Great Britain), a friendly nation (Spain), a neutral country (Switzerland) or other country (Iran, Afghanistan, China). The U.S. has different policies, treaties, and rules regarding how to interact with each and limitations on the actions we can take.

After all of this, if guardians are successful then the best they can hope for is to frustrate hackers. The hackers will investigate their failures and discover the penetration into their networks. However, the hacker may capture the guardian's weapon and techniques used in the preemptive attack and may turn them against the guardian or another party. The hacker will most likely remove the vulnerability that enabled the preemptive attack thus eliminating the guardian's threat of future attacks. The adversary may either move or change their activities to prevent future monitoring, thus causing intelligence collection efforts to go blind.

The U.S. has told the world it's okay to compromise and damage networks preemptively, and these announcements will be noticed. In 2008 Russian hackers were believed to have used thousands of compromised machines around the world to flood the Georgia public and private networks.

Is this the strategy we want the world to follow?

The premise of Active Defense is that a guardian conducts surveillance against potential future adversaries for the sake of preventing future destructive attacks and espionage. However, the victims of this surveillance can't differentiate this espionage on their networks from criminal activities or preparation for a destructive attack. We have told the world they have the right and obligation to launch preventive cyber strikes against hackers, and our active defense is nothing less than hacking others.

We need to remember that a U.S. preemptive strike against Cuban and Russian forces during the 1961-1962 Cuban missile crisis would have escalated as each side responded with greater military force. Similarly, a hacker may perform espionage that triggers a guardian into a preemptive, destructive attack, although the espionage is legal under international law. The preemptive attack may appear to the hacker as the opening shots in a destructive campaign. International law permits the victim, in this case the hacker, to respond. Civilian leaders need to keep the Pentagon on a tight leash, or risk cyber warriors getting our nation into a real war.

Bean Counters

A government strategy to deal with changing environments and incidents is to create additional policies. Many government initiatives such as the Federal Information Security Management Act, or FISMA, were knee-jerk reactions to publicized network compromises.[20] FISMA requires every government agency to collect metrics on how they maintain their networks, and report these metrics quarterly to Congress. This bureaucratic process consumed over $2.3 billion annually,[21] and provides a consistent funding stream to contractors who collect, compile, analyze, audit, and publish these metrics on behalf of the government.

Since 2002 when FISMA became law, the constant compromise of public systems shows the programs and laws are ineffective or ignored, since every government agency penetrated by hackers has either complied with FISMA or ignored the federal law. Congress and government watchdogs allowed FISMA to become an administrative *request* to generate reports rather than a Federal law to protect networks.

The Office of Personnel Management (OPM) manages federal employees. OPM created information systems to contain the sensitive personal records of the 22.1 million current, former, and prospective government employees and their family, friends, and personal references. These systems contained records of personal interviews, fingerprints, criminal histories, performance evaluations, and all the sensitive background investigations required for government security clearances. The OPM knew this information was a goldmine for cyber criminals. But it was also a wealth of information for foreign intelligence services since it contained information on intelligence operators and the classified work they perform.[22] Then OPM placed these systems on the Internet. Foreign hackers compromised the OPM systems from 2013 through 2015 and exfiltrated the sensitive information.[23]

OPM failed to implement basic security practices to monitor or protect the systems, and didn't test the systems to ensure they were safe from common hackers. Many of these systems appear to have not complied with federal laws and policies, were not authorized to be online, were not maintained once online, and their security was little more than administrative paperwork. OPM didn't monitor their systems for malicious activity. The OPM Inspector General responsible for combating fraud, waste and abuse and improving government efficiency reported these findings for years prior to the compromise, and government leaders ignored them.

OPM officials put every government employee and their families at risk possibly because the officials knew there are no consequences for systems not being compliant, for breaking the law, for ignoring government policies and watchdogs, and having a network compromised. Government failures lack consequences because the person with the authority and responsibility for deciding the consequences are the managers of the government agencies themselves.[24]

The government could replace FISMA with a simple report on government networks and systems that perpetrators compromise. Government agencies could report how they prepared prior to the compromise, how perpetrators obtained access, how others are affected by the compromise, and how actions implemented to prevent reoccurrence. This report would inform our national leadership on how they are doing and how to get better. But do government leaders want this information collected and reported?

Periodically a government spokesperson promises they can increase security through new government programs to increase monitoring, attribution, and control at the cost of reduced personal privacy. These announcements don't mention these programs won't reduce the Intelligence Community's ability to conduct espionage. Since these programs won't stop our intelligence efforts, and hackers use the same technology and tactics, these government programs will have little effect stopping other nations or sophisticated cyber criminals. However, oppressive regimes around the world will use these monitoring and identification programs to suppress dissents and track and identify malcontents. Others could be at risk due to increased online tracking and attribution including journalists protecting their sources; whistleblowers; mental or physical abuse victims seeking protection; teenagers seeking advice on contraception or medical issues; child and sex traffic victims; asylum seekers and refugees. In the end, these efforts may cause considerable harm to personal privacy and civil liberty.

Conclusion

In 2007, General Ronald Keys, commander of U.S. Air Combat Command stated that technology has outpaced policy and that policies prevent the U.S. from pursuing cyber threats in foreign countries. Keys noted that "The United States should take more aggressive measures against foreign hackers and web sites that help others attack government systems... It may take a cyber version of the 2001 terrorist attack" – meaning 9/11 – "for the country to realize it must re-examine its approach to cyber warfare."[25] However approaches coming from the Pentagon are requests to authorize offensive attacks.

Others around the world may see the problem differently. A survey of international cyber security experts ranked the U.S. as the country of greatest concern for conducting cyberattacks, just ahead of China.[26] These people see the U.S. promoting the use of offensive and destructive cyber weapons and policies to deploy those weapons.

Deterrence has been the foundation of our nation's nuclear strategy since the 1950's. Military leaders believe this strategy worked to defeat the Soviet Union during the Cold War, so surely we can simply adjust deterrence theory to deal with our cyber adversaries. Yet Washington hasn't explained how this will work.

A national strategy based on offensive cyber capabilities is wishful thinking, and every act of punishment demonstrates the failure of the U.S. cyber deterrence strategy. Perhaps it's time to stop trying to force cyberspace to fit into 1950's thinking, and look for alternative strategies?

There are many other strategies to consider. We've discussed passive defense, denial, coercion, compellence, retribution, utility manipulation, and active defense. There are many more. Perhaps an effective national strategy is a set of strategies, with each targeting specific classes of hackers.

Chapter 12. The Digital Apocalypse

"This great nation will endure as it has endured, will revive and will prosper.
So, first of all, let me assert my firm belief that the only thing we have to fear
is fear itself – nameless, unreasoning, unjustified terror which paralyzes needed efforts
to convert retreat into advance."
- Franklin D. Roosevelt (1882-1945)
Thirty Second President of the United States

"The most likely way for the world to be destroyed, most experts agree, is by accident.
That's where we come in; we're computer professionals. We cause accidents."
- Nathaniel Borenstein (1957 -)
U.S. Programmer

The Russians are Coming!

In November 2011, Russian hackers apparently broke into the Curran-Gardner Public Water District water plant control system in Springfield, Illinois and damaged a water pump. The news media heralded this incident as the first reported case of a malicious cyberattack damaging the critical systems essential for the U.S. society and economy.[1] Cyber experts were quick to proclaim the dawn of cyberwar and speculated about the coming cyberattacks on our nation's critical infrastructures.[2] These experts declared power grids would soon fail and cause blackouts; hackers would destroy the financial systems leading to a worldwide economic collapse; airplanes would fall from the sky as viruses attacked aircraft flight control systems and the nation's air traffic control systems.

The real story was much less dramatic. During the previous June a contractor who helped establish and maintain the facility control systems decided to vacation in Russia. During his vacation an employee from the water facility telephoned and asked him to examine data in the water system. The contractor connected to the control system from Russia, checked the status of the water systems and reported everything looked fine. Five months later when a water pump in the facility failed investigators suspected hackers and began looking for evidence to support their assumption of a computer attack. They examined the system logs and discovered someone had remotely connecting to the water control system from an IP address in Russia. Confirming their original assumption, they jumped to the conclusion a Russian hacker had remotely connected to the water pump and caused it to fail by repeatedly turning it on and off. Security experts and news media sensationalized the event from there.[3] The 2011 Springfield incident had nothing to do with a cyberattack, but was a series of investigation blunders and sensationalized stories.

For 20 years' security pundits have been claiming a massive cyberattack would disable banking, telecommunications, and power grids, and throw modern societies back to the Stone Age. Government officials and hackers alike refer to these catastrophic cyberattacks on national civilian infrastructures as a "Cyber Pearl Harbor," "Digital Apocalypse," "Cyber Terrorism" and "Internet 9/11." They claim that disabling or destroying a nation's critical infrastructures may bring an industrial nation to its knees and compel it to submit to an antagonist's demands.

Tinker Toys

Improving the efficiency and effectiveness of individual companies, and then combining corporate technology, operations, and processes with suppliers, shippers, and consumers through computing and telecommunications technologies has created tremendous opportunities for business and improved societies quality of life. When a retail outlet combines a modern automated inventory system with effective telecommunications and computerized shipping industries, it may create more or entirely new functionality and vastly more effective and efficient stores. This may reduce product storage and returns through "just in time" inventory control that orders inventory as the system anticipates a need, ensuring shipping companies can deliver supplies as stores need them, and eliminating the need for large local warehouses and back rooms. This may also allow companies to focus on their core competencies such as developing and selling products to consumers rather than on tasks they may not excel such as delivering product to consumers.

The result is a *system of systems* where dedicated and specialized component systems combine into a larger, more complex system that is more than the sum of its parts. This composite system may decrease costs or improve timeliness of products or services, and increase profits for businesses as they specialize and become more efficient.

These composite systems have revolutionized entire industries. When Amazon.com went live in 1995, it revolutionized book sales around the world. Amazon created this revolution through an automated information infrastructure to manage its inventory, sales, and shipping. However, Amazon also needed other businesses to provide an efficient and cost effective transportation infrastructure to transport books — and telecommunications enabled this transportation infrastructure. Online book sales would not have started had it not been for a (relatively) trustworthy online financial system-of-systems that allowed consumers to pay Amazon for books and shipping costs, Amazon to pay publishers for their books, and shippers to deliver the books quickly to customer's homes and offices. This revolution dealt a deathblow to many traditional "brick and mortar" bookstores that could not adapt and compete due to their cost of operating local stores and maintaining stock in each store.

Cyberspace has also revolutionized the building blocks of modern societies. *Infrastructures* maintain a nation's society, economy, security and way of life. These infrastructures include power, communications, water, food, finances, transportation, manufacturing, and emergency services.[4] The U.S. Department of Homeland Security defines these infrastructures as "… the backbone of our nation's economy, security and health… so vital to the United States that their incapacitation or destruction would have a debilitating effect on security, national economic security, national public health or safety, or any combination thereof."[5]

The infrastructures interdependencies make each infrastructure more effective and efficient, but also exacerbate the impact of single outages. When an incident affects one infrastructure, the effects may cascade through the dependent infrastructures. When man-made or natural events degrade electrical power and telecommunications other infrastructures are affected. Gas stations can't pump petroleum without electricity. Shipping companies lose touch with their customers and can't refuel trucks, so shipping stops. Stores quickly lose inventory. Frozen and refrigerated foods spoil in hours or days as refrigeration stops and backup generators run out of fuel. Stores may not honor credit card sales since the stores can't connect to banks for purchase authorizations. Automated teller machines (ATMs) deny people their cash due to power outages or an inability to call banks to confirm on-hand balances. Soon society itself may breakdown due to collapses in infrastructures.

Natural disasters, accidents, technical failures, and deliberate damage have always threated these infrastructures. One only has to think of the last hurricane, tornado, ice storm, or major thunderstorm to see the effect. People today are much less self-sufficient and therefore more reliant on these critical infrastructures than in the past. Many families will find themselves short of food and fresh water in days, if not hours, when there's a power outage. In 2005, Hurricane Katrina showed the effects of prolonged local infrastructures outages when it transformed New Orleans in a matter of days from a modern city into a third world crisis.

All the national infrastructures depend on vulnerable telecommunications and computing technology that adversaries may exploit. Launching cyberattacks against a nation's infrastructures has many of the same strengths and weaknesses as other offensive cyber operations. However, to create a digital apocalypse an attacker doesn't switch off or destroy computers. An apocalypse requires a hacker to create physical effects such as turning off electrical power systems, opening floodgates, causing train wrecks or disabling bank teller machines.

The Digital Apocalypse

A hacker could plan an attack to maximize its effect to citizens, such as during the hottest part of the summer or during a blizzard. Or a hacker could plan an attack to occur when their nation is planning to invade a neighboring country to keep the victim occupied with their own problems and out of the invader's way, and slowing their victim's ability to mobilize and respond in the face of a kinetic attack.

An infrastructure attack may harm people and property. Accidental power outages in very hot summers nearly always result in the deaths of the elderly and sick. Power outages in the winter may cause hypothermia since many homes don't have a backup source of heat. People may also be harmed indirectly such as the chaos that occurs in major cities when all the traffic lights and street lamps turn off during power outages.

Infrastructure outages also create massive inconvenience. Consumers and businesses may not access funds, suppliers, or consumers. Transportation including passenger and cargo ships, trucks, and aircraft may stop. The stock markets may shut down preventing the selling and buying of corporate stocks. Billions, perhaps trillions of dollars could be lost per day. Public and private transition and reliance on just-in-time logistics increases our reliance on these infrastructures. A small outage in power, transportation, or banking will have a more significant impact if customers don't have supplies on-hand.

Regrettably, some people will riot and loot as time passes and they consume their food, heat, and grow more frustrated. One only has to look at New Orleans, New York, and Los Angeles for historical examples of the effects of outages.

The 2005 Hurricane Katrina was a dark spot in the nation's preparation and response to a natural disaster, but in a few years Katrina will be a footnote in history. Will a future cyberattack also be an apocalypse or a blip in history?

Elmer FUD

On November 6, 2008, retired Vice Admiral John "Mike" McConnell, then the Director of National Intelligence, briefed President-elect Barrack Obama on the threats to our national security. He noted that the U.S. was vulnerable to cyberattacks. Referring to the terrorist attacks of September 11, 2001, he noted that had the nineteen terrorists been "cyber smart" they would have created an order of magnitude greater impact than destroying two World Trade Center buildings and damaging the Pentagon. McConnell told the president-elect that the Bank of New York and Citibank each handle $3 trillion daily of financial transfers. The U.S. GDP is $14 trillion. If the terrorist had destroyed the bank data, there would have been a financial crisis.[6]

McConnell confused the Gross National Product (GDP) and the total quantity of commercial and personal financial transactions when he briefed the incoming president. The GDP measures the monetary value of all the finished goods and services produced within a country's borders but he was comparing it to the financial transactions of the Bank of New York and Citibank that include processing financial transactions for citizens, commerce, and governments of foreign countries. If we believe these two banks transfer over $1 quadrillion per year, calculated by McConnell's $3 trillion multiplied by 365 days per year, then the estimated one day loss represents 0.3% of the annual financial transactions for these two banks. However to prevent the loss of critical data due to natural and man-made disasters banks typically store financial transaction information offsite, so past information would not have been lost. Financial institutions could store transactions until systems are back online when the banks could then process the transactions. A cyberattack could create a large loss in the short term – but a financial crisis?

McConnell used a false analogy, better known as comparing apples to oranges, when he compared the 9/11 terrorsits with a cyberattack. Let's look at another example. The U.S. Senate blamed the 2007 to 2008 U.S. financial crisis on "high risk, complex financial products; undisclosed conflicts of interest; the failure of regulators, the credit rating agencies, and the market itself to rein in the excesses of Wall Street."[7] This economic collapse cost the United States over $11.5 trillion, including:[8]

- $648 billion in lost consumer income,
- $73 billion in the government response to the crisis,
- $3.4 trillion in lost real estate wealth,
- $7.4 trillion in lost stock wealth.

Our nation's banking and financial policies resulted in nearly four times more damage than McConnell's hypothetical cyberattack against the banking industry.

McConnell's brief to the future leader of the free world was an example of what marketing professionals call FUD — *Fear, Uncertainty, and Doubt.*[9] FUD is a strategy to influence decision makers by scaring them with questionable, exaggerated, or embellished information, and using colorful phrases like 'war' and 'terrorism' to support their opinions and evoke emotional responses. Some believe McConnell's brief to Obama was sensationalism to promote an agenda - to increase funding to the U.S. Intelligence Community cyber programs.

McConnell became the Executive Vice President and Vice Chairman of the consulting firm Booz Allen Hamilton where "... his primary roles include serving on the firm's Leadership Team and leading Booz Allen's rapidly expanding cyber business."[10] Reportedly, McConnell received a total annual compensation from Booz Allen Hamilton of $4,659,255.[11]

In July 1996, President William Clinton signed Executive Order 13010 establishing the President's Commission on Critical Infrastructure Protection that published "Critical Foundations – Protecting America's Infrastructure." The report identified threats, vulnerabilities and recommended mitigation actions. A major observation was a "general lack of awareness of vulnerabilities" to physical and cyberattacks. The report concluded that the vulnerabilities would impact national and economic security if not addressed within 3-5 years.

In May 1998, the White House published Presidential Decision Directive-63 (PDD-63) conveying the President's "intent to swiftly eliminate any significant vulnerabilities of our infrastructure from physical and cyberattack." Clearly this didn't happen.

A challenge that wasn't addressed was the sensitive nature of the vulnerabilities threatening the critical infrastructures. The government organizations with the most knowledge of vulnerabilities provided little on how vulnerable the infrastructures were in fear the information would become common knowledge. The government drafted a classified version of PDD-63 and restricted access to this document to people with government security clearances. The classified version contained broad hand waving but few specifics on critical infrastructure vulnerabilities. Even so, the vast majority of civilians that own and operate the infrastructures couldn't access and read the classified document, and the unclassified version was dumbed down for the sake of political convenience. Few took PDD-63 seriously.

Today Homeland Security Presidential Directive-7 states that the Department of Homeland Security (DHS) will coordinate the protection of U.S. critical infrastructures from terrorist attacks.[12] This policy suffers from two critical challenges. First it only gives DHS authority to protect against terrorist attacks while the threat to critical infrastructures includes terrorists, foreign militaries, and cyberspace hackers. In April 2015, the Department of Defense also declared itself responsible for protecting the homeland in cyberspace. This segregation of responsibilities with each department pursuing its pieces of the missions, budgets, and personnel exacerbates the current political challenges.

Second is the vast majority of the critical infrastructures are owned and operated by private industry, although they may have government oversight and government regulations in their operations. DHS must work collaboratively with the commercial industries that own and operate these industries. This occurs through information sharing, exercises, assessments of sector vulnerabilities and the consequences if those vulnerabilities are realized, and managing a national response during a catastrophe.

Is an attack against our critical infrastructures the end of the world or marketing? To understand let's look at one critical infrastructure that's in the media more than any other — the U.S. electrical power infrastructure.

Power

The North America electrical power infrastructure has been called the largest and most complex machine ever built.[13] It includes electrical production, transport, distribution, and support infrastructures. Public and private companies own and operate the electrical power system with oversight from commercial entities and government agencies.

The companies representing the electrical power infrastructure have a very detailed understanding of the threats to this infrastructure. These threats include nature (environment, weather, vegetation, animals, and humans), mechanical (equipment age and failure), and electrical (transmission capacity and load management). And they designed their infrastructure to deal with one overarching concern, the reliability of the power systems — the ability to prevent and recover from degradation and outages.

Like all industries they are concerned about the likelihood of a threat, and the impact should it occur. And like all industries they have limited resources to deal with these threats. They examine the probability of hurricanes, thunderstorms, high winds, and trees falling and compare them to the consequences if these occur - and how to prevent or reduce the impact of these consequences. Sometimes, they accept the risk of these threats.

The actual cost of a cyberattack depends on the calculus uses to calculate risk, and all the factors and assumptions taken into consideration. However, there is little historic data associated with a cyberattack against a power system.

The electric industry has several watchdog and government groups that keep an eye on the situation. One is the Critical Infrastructure Protection Standard (CIP) of the North American Electric Reliability Corporation (NERC). The NERC is comprised of industry members who set standards that may be approved through a vote. The Federal Energy Regulation Commission, or FERC, then ratifies these standards. The FERC is a government body that provides oversight of electrical power. The NERC then audits industry members to ensure they achieve those standards and can fine members for non-compliance to those standards.

In 1996 FERC issued Order 888 and 889 that required common standards and open access to the national power grids to promote wholesale competition.[14] These orders helped to open the power system to smaller power companies and drive down the cost of power. However, the resulting competition within the power industry has forced power companies to reduce operating margins, which has reduced the likelihood of implementing controls against a theoretical threat. Likewise, common standards, open access and the worldwide connectivity of cyberspace may have enabled malicious individuals to affect local power infrastructures and the other interdependent infrastructures from across the globe.

Flipping Switches

Supervisory Control and Data Acquisition Systems (*SCADA*) is a term for a broad range of industrial control technologies for electronically manipulating physical devices. In power systems these technologies allow engineers to manage Remote Terminal Units (*RTUs*) that control the physical relays that protect generators and control power generation from control centers.

The Digital Apocalypse

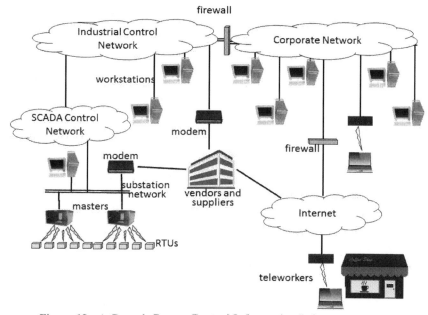

Figure 19 - A Generic Power Control Information Infrastructure

These control centers control power distribution by reading data their sensors send them, and transmitting commands to relays and transformers.

Under some circumstances utility companies connect production, distribution, and control to the company's enterprise management and commercial practice networks. Power companies interconnect these networks to reduce operating costs and to join their business, management, power, sales, and power management to enable a more efficient system-of-systems.

Executives may also connect the power control infrastructure and corporate information systems to other utilities, supporting vendors and contractors, remote maintenance and administration systems. These networks are typically protected by the same security controls and practices that everyone uses. And hackers have a long history of bypassing and exploiting these security controls.

The 2011 Springfield event was an example of a SCADA system within the water infrastructure. The water company installed technology that allowed remote maintenance personnel to provide after-hours maintenance and respond to potential outages.

Some attacks against a power system may fizzle. A hacker may trip a breaker via an RTU, but if the power company detects the event they can transmit commands to reset the systems. Other attacks may require the power company to dispatch a technician to reset a substation or relay. While the end result may be a temporary local power outage, the reset would restore the region, resulting in less-than desirable effects but announcing to guardians that hackers have gained access to the power system.

In 2000, an Australian hacker spent three-month attacking the Australian Maroochy Water Services and caused 800,000 liters of raw sewage to spill into waterways, hotel grounds and canals. In this case an engineer who had installed the system conducted the attacks after being denied a job with the waste management company. He was sentenced to two years in prison.

The 2004 U.S. Northeastern regional power outage was caused by defective software. Some have called this a major cyber event, however it only affected the most densely populated eastern sector. The actual cause of the event is unclear with some claiming hackers or cyber worms either caused the incident or was responsible for the scale of the outage. However the 2004 outage demonstrates the potential impact of regional outages.

In 2007 the Department of Energy sponsored the Aurora experiment at the Idaho National Laboratory. In this government-sponsored demonstration, government hackers sent remote commands across a network that changed the operations of an electric generator and caused the generator to shake itself apart. The experiment demonstrated a hacker could use a cyberattack to damage generators rather than just turn them off. Since the U.S. doesn't have a ready reserve of generators, transformers, and other large, costly electrical equipment a large-scale attack against multiple power systems can cause prolonged outages as power companies scramble to find, buy and ship, or cannibalize power generation and transportation equipment.[15]

On December 23, 2015 Ukrainians lost electrical power when hackers attacked three Ukrainian electrical distribution company control systems within 30 minutes of each other. The hackers conducted a sophisticated and coordinated attack that caused power outages not by attacking power production, but by disconnecting power switching stations and control systems.

First, hackers performed long term reconnaissance of the power systems to learn the systems configurations. Next, the attackers used sophisticated spear phishing emails containing Microsoft Office documents with variants of BlackEnergy malware. After gaining a foothold in the energy companies' information networks the hackers harvested credentials and gained access to the Indiustrial Control System (ICS) network. From there the hackers attacked uninterruptable power supplies (UPS), and devices at substations using custom malware that rendered device hardware inoperable. Next the hackers used the company telephone system to flood power company call centers to deny customers the ability to report outages and increase their frustration, and deny the power companies from understanding the scale of the outages.

This attack caused an outage of over 225,000 customers for several hours as power operators were forced to use legacy manual control systems to restore power distribution. Electrical power was quickly restored but with degraded service and forced to continue using manual operations.

The perpetrators and their motives are unknown, however analysts blame the cyber attacks on Russian government hackers. Whoever was responsible, this was a clear demonstration that hackers could synchronize a cyber attack with criminal or military kinetic operations

This scenario also demonstrated that impact assessments are relative. At the macro level this was a minor outage. However the outages were certainly perceived as critical to the power company customers, and the power companies surely perceived this attack critical to their reputation to reliably service their customers.[16]

It should be noted that while a cyberattack against a U.S. power systems is possible, hackers will not take down the U.S. national power grid. This is because a national powergrid doesn't exist, despite what the government, defense contractors, former directors of the CIA, and action movies show. In North America there are five major power grids covering Texas, western U.S., eastern U.S., Alaska, and Quebec with minimum interconnections between these five systems. Causing outages in one region will have minimal impacts in the other regions. However, the Ukrainian power companies could revert to manual control. Many U.S. power companies no longer have the same option for manual control due to the U.S. automation and reduction in response technicians available for a large-scale manual response.

Infrastructures and the Nation State

Modern militaries rely on civilian critical infrastructure — electrical power to operate bases; fuel to operate military vehicles; civilian shipping to supply forces.

A government's reliance on critical infrastructures to support their military forces and defense industries has resulted in foreign nations legitimately targeting these infrastructures. While it is a war crime to target civilians and their infrastructures deliberately, international laws permit nations to attack their opponent's infrastructures and industries as legitimate military targets if they support their military. These attacks will undoubtedly kill and injure civilians that work or support these industries and create outages for the civilian populations that also rely on these infrastructures. Our decision to tie military capabilities to civilian infrastructures has made these civilian infrastructures legitimate military targets and those who wage war labeling the destruction of these infrastructures a *military necessity*.

The U.S. supports this view. In 1991, Marine Brigadier General Richard I. Neal described coalition forces pounding the Iraqi city of Basra and causing massive collateral damage. Neal explained that, "Basra is a military town in the true sense, it is astride a major naval base and a port facility. The infrastructure, military infrastructure, is closely interwoven within the city of Basra itself." Coalition forces destroyed targets in and around Basra as part of an "intensifying air campaign against all echelons of forces, from the front lines and all the way back..."[17]

As technology evolved and nations have become more reliant on infrastructures the infrastructures have become critical to the survival of a nation. The converse is that a cyberattack on a nation's critical infrastructure may be perceived as an act of war and justify a military response.

If critical infrastructures are vulnerable to sophisticated hackers and a cyberattack may generate significant impacts, why haven't we seen more infrastructure attacks?

First the absence of a report does not mean attacks have not occurred. Hackers have launched attacks that failed. Alternatively, a successful attack may look like a mechanical failure from the point of view of an outside observer. Or perhaps the victim of a successful attack may not have an incentive to announce the true cause of an outage or degraded service when this announcement may encourage other hackers, and would gain the interest of governments, media, and private watch groups.

Second is that electrical incidents occur every day in the power industry. Vegetation, animals, weather, and equipment failures conspire to cause outages. Our electrical power industry is exceptionally well prepared and trained to deal with these issues. An unskilled or under resourced hacker may be able to penetrate a power system and flip a relay. However, our power engineers may simply respond by resetting the device or routing power around the issue, resulting in no visible impact to customers.

Third, a victim may view an attack against their critical infrastructure as an act of war or domestic sabotage, and a situation may not have occurred that has justified a nation to attack another nation's infrastructure. Clear thinking amateur hackers may not want to be labeled as saboteurs and gather attention from law enforcement and paramilitary organizations that would certainly respond to an infrastructure attack.

Fourth, if a hacker is capable of degrading an infrastructure they need to consider if they receive more utility by temporarily disabling systems or to continue to exploit access to the systems. A one-time attack against an infrastructure may announce the system is compromised, and the victim's response may cause the loss of all future collection. The specter of Coventry raises its head once again.

Hackers could also use the intelligence they are collecting to improve the impact of a kinetic attack. Why turn off a SCADA control systems and disable power for a few hours, when they can download schematics to learn the details of the switching station, then throw a steel pipe or drop a carbon-fiber bomb on the switching station to disable the system for days as the power company is forced to troubleshoot, purchase, transport, and replace transformers?

Conclusion

Infrastructures are the foundation of society and we've made cyberspace the lifeblood of infrastructures to enrich our personal and private life. However cyberspace also enables adversaries and their malicious agendas.

Information-age nations are the most vulnerable to a digital apocalypse since they are the most reliant on vulnerable, cyber-enabled technologies. The

The Digital Apocalypse

Director of National Intelligence believes the "level of technical expertise and operational sophistication" to conduct a major cyberattack is out of the reach of most actors at this time.[18] Under most circumstances nations and individuals don't want to create catastrophic cyberattacks, they want cyberspace to flourish and to exploit the information they obtain online; to make money, learn national and corporate secrets, and manipulate individuals and organization. Nations such as Russia and China "... are unlikely to launch such a devastating attack... outside of a military conflict or crisis that they believe threatens their vital interests." Less-developed, and less-reliant nations have the least to lose, and the most to gain by using cyberattack technologies.

The Director of National Intelligence believes that smaller nations or non-state actors may deploy less sophisticated attacks "as a form of retaliation or provocation."[19] Regional conflicts that go back centuries, tribal wars, and wars for the very survival of a group may motivate a devastating cyberattack. As the world becomes more connected attack technologies and hackers are also increasingly available for hire resulting in inexpensive cyber warfare resources.

There are adversaries and instances where an organization would want to disable or degrade our infrastructures. Under the direst circumstances a nation will attempt a catastrophic cyberattack — one where its own survival is at stake. A cataclysmic cyberattack will occur when nations are about to go to war — a real bullet-shooting, bomb-dropping war.

Chapter 13. Digital Terrorists

"We often give our enemies the means to our own destruction."
Referring to an eagle that dies from an arrow whose shaft had been feathered with one
of its own plumes.

- Aesop

"It would not be America if the country were secure.
It would not be America if its computer network were impenetrable...
Any man-made product contains weakness because man himself is a weak creature. So
it is with the Americans, who boast they are a strong nation."

- Imam Samudra (1970 – 2008)
Terrorist[1]

Terrorism

Terrorism is violence and intimidation aimed at civilian non-combatants to support political and social change.[2] The terrorist's goal is not violence, but the psychological reaction to violence.[3] Terrorist tactics may give the weak, angry and disenfranchised the possibility to overthrow a government or absorb a geographical region by generating fear, panic, and chaos. Cyberspace has provided terrorists both the means to support their operations and new means to create chaos.

The properties that makes cyberspace attractive to individuals, businesses, and governments also makes cyberspace attractive to malicious individuals and groups. Every significant terrorist group has learned about the benefits of cyberspace and has an online presence.[4] Obvious benefits include connecting and maintaining information with current and potential supporters, swaying public opinion to their causes, and demoralizing populations.

In the past, terrorists needed to find a publisher or news media willing to publish their discourse. Today cyberspace enables anyone to publish their opinions with little or no government censorship or control, enabling terrorists to create a rapid, dynamic, and inexpensive propaganda machine to raise awareness of their perceived plight. Shockingly, today terrorists can shape traditional mass media that use the unregulated and uncensored Internet as a primary information source. In July 2005, al-Qaeda leader Ayman al-Zawahiri wrote to Abu Musab al-Zarqawi the leader of al-Qaeda operations in Iraq that

Digital Terrorists

"We are in a battle, and more than half of this battle is taking place in the battlefield of the media."[5] A simple search[6] for 'Muslim fundamentalist' will return numerous "jihadist"[7] websites, images, stories, and propaganda.[8] Terrorist groups use these materials to recruit new members to their cause, inspire those interested and involved, or to indoctrinate and radicalize potential sympathizers.

It's alleged that the November 2009 Fort Hood shooter Nidal Malik Hasan, Christmas 2009 Flight 253 underwear bomber Umar Farouk Abdulmatallab, and May 2010 Times Square car bomber Faisal Shahzad became radical terrorist in part due to their access to online terrorist information and communications.[9]

Like most modern organizations terrorists use cyberspace to train their members. Books such as *The Terrorist Handbook* and *The Anarchists Cookbook* provide easy to understand instructions on making homemade bombs. *The Mujahadeen Poisons Handbook* published by the Hamas provides instructions on homemade poisons and gases. *The Sabotage Handbook* provides instructions on planning assassinations and avoiding surveillance.[10] Terrorist organizations publish newsletters keeping their members appraised on the latest military and technical tactics and techniques. Just as others use cyberspace for digital training and to share training materials, terrorists use cyberspace to train their operatives to pass through security checkpoints and bypass law enforcement surveillance.

The brothers Saïd and Chérif Kouachi that perpetrated the January 2015 Paris attack against Charlie Hebdo are believed to have received their radicalization and training online.

Cyberspace offers an attractive fund-raising vehicle for terrorists and their supporters to search, identify and engage prospective donors, and transfer, conceal, and launder funds. Terrorists have also contributed to cybercrime becoming a larger financing enterprise than international drug trafficking. It's believed that the 2002 terrorist bombing in Bali that killed 202, most of them foreign tourists, was partially funded through "carding" credit card fraud. Imam Samudra, who engineered the attack, published a 280-page jailhouse autobiography with a chapter called "Hacking, why Not?" where he provided details on performing credit card fraud to fund terrorist operations.[11]

The anonymity and simplicity of cyberspace makes it an ideal media to communicate and coordinate with other terrorists around the world through coded plans on outwardly benign websites and digital forums. One online forum, al-Ansat enables 4,500 extremists to communicate between themselves.[12] Terrorist have buried messages within games and images to hide that people are communicating, or encrypt messages hoping governments won't read the content of messages.

Terrorists have used cyberspace to conduct surveillance and intelligence collection against potential targets. In 2003, the Pentagon announced that an al-Qaeda training manual recovered in Afghanistan stated that by "using public sources openly and without resorting to illegal means, it is possible to gather at least eighty percent of information about the enemy."[13] In one case an American terrorists took videos of targets within the U.S. and shipped them to

other terrorists so they could plan operations.[14] ████████████████████
██ In
2015, the Islamist militant group and political party Hezbollah was believed to
be operating a cyber spy organization targeting Israel, the United States, Canada,
Russia and British government and military.[15]

It's ironic that the free and open nature of cyberspace is used and abused by
many who are themselves hostile to American freedoms, uncensored thought,
personal expression, and diversity.

Cyber Terrorism

Strategists refer to a conflict between two or more forces that differ significantly
either in size or technology as *asymmetric warfare*. The weaker force is driven to
unconventional tactics or weapons. The weaker force may not attack the
stronger force directly; rather they attack that which directly or indirectly
provides the stronger force its power, seeking to create large effects with little
effort.

Asymmetric advantages are not something new. Any time someone receives
more benefit from an action than the effort they put into an action they receive
an asymmetric advantage. In the third century BC Archimedes discussed the
benefits of the mechanical lever and block-and-tackle pulley systems that
provides a leverage advantage. In the nineteenth century anarchists and
revolutionaries believed the recently invented dynamite would provide them an
asymmetric advantage and balance the perceived inequities between the
overbearing governments and the oppressed.[16] A modern guerrilla (or insurgent
or terrorist depending on your perspective) may use of a $100 improvised
explosive device (IED) to defeat a $7.5 million M1 Abrams main battle tank.

Today some believe a modern societies' reliance on vulnerable information-
based technologies provides terrorists with a means to equalize the power
between themselves and oppressive governments at little risk to the terrorists.

Creating digital chaos requires a computer and a connection to the Internet.
The vulnerabilities in cyberspace and ubiquity of hacking instructions and
downloadable cyber toolkits and malware ensures even the poorest of groups
can punch a super power in the nose. Cyberspace can provide careful terrorists
with anonymity to ensure their safety while simultaneously giving them the
ability to claim credit for any attack in the name of their cause. Our reliance on
insecure technology, our well-publicized fears, and the government and industry
hype regarding a cyber catastrophe may convince terrorists that a cyberattack is
a viable means to deal with perceived inequities and injustices.

In response to a perceived western economic and military expansion
worldwide terrorists may perceive cyber as a low threat alternative to striking
back.

While a terrorist organization may benefit from attacking a military
organization, an attack against a military organization is not terrorism. Terrorists
seek to attack highly visible *civilian* target that reflects the terrorist's motivations
and ideologies and create a sense of fear and dread within the population to

foster change. Terrorists may be motivated to strike political targets, financial institutions, multinational corporations, religious groups, schools, or anyone the terrorists view as collaborators with their perceived oppressors. The desired effect may not be a political revolution, but retribution out of frustration that can place the terrorist's goals on the international stage.

However, we've noted earlier that most cyberattacks result in only temporary effects. These effects may be very costly to victims and cause tremendous stress and discomfort, but they are not likely to rise to the level of terror. Terror requires something more.

The FBI reports that terrorist attributed cyberattacks have been limited to unsophisticated email of malware to ideological foes, defacing websites, and flooding system disruptions. A limited yet devastating attack that degrades, damages, or destroys a portion of a nation's infrastructure is possible, but hackers would need to acquire the necessary skills and tools. The FBI notes that resourced terrorists need not possess cyber warfare skills since they may purchase the skills and weapons online.[17] Some argue that this would require terrorists and hackers to get beyond their ideological differences. However, terrorists may acquire the necessary skills and tools by threatening a hacker or their loved ones, or using a third-party mediator to hide the terrorist's affiliation in *false flag operations*. In either case sophisticated skills and tools are available.

A terrorist group may see a devastating and visible infrastructure attack as a viable means to draw attention to their plight. While terrorists may see an attack against a nationwide infrastructure such as the air traffic control system as desirable, a more likely scenario is that a hacker could affect a city or region. The infrastructures interdependencies could cause even a limited infrastructure attack to result in the loss of life and billions if not trillions of dollars of direct and indirect costs. However, a terrorist attack against something like the stock market may be perceived as affecting a societies elites and not the common person. This may limit the impact the terrorist is seeking. On the other hand a massive, non-discriminate cyberattack may cause previously sympathetic supporters to become unsupportive to the terrorist's cause.

Terrorist commentators like to proclaim that cyberattacks are the tools of the terrorist. In reality, terrorist aim for bloodshed, destruction and death. While non-lethal cyberattacks may allow terrorists to spread their word without the risk of blowback, terrorists are interested in mass casualties, not mass disruptions. Terrorists have become reliant on cyberspace and will need communications to conduct surveillance on potential victims, to publish their messages, and to allow victims and observers to spread the fear that is so important to the terrorist.

Turning off automated teller machines, bank accounts, or 911 systems may cause chaos, but wouldn't cause a nation's people to surrender. And terrorists know the world's intelligence organizations may intercept and track their attempts at developing or purchasing cyber weapons or skills and may cause uninvited visits by paramilitary organizations or armed drones.

Terrorists are using cyberspace to get their message out, recruit members and funds, communicate and coordinate operations, obtain intelligence, and complement kinetic attacks. However, the Coventry Argument may deter them from bringing attention to their cyber skills. While terrorists are using cyberspace and have even had success with limited cyberattacks, planning a large-scale cyberattack may represent too much risk for little gain. And a terrorist's use of cyberspace to support their operations also makes the terrorist vulnerable

Dens of Terrorists

The website of the Egyptian Islamic Jihad, a violent group of al-Qaeda contained a 45-page defense of suicidal terrorism. Terrorist supporters post horrendous videos of killings to foster support and compel the U.S. and its allies to leave the Middle East, while demonizing and delegitimizing their victims.

Our reaction is intense and immediate. American politicians call on the military, Intelligence Community, and law enforcement to put an end to these "dens of terrorists." The politicians don't understand that government cyberattacks against sites erase the contents of the sites, but only provide a temporary and limited solution. Terrorists may store these file in virtually infinite other locations, and they can upload and be back online in moments.

An attack conducted by the U.S. government must ensure the website is not owned by a U.S. corporation or U.S. citizens. The information posted may be protected under the U.S. citizen's First and Fourth Amendment rights, since we have freedom of speech and protection from unreasonable searches and seizures.[18]

There may be unintended consequences of directly attacking a terrorist website. An attack against a single site may simultaneously degrade or damage several unrelated sites residing on the system.

If a terrorist organization is recording all the activities occurring on their websites, then an attacks against these sites may arm terrorists with the attack tools. The terrorists could then use these weapons against others.

However, we are not restricted to temporarily shutting down websites. Intelligence, military, or law enforcement agencies may change the data on the sites to manipulate hackers or their support infrastructure. Terrorist websites and online tools are also targets for the world's law enforcement, intelligence, and military forces to monitor the people behind the sites and those that visit, post information, or donate to those sites. Here the Coventry Argument may interfere with governments bringing down a site if intelligence, military, or law enforcement agencies are obtaining significant intelligence from the site.

Conclusion

Vendors, consultants, and other experts generate *pretraumatic stress* by perpetuating fear, uncertainty, and doubt regarding what a terrorist *could* do until the public believes the attacks *will* occur. Exaggerated reporting includes the possible disappearance of money, wholesale electrical failure, changing medical records to kill people, and death.[19] These overstated and over generalized reports further the speaker's goals of selling readership, consulting opportunities, or security products while simultaneously supporting the terrorist's goals of spreading dread and anxiety.

Protecting our nation though preemptive attacks against hacker and terrorist groups is both an ineffective and inefficient use of resources and provides a false sense of security. While we look for means to monitor, prevent, and defeat those that mean us ill, we must be careful to not erode the properties and values of our society that make us great. Cyberspace is an imperfect embodiment of the ideas of free and open communications. It enables anyone to say as they wish without censorship, but like all freedoms, it can cause harm when abused.

Government spokespeople are quick to note terrorists use the Internet to communicate, recruit, train, and share information and recommend additional restrictions, such as ending anonymity through increased online surveillance will prevent criminals and terrorists. Likewise, government officials use horrific terrorist attacks to argue that strong encryption technologies prevent law enforcement and intelligence agencies from tracking terrorists, and should be eliminated. However, these are the same important features the Internet offers everyone. For example, strong encryption enables secure business and personal communications, and financial transactions.

We must be careful not to overreact to government officials and their exploitation of terrible international events to pursue their agendas, and hand terrorists a victory by succumbing to their threats at the expense of our freedoms. Overzealous regulations to manage a small problem could destroy the Internet. A centralized and controlled network is not the way to defeat a decentralized terrorist enemy. The Internet represents U.S. values of open and free exchange of information. Freedom will defeat terrorists by eliminating their base of recruitment through openness, participation, and distribution of authority.

Chapter 14. Secrecy

"Three things cannot long stay hidden:
the sun, the moon, and the truth."

- Buddha

"At times, in the name of national security,
secrecy has put that very security in harm's way."
- Daniel Patrick Moynihan (1927 – 2003)
Secrecy

Secrecy

Governments create secrecy policies to prevent the disclosure of information that could damage national security. Written records for protecting sensitive information dates back to the Egyptian hieroglyphs. However, the combination of advanced information technology and global, near instantaneous communications has created a need to relook information protection and address a fundamental flaw in our thinking today. We need to consider if not sharing information could cause greater damage to national security.

National Security Information

The Art of War is arguably the oldest and most successful book on military strategy in the world. For the past two thousand years it has remained an important guide on military and business tactics alike. The fifth century BCE Chinese military strategist and philosopher Sun Tzu is often quoted when people discuss the need of the state to protect its secrets. But what is secrecy?

Secrecy is the expenditure of effort to prevent an adversary from knowing the truth to provide an advantage. Individuals, corporations, and nations want their capabilities and weaknesses private so others can't take advantage of them. Likewise, adversaries want to learn things about friends and enemies to obtain an advantage — to learn other's secrets.

The U.S. government secrecy program suppresses government employee and contractor's freedom of speech for the good of the state.[1] Prior to 1940, the U.S. had numerous policies for protecting information regarding military capabilities and facilities. President Franklin Roosevelt consolidated these policies in 1940 with Executive Order (EO) 8381 directing the protection of sensitive information in the name of *national defense*.[2,3] Since this order there has been tremendous growth in the reasons for protecting secrets, and the apparatus used to protect our national security.[4] The latest presidential directive, EO 13526, issued by President Barack Obama on December 29, 2009, states *"...national defense requires that certain information be maintained in confidence in order to protect our citizens, our democratic institutions, our homeland security, and our interactions with foreign nations."*[5] This presidential order identifies broad categories of information that must be protected, calling it *national security information*, which includes government owned information related to national defense, foreign relations, intelligence activities, weapons of mass destruction and defense against transnational terrorists.[6]

When a government official decides to protect this information, it becomes "classified information" and is given one of three increasing *classification levels*, either *confidential, secret,* or *top secret* based on the "damage," "serious damage," or "exceptionally grave damage" to national security that could result if the information became public knowledge. The government also uses over a hundred additional caveats, compartments, and labels to further restrict the release of information, with some government programs so sensitive their existence, names, and budgets are restricted to a very small community.

Using a myriad of other policies the U.S. government designates much more unclassified information similar protection and controls as classified information, collectively called Controlled Unclassified Information (CUI).[7] For example, the Computer Security Act of 1987 defines requirements to protect information pertaining to government information systems, and includes "any information, the loss, misuse, or unauthorized access to or modification of which could adversely affect the national interest or the conduct of Federal programs, or the privacy to which individuals are entitled..." The government protects numerous other classes of information including law enforcement information (called Law Enforcement Sensitive), business proprietary information, personally identifiable information, and information related to international trafficking in arms (ITAR), and export controlled information. Discussion of all of this information could take up an entire book unto itself — so we'll focus on classified information.

The government classification process occurs under the watchful eyes of over 2,300 government officials called Original Classification Authorities (OCAs) given authority to designate classified information.[8] While the quantity of information OCA's have deemed classified information is difficult if not impossible to determine, the government reported over 92 million additional "classification decisions" in 2011.[9]

Classified information includes information about military strengths and weaknesses that must be protected to ensure adversaries can't defeat our military forces. It also includes information that could expose our intelligence *"sources and methods."* Preventing the loss of this sensitive information may prevent adversaries from eliminating an information source and causing agencies to "go blind," or from putting deliberately deceptive information into intelligence collection processes to deceive the intelligence apparatus. In fact, protecting sources and methods of classified information is the top reason cited within the government for protecting information.[10]

Since classified information is not available through open sources, it must be the government's most important information, and there should be a well understood and implemented process for securely sharing this critical information across the government to ensure effective and efficient government operations. This is not the case. While a tremendous number of government policy documents describe how to deal with classified information, the government does not have a clear process for defining the specific information that is classified national security information.

The challenges begin with the Executive Order. A Director of National Intelligence study found that the President's Executive Order requires government officials "be able to identify or describe the damage to national security that would result in a classification decision" but doesn't require government authorities to define the damage. The document notes there isn't common and consistent terminology across the government regarding security classification. The Order lacks definitions, examples, or guidance for the categories of classified information, or explanations for what constitutes "damage," "serious damage," and "exceptionally grave damage." The lack of clear definitions has resulted in subjective interpretations across the government as agencies and individuals independently interpret these policies, resulting in a confusing, decentralized and subjective process for dealing with our nation's most important and sensitive information.

Furthermore, the decentralized process for defining classified information confuses users of the information. The decision to *classify* specific information is contained in *security classification guides* approved by one of the 2,300 OCAs. Government authorities draft classification guidance based on their subjective interpretation of the policies resulting in inconsistencies and contradictory classification rules that confuse users and slow or prevent information sharing. Likewise, the government does not maintain a central registry of these guides, nor is there a standard for format, content, or terms.[11]

Under most circumstances these guides are themselves classified, and often government employees are unaware a specific guide exists, resulting in guides that conflict with one another, further hindering officials from understanding what information is supposed to be protected. If a government official or contractor can't find a guide related to a specific topic, they might not know they possess classified information until they've violated a guide and released sensitive information, referred to as a *spill*.

If an individual can find guides related to a topic, they may discover multiple guides that declare the same information different classifications due to the ambiguity in language. If a government bureaucrat names a project based on what it does, say *data protection*, then it might sound like a commercial system and would be *Unclassified*. But if they name the same project by what it could be used for, say *counter espionage*, then it may be classified *Top Secret* - and have numerous caveats and compartments that further restrict sharing. Similarly, the government may use a euphemism to describe technology such as *signals intelligence* where commercial vendors may call the same technology *entity analysis*. A government manager could call a program to detect malicious software *antivirus* or *malicious adversary binary threat mitigation* depending if they wanted the project and funding unclassified or protected from government oversight and rigorous technical assessments. Since the government has never defined a hierarchy to these guides, government policies force managers to classify specific information at the highest classification found across multiple guides, further limiting information sharing and the spirit of the Executive Order.

A Director of National Intelligence study found that the guides "provide little insight into the reasons for setting classification [decisions] and limited guidance for discriminating between classification levels" and that the government lacks standards for defining what must be contained within the Security Classification Guides. Where there is conflicting guidance the study found "it is difficult to discern which guide or level should take precedence, leading to over-classification in many cases."

As far back as 1994, the government understood the primary difficulty to information sharing has been in determining who holds authorities to compel sharing of sensitive classified information in an environment of distributed classification authorities where the classification system is "cumbersome and confusing," "inherently subjective," and "more complex than necessary."[12]

From a pragmatic point of view government employees know there is little risk of being punished for not sharing information unless there is a major incident and subsequent investigation like the 9/11 terrorist attacks. However, government officials and contractors know sharing information another government official has deemed classified information carries strict administrative and criminal punishment, including the possible loss of their clearance, their job, and imprisonment. Therefore, it's in the best interest of government officials to err on the safe side by not sharing information.

This decentralized classification process undermines information sharing with the guardians who defend public and private information systems. However, the real threat is the dysfunctional classification policies and processes prevent sharing our nation's most important information within the U.S. government, even with those within the government who have a legitimate "need to know." While EO 13526 states that government officials will restrict the least quantity of information necessary to protect national security and the Director of National Intelligence has announced transitioning from a "need to know" to "need to share" to "responsibility to provide,"[13] the ineffective classification system sabotages the vision.

The real irony is that our national propensity regarding secrecy has made us less secure.

Economics and Warfare

Elements of national security and national power are directly related. The preamble to the U.S. Constitution defines the role of the Federal government to enhance security at home and abroad, promote economic well being, and promote democracy and human rights.[14]

However, the U.S. government cannot "classify" information related to our national economy or private businesses unless it pertains to national defense. A prerequisite for living in a free and open society is having information that could damage our national economy, and thus our national security, open to the public.

In today's interconnected world, economic security is as important as military security, and economic information and systems are critical to the U.S. security even if the government doesn't protect these. But let's look at this issue in another way. If economies are critical to a nation's power, then exploiting a foreign nation's economic information and information systems would interest a nation's intelligence and military forces — and thus are a national security concern. To paraphrase, our national economic information is free and open, however, our ability to access and collect on foreign economic systems may be a national security issue. This connection between a free and open U.S. economy, and the desire to collect information and manipulate other nation's economies has created tremendous opportunities for our opponents.

Hypothetically, our government may have knowledge of a zero-day vulnerability in an adversary's information system that would allow U.S. intelligence or military forces to conduct espionage or destructive attacks during a conflict. Since knowledge of this vulnerability enables our intelligence and military forces to conduct these actions, our government would protect this knowledge under EO 13526 as intelligence methods and/or military capabilities, respectively. However, the desire to keep vulnerabilities secret is not sufficient to do so.

Historically, if both parties who know a secret can maintain the secret, and the techniques both parties use to communicate and store information about the secret maintains the confidentiality of their information, the information will retain its secrecy. That is, if national security information is protected then it will remain unknown to our adversaries.

However, organizations can learn secrets in scientific and engineering fields without the use of spies, breaking into information systems, or eavesdropping. For example, foreign nations have built nuclear weapons without access to secrets by using independent scientific and engineering efforts.

Similarly the U.S. government may classify information regarding cyber vulnerabilities in commercial technology, however others can learn these secrets without resorting to spycraft. This may happen through at least three means. First, an adversary may stumble on the vulnerability unintentionally. Second, an adversary may discover the vulnerability through *reverse engineering*, analyzing a system's structure, functions and operations to understand how its component parts work and interact. Third, an adversary may discover the vulnerability through system testing techniques such as fuzzing or robustness testing; presenting invalid, unexpected, or random data to a system hoping to create an unexpected response that may indicate a vulnerability. There's a vast hacker underground that discovers new vulnerabilities daily and share these doors through cyberspace to the community.

Classifying information about a door into an adversary's network doesn't prevent vendors, adversaries, guardians, or the public from discovering the vulnerability. The vulnerability exists, only some people are not aware of its functionality. At best classifying the vulnerability delays the independent discovery of the information. The government has no idea when an adversary may discover the "secret" vulnerability. This is potentially a common occurrence where national critical information and control systems are built from commercial systems.

Let's assume a U.S. intelligence service discovers a previously unknown vulnerability in a commercial word processing application used by a foreign nation. The U.S. military or intelligence services may want to use this vulnerability to obtain access to the foreign systems to gain intelligence or to prepare the foreign system for a future offensive attack. In either case, the government would consider knowledge of the vulnerability an *intelligence method* and requires the Intelligence Community to classify the vulnerability and not share it with the vendor or U.S. guardians, denying them knowledge of a known open door into their system.

Likewise, knowledge of this cyber vulnerability would be further compartmented to the U.S. cyber espionage and attack organizations and not released to the guardians that defend the military, government, or public enterprise networks. Their reasoning is that our guardians would react and alert adversaries of the vulnerability who would remove the vulnerability and prevent future access to their systems. This would cause the loss of future intelligence or military operations.

Another justification used for classifying information about a vulnerability is that adversaries could use this to compromise U.S. and allies' systems that haven't updated their systems. This vulnerability would therefore represent a threat to U.S. government systems.

The result is that the U.S. government classifies vulnerabilities and denies our guardians information about a vulnerability that the enemy may already know, or may discover on their own. This is deliberately withholding information that may cause damage to U.S. national security.

If later our intelligence or military uses malware against an adversary that exploits this vulnerability, the victim can reverse engineer the malware with readily available commercial tools to discover how it functions, and then turn it back on the U.S. And our guardians are still unaware and vulnerable to the malware, and the potential damage it can create.

The Paradox

Clearly secrecy is a major tool in protecting national security. However, there are numerous instances where our government's secrecy causes greater harm than it protects.

From December 1941 through the summer of 1942, the Germany navy launched Operation Drum Beat, a daring operation to send German U-boat submarines to the U.S. Atlantic coast to inflict massive damage to the U.S. merchant ships. German submarines sank 609 ships totaling 3.1 million tons while suffering the loss of 22 U-boats. The losses during this six-month period off the U.S. eastern seaboard represented one quarter of all shipping sunk by U-boats during the entire Second World War. Secrecy and the U.S. "Loose Lips Sink Ships" propaganda campaign were not meant to protect American shipping, but to maintain U.S. morale. The U.S. policies resulted in increased loss of shipping and life, in what has been called the Second Pearl Harbor.[15]

Similarly, the Bipartisan 9/11 Commission found that over classification and compartmentalization made the nation less secure and led to the successful terrorist attacks on September 11, 2001. This continues today.

U.S. drone missile attacks in ███████████████ Yemen are often observed and reported by the local media and populace and posted within hours on social networks. The U.S. government claims many of these reports include exaggerations of the civilian casualties, hampering the U.S. attempt to win over the local populace. Despite that civilians observe these attacks and the media discuss the attacks, any information regarding drone attacks is classified in U.S. government channels, forcing the U.S. ambassador and diplomatic staff to remain quiet. U.S. leaders can't address the exaggerated collateral damage or announce the terrorists being "put out of action" because of the drone attacks.[16] Our national secrecy policies are enabling our adversaries to win the propaganda war in the Middle East.

Guardians and benign hackers also struggle with releasing information, typically called "responsible disclosure." When a hacker learns of a vulnerability they keep the knowledge private until the vendor of the vulnerable product releases a patch that removes the vulnerability, and the resulting information could no longer cause any harm if released.

Some guardians believe that keeping vulnerabilities secret leads to a less secure world. They believe the community should share vulnerabilities and defense capabilities so guardians can understand the true state of their systems. The commercial antivirus community is a good example of public and open security.

While the defense community knows how the antivirus tools work, so do hackers. Before a hacker releases a new piece of malware onto cyberspace, they can try their 'new' malware against antivirus products and see if the control will detect or defeat their malware. The hacker can load their malware into one of the commercial test suites that will run the malware against all the commercial antivirus tools and determine if any of them will detect the malware.[17]

Secrecy

Microsoft protects it software source code as a trade secret. Of course, hackers and guardians can reverse engineer the code to discover how it works and its bugs. Or they can wait until a patch is released and compare their system before the patch to the system after the patch, to see what was changed, and then analyze the change to determine where the original bug was located within the code and how to defeat unpatched systems, knowing it takes people time to patch their systems. There hasn't been a shortage of patches on Microsoft systems although they keep their source code secret. But then again, since 2003 Microsoft has shared their source code with foreign intelligence services including the NSA, Chinese PLA, and Russian intelligence (FSB) under their Government Security Program (GSP).[18]

Our National Security

The government created our secrecy programs to blind our adversaries and provide us with an advantage. However, with the creation of cyberspace our secrecy policies prevent us from clearly seeing threats and reacting before our adversaries.

We classify information regarding networks vulnerabilities and how hackers have successfully compromised them. However, the hackers that did the compromising, whether criminal, amateurs, or foreign intelligence services understand how unprotected the networks are since they are the perpetrators compromising them.

It's important to realize that nations deal with secrecy differently. Due to our open society and capitalistic beginnings, the U.S. government doesn't protect economic information, unlike many other countries like China and France. And other countries may be more restrictive in protecting information, such as the United Kingdom, Ireland, and India which have laws typically referred to as an "Official Secrets Act" forbidding private citizens from sharing sensitive government information.

Secrecy prevents the American people and our leaders from understanding the vulnerabilities and previous compromises in our systems. And the result is that our national leaders, private industry, and citizens don't understand the true threat that has perpetuated our continued losses in cyberspace while budgets and government fiefdoms continue to grow in the dark.

Digital Gold Mine

Our propensity for national secrecy in everything related to cyber conflict has also created a growing industry to protect that secrecy.

An investigation by the Washington Post estimated that there were over 854,000 people that possess Top Secret security clearances.[19] Personnel who can obtain the required clearances, many of which require either the counter-intelligence or more stringent lifestyle polygraph demand much higher salaries. This has created a demand that is especially true in the computer security field — there just isn't enough trained security personnel with clearances — and those who are cleared can demand significant salaries. As a result, companies are hiring people who can pass the rigorous security vetting process, sending them for computer certifications to make them marketable, and advertising them to the government as cyber security experts to draw the higher salaries and profits.

But people are just the beginning. Classified programs need special secured facilities — from secret vaults to Special Compartmented Information Facilities called SCIFs, to the most secure Special Access Projects Facilities - SAPFs. They need separate and disconnected information networks — typically one for each program they are assigned, and special safes, shredders, and handling techniques. This support infrastructure — the facilities, information systems, financials, and document tracking also requires cleared and trained security personnel. While the actual cost to protect classified information is itself classified, a 2011 government estimate of the annual cost for 41 executive branch agencies including the Department of Defense was $11.36 billion. This estimate represents a small portion of the actual cost, since it didn't include the costs of the Central Intelligence Agency, the Defense Intelligence Agency, Office of the Director of National Intelligence, National Geospatial-Intelligence Agency, National Reconnaissance Office, and the National Security Agency. These agencies are the largest within the Intelligence Community and their budgets are themselves classified.[20]

Senator Patrick Moynihan noted in his 1998 book that secrecy is a means to hide incompetence and bureaucracy and to insulate government bureaucrat's careers. It prevents oversight, protects government budgets, mismanagement, and sometimes illegal activities. He notes that classification and secrecy are exempt from the democratic process and government oversight.[21]

If information is power, then an agency or individual having information makes them more powerful, and sharing information does not. Intelligence has become the currency in cyberconflict.

Conclusion

Under existing government policies it's impossible for a U.S. government agency to determine if not sharing information will cause more damage to national security than releasing the information. When combined with the punitive measures taken when a government official or contractor deliberately or accidentally releases national security information, there is little hope of the government releasing information pertaining to cyber vulnerabilities or incidents.

The National Security Act of 1947 explicitly prohibits U.S. intelligence agencies from operating in a law-enforcement or internal security capacity. While U.S. intelligence and military organizations may learn of vulnerabilities in commercial systems used by foreign entities, they are forbidden from collecting information on U.S. entities and can't investigate the systems used by domestic commercial entities. It makes little sense for U.S. intelligence and military organizations being responsible for determining what information should be shared. An individual or organization that can investigate domestic systems, and our deepest intelligence and military secrets must determine the cyber information that must be shared to prevent damage to our nation.

Technically there may be no difference between professional criminals breaking into corporate information systems to steal intellectual property, hobbyists breaking into personal computers just to see if they can, or national intelligence services breaking into foreign computers to steal foreign intelligence information. They are all reading others' information, and may even use the same hacker tools. When government leaders permit cyber secrets that enable a government organization to cause mischief to their adversaries, these government leaders may also enable others, such as criminals and foreign threats, to cause mischief against us.

Our nation has turned to the Pentagon and the Intelligence Community to operate our government cyber operations in the belief they know best. The obvious result has been secrecy in everything related to cyber operations. However, these national secrets are openly discusses in the hacker community daily. The result is that our national policies regarding cyberspace and cyber operations have enabled a growth of foreign espionage and cybercrime. Our nation is flailing in cyberspace not despite our national policies, but because of them.

Chapter 15. The Great Equalizer

*"For every complex problem
there is a solution that is clear, simple, and wrong."*
-H.L. Mencken (1880 –1956)
journalist, critic and scholar

*"Peres Law: If a problem has no solution, it may not be a problem, but a fact —
Not to be solved, but to be coped with overtime."*
- Shimon Peres (1923 -)
9th President of Israel

Strong Muscles, Brittle Bones

In 2009 President Obama proclaimed, "Our technical advantage is key to America's military dominance."[1] This technical advantage is reliant on the cyber technology proliferating our military to produce capabilities we once only dreamed possible. The Pentagon has replaced armies of armored vehicles, infantry, and support troops with smaller, highly mobile forces supported by stealth aircraft, precision artillery, satellites and drones. In January 2012, President Obama announced further reductions in U.S. military forces, relying on the advanced technology to offset a size discrepancy with a foe.[2]

U.S. military visionaries overlooked two significant facts from the 1972 Yom Kippur War. First, the primary reason the Arab attack surprised Israeli intelligence and leadership was Israel's reliance on technology and what their technology was telling them.[3] Second, Israel defeated the technologically superior and larger Arab coalition due to nontechnical reasons; Israeli troops had superior training, leadership, and morale. Israel not only endured but defeated and embarrassed the Arab nations. Technology is not a panacea nor does it guarantee success.

We can see this principle repeated in the U.S. defeat in Vietnam, the Soviet Union's defeat in Afghanistan, and Russia's defeat in Chechnya.[4]

The problem isn't the Pentagon's use of vulnerable digital technology to glue its forces together. The problem isn't the hackers. The problem is military leaders, politicians, and the American people who misunderstand the nature and significance of cyber conflict. And our leaders have built our current policies and plans on these misunderstandings.

161

The Great Equalizer

"But he isn't wearing anything at all!"

Hans Christian Andersen wrote *The Emperor's New Clothes* in the nineteenth century about a vain emperor manipulated by swindlers into believing he wears the finest clothes invisible to the unfit or simple-minded. No one dared comment as the king proceeded naked through his kingdom, or others would judge them unsophisticated. It isn't until a child unencumbered by adult fears speaks the truth that the emperor realizes he's been swindled, and his advisors are untrustable. And just as the emperor and his ministers didn't want to be perceived as incompetent, leaders today don't ask questions because they don't want to be perceived as simple-minded or anti-technology luddites.[5]

The lack of understanding causes leaders to fall back on what they know: mythology, traditional warfare, Cold War theory, and bureaucracies while trying to create a twenty-first century, high-tech military, government, and nation.

The greatest cyber myth is that technology can protect us. Cyber security involves people; people creating technology, and people trying to use cyberspace to accomplish their goals. People make mistakes — in software, in configurations and in operations. And hackers will exploit systems and the people who rely on those systems.

Governments, colleges, vendors, and training firms perpetuate the myth by overselling the cyber security field. These "security experts" have misled leaders into exposing their sensitive information online and to rely on ineffective defenses. And cyberspace is teeming with individuals motivated to cause mischief.

Every successful network compromise was a risk someone took based on the information they possessed. Public and private policies often require executives prove they have "adequate security in place" before placing technology into cyberspace. Executives need to ask themselves, "adequate for what?" Management must accept and acknowledge guardians can't provide perfect security, and may not keep resourced and motivated hackers out before they approve the development and deployment of technology or information into cyberspace.

Just one example is placing information and systems on isolated networks[6] to limit hacker's access and potential damage, rather than installing security controls to make a leader feel good but not prevent a potential catastrophe. This isn't saying we should remove everything from information networks and return to typewriters and metal filing cabinets. Cyberspace has improved our lives. But before we expose mission critical and life threatening information on the Internet, we must be sure it's a deliberate and informed decision. And informed decisions begin with information.

Throwing Stones in Glass Houses

On May 29, 2009 in the East Room of the White House, President Obama stated, "It's the great irony of the Information Age - the very technology that empowers us to create and built also empowers those who would disrupt and destroy." Was President Obama speaking of foreign threats, or his own military and intelligence complex? A survey of cyber security experts "ranked the U.S. as the country of greatest concern in the context of foreign cyberattacks, just ahead of China."[7]

The Pentagon has built their technical advantage on the premise of *information superiority* – the ability to dominate adversaries in cyberspace using offensive digital warfare and cyber espionage.[8,9] However, basing a strategy on offensive cyber capabilities has two critical flaws. First, adversaries on a future battlefield may not be vulnerable to a cyber punch. Our future skirmishes and wars may be against less industrial nations, terrorist groups, and transnational criminals where offensive cyber operations may not be effective.

The second is a fact all fighters understand — brute strength will not guarantee a win when a fighter has a glass jaw. Our warfighter's reliance on advanced technology weapons is misplaced if this belief is based on a vulnerable and repeatedly compromised cyber battlespace where adversaries obtain the plans to those systems, access and disable those systems, or turn those systems against the warfighters. As the Pentagon loses control of the information and systems, they lose the amplified military capabilities promised by these technologies. Worse, their performance defending their portion of cyberspace and their adversary's successful use of espionage and offensive cyber weapons may embolden adversaries to believe they can defeat our kinetic forces.

Cyberspace may become *the great equalizer* that allows adversaries to dominate the U.S. armed forces by exploiting weaknesses in systems the Pentagon deliberately placed in cyberspace.

Our government spends tremendous resources discovering doors into other nation's networks and keeps knowledge of these doors to themselves. The rub is that the Pentagon and Intelligence Community use the same technology foreign intelligence agencies, hackers, and criminals use to enter our public and private networks. Government secrecy regarding vulnerabilities in commercial systems is self-deception between our government hackers trying to break into other's networks, and the public and private guardians trying to defend our networks. And our government hackers control access to sensitive cyber information.

The government secrecy policies are the most significant threat to making informed decisions. It's obvious those in the U.S. government who execute destructive digital attacks and espionage have kept their capabilities secret from those responsible for defending public and private networks. Hiding our offensive successes and defensive failures has left our guardians ignorant of what skilled, resources, and motivated hackers can perpetuate against them. We do not need to study hackers to understand what they can do; we need the Government to share their capabilities with the guardians.

The Office of the Director of National Intelligence, or ODNI, manages the government classification program. A 2008 ODNI information classification policy review found the current system impairs cooperation and performance and poses a risk to our national security. However, the ODNI hasn't addressed the issue despite the risk to national security. Information is the currency of bureaucrats, and bureaucrats will fight to keep control of the information and information sharing processes they possess. Change creates animosity in a city where leadership is defined by consensus building and status quo. And no one within the ODNI is prepared to deal with fighting the intelligence, military, and government agencies as they protect their interests.[10]

The U.S. information classification process is a national crisis. Our government will never obtain information superiority when government officials restrict critical information other officials need to make informed and effective decisions.

The government must balance its ability to conduct espionage against foreign nations, terrorists and criminals with its ability to defend our nation's information systems from those same threats. Our nation's reliance on the NSA to provide security in cyberspace is contrary to the NSA's primary mission to collect foreign intelligence. The collection mission relies on the NSA to maintain secrecy regarding the means for conducting this collection. This secrecy ensures the ultra-secret cyber espionage community keeps our own defenders uninformed of known vulnerabilities in their systems — as foreign nations and criminals exploit these same vulnerabilities and steal our information. The result is the government's increased preponderance for intelligence and continued sacrifice of economic, political, and military safety.

Alternative Reality

Cyber experts and those pandering the latest cyber tools, processes, policies, and gizmos are quick to announce that the U.S. is under attack, losing its intellectual property and technological edge, and someday will suffer a catastrophic cyber Pearl Harbor that will throw it back to the Stone Age.

It's gotten so commonplace that during the March 10, 2016 republican presidential debate Ohio Governor and Presidential Candidate John Kasich responded to a question regarding Chinese government sponsored cyber espionage. He told the world that the next commander-in-chief must ensure the U.S. can fire back against state-sponsored hackers.

"[W]hen it comes to the issue of cyberattacks, we're going to have to beef up the Cyber Command. And they need to understand that if you attack us, we will defend ourselves, everything, including our grid. But if you do it, we have the capability to take out your systems. The president has not given the Cyber Command that authority. I will." Later Governor Kasich announced, "They have to stop hacking everything we have in this country, or we'll take out their systems."

However, let's look at this situation from another way. Chinese military strategist and philosopher Sun Tzu pointed out over 2500 years ago that the supreme art of war is to subdue the enemy without fighting.[11] Perhaps the real purpose of the rampant cyber espionage and minor attacks is to cripple the U.S. economically and force us to lose trillions of dollars of intellectual property and national security information, while simultaneously spending hundreds of billions on ineffective security programs and technologies.

In the 1980s President Ronald Reagan pronounced the Strategic Defense Initiative, or SDI, would protect the U.S. from a Russian first nuclear strike. While the U.S. invested in advanced technology to develop SDI, Russia drained its coffers trying to maintain parity with the West. Some believe SDI was part of a White House strategy to collapse the Soviet economy and end the Cold War.

Perhaps the real purpose of most cyber espionage and attacks isn't to prepare for a destructive attack against the U.S. in cyberspace, but to cause the U.S. to spend itself out of the world economic leadership? In this case we must look for alternative solutions because we are not in a cyber war but an economic war. Rather than escalating a cyber espionage incident with a destructive retaliatory attack against a foreign populous we need to consider preemptive actions to secure our systems and prevent the economic hemorrhage, and retain our technological, financial, and economic world leadership.

Conclusion

The U.S. is not winning in cyberspace, we are at best walking wounded. The rapid rise of information technology and cyberspace has created an environment where personal privacy, civil liberty, confidentiality, intelligence and surveillance are all in conflict. Yet, the U.S. will not win this cyberwar because what is occurring in cyberspace isn't warfare.

Cyberspace has become an environment we rely on, yet we can't defend. It provides amazing benefits, and at the same time a risk to our military, political, economic, and personal security. We need to get beyond the myths and wishful thinking, and understand how cyberspace operates before our warfighters suffer a catastrophic loss on a battlefield, a battle we lost long before bullets fly.

The Great Equalizer

Thought Questions

Introduction
1. What are the differences between the author's and senior military leader's perspective? What was the result of the apparent miscommunication?

Chapter 1. The Vision
1. Compare and contrast the lessons U.S. and Arab military strategists learned from the 1973 Arab-Israeli War regarding the use of advanced technology on a battlefield.

Chapter 2. The Perpetual Struggle
1. How can we resolve the apparent discrepancy between the societal benefits of worldwide connectivity and communications with the threats conceived by those who want to use cyberspace as their private battlefield?
2. What constitutes sovereignty in cyberspace and what responsibility does a nation have for the actions occurring on computers in their sovereign territory?
3. What constitutes free speech in cyberspace?
4. What constitutes a national response in cyberspace?
5. Is there an inherent flaw in the design of computer systems that means we can never make them secure? Defend your perspective. If so, what should we do in light of this revelation?
6. Why is general purpose computer an issue for guardians and cyber defense?
7. How can vendors support backwards compatability and still build secure systems?
8. Explain the impact of "attack surface" when compared to the "usability" of our systems.

Chapter 3. Groundhog Day
1. How might the outcome of the First Persian Gulf War have changed if the hackers had bribed disgruntled individuals with access to important information and systems, stopped or redirected vital supplies being shipped to Southwest Asia during the buildup and execution of the Persian Gulf War, and been able to defeat the U.S. weapon systems, while simultaneously taking down the U.S. command and control information systems? What other actions could the hackers have done to impact the United States and the coalition?

2. Cliff Stoll's book, *The Cuckoo's Egg,* noted that national leadership knew about the potential for digital espionage and destructive attacks in the 1980's. Certainly our leaders took actions to protect us from adversaries who would want to conduct this mischief? How can this cycle continue for over 25 years?

3. The Geneva Convention requires military service members captured on the battlefield to only provide their names, ranks, and service number. What are the implications of cyberspace during an interrogation and how might the U.S. military deal with these issues?

4. How does the apparent loss of intelligence appear to impact senior leadership's decisions related to cyber defense?

5. Given the case of Buckshot Yankee, what circumstances might motivate so many service members to violate a known security policy?

Chapter 4. The Guardians

1. Many believe cryptography (methods to send and receive messages securely) and strong authentication (methods to verifying the identity of a user or device) will provide "sufficient" confidence or trust for remote communications. How do the variable security policies and enforcement across agencies or corporations hinder these goals, and how can hackers defeat or bypass these tools?

2. Many within the security community view "security by obscurity" (using secrecy in the design of security tools) as a flawed concept. How might obscuration help and/or hinder guardians and hackers?

3. Compare and contrast cryptography with security by obscurity.

4. Some government officials have argued the continued loss of sensitive information from U.S. government and corporate networks to foreign hackers is the cost of doing business in cyberspace. What are your thoughts? Defend your arguments.

5. In June 2015 the U.S. government reported an advanced persistent threat penetrated the Office of Personnel Management and exfiltrated the records of at least twenty-one million current and former government employees. This information is now either being analyzed by a foreign intelligence service for key information they can exploit, or being shared or sold to other hackers. What was the benefit of OPM placing all of this information in cyberspace, and what was the ultimate cost? How could the government improve the system?

6. Discuss malware and anti-malware developer's incentives, and how they differ and intersect.

7. Discuss how "bug bounties" function and whether they improve or incentivize hacker behavior.

Chapter 5. The Antagonists

1. One report states the 2008 Georgia attack was, "…too large, coordinated, and sophisticated to be the work of independent hackers." In the next paragraph the report states, "High technology and online skills are now

available for rent to a variety of customers, including private individuals and terrorist organizations, and can partially destabilize a countries whole economy and crucial security infrastructure" If hacker skills are available through money (buy someone with the skills), ideology (convince someone to perform an act for their beliefs, such as political or religious reasons), coercion (force someone to do something against their will), or ego (to show others they can) what does this tell you about categorizing threats groups (nation states, terrorists, criminals, hackers)?

2. How do thee author's description of hackers differ from media descriptions?
3. How can guardians and senior leaders deal with APTs?

Chapter 6. Attribution and Anonymity
1. Cyber intrusions have reached near pandemic proportions in government, military, and key industries. Are the sometimes-brazen attackers better at hiding their tracks, or is something else occurring to explain this lack of government response to unending compromises?
2. Government bureaucrats like to say the U.S. should reengineer the cyber environment. However, cyberspace is no longer a military or even government environment. It's built and managed by private enterprise and required for trillions of dollars of national and international commerce. How could we reengineer cyberspace to prevent malicious activities but preserve its positive features?
3. Would perfect and complete attribution be desirable? Would we want an oppressive regime to have perfect attribution? Would we want to suppress expressing ideas? Don't we want to protect personal privacy? Would we want our espionage activities attributed by our adversaries?
4. Governments may want their intelligence and/or law enforcement agencies to have the ability to track anyone responsible for malicious cyber actions. However, these same agencies don't want to be tracked by anyone else. Does this make sense? What are the implications?
5. Provide your support or criticism of the author's perspective that the technology that makes systems usable for users also makes them usable for hackers.
6. Is cyber attribution possible in all cases? Defend your decision.
7. What is an ISP's perspective for cooperating with a law enforcement investigations?
8. The author provides multiple possible scenarios regarding the Stuxnet incident. Choose a possible culprit and provide arguments, with supporting publicly available references.
9. If attribution is as difficult as the author proposes, then how should public and private organizations respond?

Chapter 7. Geeks in the Wire – Information Collection

1. Who decides to preserve cyber intelligence over alerting defense organizations of a vulnerability? Prior to the decision how can the leaders understand the implication of those decisions or indecision?

2. What are the implications if an individual (or organization) uses cyber espionage to determine the physical location of a senior leader and then provides this information to another who assassinates the leader?

3. Some argue the continued collection of sensitive information off government and corporate networks is the cost of doing business in cyberspace. What are your thoughts?

4. Recently a member of the U.S. Intelligence Community complained, "We make too much of the information we put on the network being taken by users of the networks - information put on the Internet is taken by users of the Internet." They apparently believe decision-makers would have placed important, sensitive information on isolated networks. Legitimate owners of the information thought they were restricting the information to a subset of the Internet users. What are your thoughts?

5. What are the implications if a U.S. citizen's data being "in the cloud"? Does cloud computing enable U.S. intelligence to collect on U.S. citizens?

6. Perform an open source analysis of person of interest. The analysis cannot be a family member; think a peer or celebrity. Present a detailed analysis of the person to include their background, interests, genealogy, real-estate tax records, social groups, contact information, and social media. Present an analysis of this information.

7. Perform Task #6 above. Now perform the same analysis of the person's next layer of friends, contacts, and organizations.

8. What are the implications when foreign nationals are prosecuted for hacking into U.S. defense contractors and harming our national security?

9. If information is so readily available that classified conclusions can be made from public information, then what are the implications to the government classification system?

10. Does the phrase "loose lips sink ships" have any meaning today?

11. In the current environment anyone could mark a document "top secret" and the new media would report it as another information leak. What is the impact to government leaders and the public?

12. How does the current activities related to intellectual property theft relate to the United States-United Kingdom intellectual property conflict (1780-1824)?

Chapter 8. Equities

1. Regarding the Comprehensive National Cybersecurity Initiative (CNCI): The idea research, operations, and defense of our nation have been placed into the hands of the Intelligence Community should cause everyone to pause. How would you design a national cyber program?

2. Recently the U.S. Secretary of Defense authorized the use of social networks for troops as a recruiting tool. What are the implications from an intelligence collection point, and how might the DoD accomplish both goals of allowing troops to communicate and protect troops from themselves?
3. Leaders often hire "white hat" hackers to assess the security of systems. Usually the leaders restrict the hackers to using common hacker tools and techniques. What does this tell you about the security of systems against dedicated and resources adversaries that are not restricted?
4. Does the Coventry Argument apply to cyber espionage?

Chapter 9. Insiders

1. The news media debated Private Manning and his release of classified information on WikiLeaks as being espionage, or an act of civil disobedience. The more important questions are why Private Manning was not detected accessing information he had no need to access, and who else did the same thing but provided the information to foreign intelligence services rather than a hacker's website?
2. The owners of Internet services (such as email and cloud-data storage services) may have access to the information the customers provide them. Make a list of the services you or your organization uses, the information you provide the service, and how you can reduce your risk. Remember search engines, social networks, messaging, email, and data storage.
3. What insider information do search engines like Google, Yahoo, and Bing collect based on the search queries coming from Internet addresses associated the White House, Pentagon, NSA, investment houses, and police departments? How can these organizations reduce their risk?
4. How can an organization mitigate their risks in the use of cloud service providers?
5. Can we expect intrusion detection systems to work effectively given their demonstrated history?

Chapter 10. Shadow Boxing - Digital Attack

1. What are the ethical issues in logically decapitating a nation by taking down the countries communications systems so they can't capitulate, surrender, or deny a claim from an adversary?
2. At what threshold would a military commander be justified, allowed, or comfortable launching a cyber or conventional retaliatory attack given the potential sophistication of state-sponsored cyberattacks?
3. Define a domain, as it's used by the Department of Defense. Consider that when an aircraft crashed from the air domain (into the land domain) the air domain remains (and the land domain may be changed). Now consider when a computer or routing system is damaged, the cyber domain changes.
4. If cyberspace is a domain, such as stated by Deputy Secretary of Defense Lynn, is it a battlefield? If it's a battlefield, then according to the Geneva Convention I Articles 33 and 35 the title to movable public property

belonging to an enemy state and captured by armed forces, regardless of the military characteristics of the property, belongs to the capturing army. This has traditionally been interpreted to mean weapons, ammunition, food, and money. Private property is immune from capture except property having a military use. What are the implications in the digital domain where information and software is easily copied?

5. If supply chain attacks are possible when should this change how a battle commander relies on their technology? How does this impact a country that relies on technical superiority?

6. How does national sovereignty impact the attribution challenge?

Chapter 11. Strategies

1. A national strategy may be to use kinetic responses to deter cyber actions. This is dependent on external factors and attribution. Please comment on the strengths and shortcoming of this approach and potential solutions or alternatives.

2. The Pentagon has been expressing the desire to "dominate cyberspace." Their adversaries have been announcing they are trying to deter us, and we aren't listening – what is the next step if deterrence fails. What should be the national strategy? What should be done?

3. The Commander of U.S. Strategic Command, the senior military officer responsible for the defense of the military networks and advisor to the President, has made the statement "we have the capability to shut down people that attack our networks in real-time." Is this statement credible? Why? Who is the intended recipient of this message?

4. How might a defender shift the asymmetric advantage from the attacker to the defender?

5. How might a defender increase an adversaries work effort? How might they define and measure success?

6. The Pentagon's networks are performing exactly as they were engineered – how might we reengineer the environment so it possible to deter or compel adversaries to behave.

7. Note similarities, differences, and challenges in deterring an individual, members of organized crime, third world nations, and industrial/information-based nations. Is there a viable strategy possible when attribution is difficult and after the fact?

8. How should another nation deter U.S. cyber espionage and/or aggression?

9. What are the effects a guardian is pursuing when using an active-defense strategy?

10. How might the government improve cybersecurity without harming its offensive intelligence and military cyber operations?

11. If foreign state and criminal hackers use the same technology and procedures as government hackers, then how should the government structure existing and future cyber security programs to deal with this issue?

12. Review public government statements regarding the causes of the 2014-2015 OPM intrusions. Which federal laws, policies, and executive orders did government leaders apparently ignore? How might the government improve its security in light of these insights? How might these revelations affect private citizens and industry interaction with the government?

13. Describe a strategy, or set of strategies, that a nation could implement to protect its citizens from cyber intrusions as well as other national threats. Describe the strengths and weaknesses of this strategy over existing strategies.

14. Select another nation and select a strategy or series of strategies that support that nation's specific national goals. How might this nation's strategy impact other nation's strategies?

Chapter 12. Cyber Pearl Harbor and the Digital Apocalypse

1. Consider the following questions as ethics issues rather than legal or technical issues:
    a) Is it ethical to damage or degrade another country's critical infrastructures? Consider the stock market, air traffic control systems, and emergency services like 911.
    b) What are the issues with damaging or degrading a system that may cripple a larger worldwide system, either electronically or through perception? Consider the worldwide financial system.
    c) Attacking a purely civilian infrastructure may cause the death of civilians. Consider air traffic control, and hospitals. What are the legal and ethical ramifications? How might we respond to an attack against these?

2. The U.S. government is actively pushing for transitioning to the "smart grid" that will connect individual devices to automated power control and billing systems throughout houses and offices. They promise the Smart Grid will reduce costs to consumers because the electricity producers will manage demand peaks and consumers will take advantage of lower costs during low peak times. What are the security implications of this effort?

3. Compare and contrast the impact of the Armaco attack with Hurricane Katrina. What if an adversary deliberately timed a destructive attack around a major natural disaster such that both occurred at the same time?

4. How can the government motivate companies to increase security when increasing costs may reduce their short-term competitive advantage?

Chapter 13. Digital Terrorists

1. List all the unconstrained actions nations can take in cyberspace to attack terrorists and terrorist's goals. What are the implications of each to rest of the citizens in cyberspace? Which would you recommend implementing?

2. The author suggests there is an asymmetry in cyber that gives the advantage to terrorists. What actions can be taken to reduce this advantage?

3. What is the impact of the fear, uncertainty, and doubt that is put forth by vendors, consultants, and other experts?

Chapter 14. Naked and Unprotected - Secrecy
1. How would you change existing government policies regarding secrecy?
2. How would you draft a mandatory information sharing policy?
3. How can the government effectively share vulnerability information without reforming the entire classification process?

Chapter 15 – The Great Equalizer
1. Make a list of the major government players in cyber conflict, and their interests and concerns regarding cyberspace. List the requirements for each player if they were allowed to "reengineer" the Internet?
2. How would you organize and operate a national cyberspace center? What would be the requirements for the director?
3. The SDI investment in basic research to universities, national laboratories, and industries led to ground breaking technology in numerous fields including high-energy physics, materials, supercomputing, and computer algorithms. How might a national "Cyber SDI" research program be organized? Who would lead the program? What might be its goals? American military strategy comes from the perspective that the U.S. forces will be technologically advanced over our adversaries. The author suggests the size and composition of our military is premised on that assumption. However, if our technology is vulnerable to attack, how might we alter our current polices or plans?

References and Notes

Chapter 2:

1. DARPA has switched its name back and forth between DARPA and ARPA. It appears the name has settled on DARPA.

2. Others around the world including British and French scientists were also researching alternative means to communicate.

3. A common myth is that DARPA created ARPANet as a communications network to survive a nuclear strike. See Barry M. Leiner et al., *A Brief History of the Internet*, at http://www.internetsociety.org/internet/what-internet/history-internet/brief-history-internet

4. For security reasons the U.S. military-only portion of the ARPANet separated from the overall ARPANet in 1983 and became MILNET, a private network with connections to the larger network.

5. J. Goldsmith, and T. Wu, *Who Controls the Internet?*, New York, NY: Oxford University Press, 2006.

6. W. Gibson, *Neuromancer*. New York, NY: Ace, 1984.

7. T. Scott, "March 17, 1948: William Gibson, Father of Cyberspace." *Wired*. Available: http://www.wired.com/science/discoveries/news/2009/03/dayintech_0317

8. Dalberg, *Impact of the Internet in Africa*, April 2013. Available: http://www.impactoftheinternet.com

9. The USA Patriot Act of 2001 defined critical infrastructure as "systems and assets, whether physical or virtual, so vital to the United States that the incapacity or destruction of such systems and assets would have a debilitation impact on security, national economic security, national public health or safety, or any combination of those matters."

10. There are many other information fields in an Internet message, but for the purpose of this discussion we focus on these three fields.

11. By the late 1990s it was obvious the roughly 4.3 billion unique IPv4 addresses were not enough for the growing Internet. To alleviate this problem engineers developed IPv6. This newer protocol has 3.4×10^{38} (34 with thirty-seven zeros following) unique addresses. IPv6 is slowly being deployed across the Internet, but often requires replacement of software and hardware. The IPv6 protocol does not address the security concerns of IPv4.

12. World Internet Statistics. Available: http://www.internetworldstats.com. Accessed: Aug. 6, 2013.

13. U.S. Navy Rear Admiral Grace Murray Hopper is credited with popularizing the term 'computer bug' after a moth caused her computer to malfunction.

14. S. McConnell, *Code Complete*, Second Edition: Microsoft Press, 2004. pp 521-522. This text provides an excellent technical discussion on the source of errors in computer code, and how to eliminate them.

15. These numbers are interpolations based on estimates extracted from informed experts and empirical data.

16. The U.S. government defines a vulnerability as a "Weakness in an information system, system security procedures, internal controls, or implementation that could be exploited or triggered by a threat source." United States, *NISTIR 7298, Revision 2, Glossary of Key Information Security Terms*, May 2013.

17. Other threats to information systems include natural and physical threats (such as fires, floods, power failure, smoking and soda spills, that can be reduced through policies, preventive actions and damage minimization); and unintentional threats, due to ignorance and accidents (such as erasure of data or incorrect data entry). D. Russell and G.T. Gangemi, *Computer Security Basics*, Sebastopol, CA: O'Reilly & Associates, 1991.

18. CNN, *Fake Tech Gear Has Infiltrated the U.S. Government*, Nov 8, 2013. Available: http://money.cnn.com/2012/11/08/technology/security/counterfeit-tech/index.html. Accessed: Nov 17, 2015.

19. B. Krebs. *Target Hackers Broke in Via HVAC Company*, Feb 14, 2014. Available: http://krebsonsecurity.com/2014/02/target-hackers-broke-in-via-hvac-company/. Accessed: Nov 17, 2015.

20. E. A. Harris. "Data Breach Hurts Profit at Target," *New York Times*. Feb. 26, 2014. Available: http://www.nytimes.com/2014/02/27/ business/target-reports-on-fourth-quarter-earnings.html?_r=0. Accessed: Nov 18, 2015.

21. M. Parks. *Target Offers $10 Million Settlement In Data Breach Lawsuit*. National Public Radio. March 31, 2015. Available: http://www.npr.org/sections/thetwo-way/2015/03/19/394039055/target-offers-10-million-settlement-in-data-breach-lawsuit. Accessed: Nov 18, 2015.

22. The White House. *Remarks by President Obama in Press Conference after G7 Summit*. June 8, 2015. Available: https://www.whitehouse.gov/the-press-office/2015/06/08/remarks-president-obama-press-conference-after-g7-summit. Accessed: Nov 18, 2015.

23. These terms are not universally accepted and discussions of these topics often turn into religious arguments between the terms and the underlying issues. MITRE defines a vulnerability as a mistake in software that a hacker can use to gain access to a system or network, and an exposure to be a system configuration issue or mistake in software that allows access to information or capabilities. Available: https://cve.mitre.org/about/terminology.html

24. There are exploits in modern networked televisions and automobiles.

25. This is not to say the profit motive is bad, simply that readers must realize that it's a key motivation.

26. A discussion of undecidability is beyond the scope of this book. In non-technical language: it has been mathematically proven that it is impossible to create a general-purpose computer that can take as input any computer code, and tell if the code is malicious. See http://all.net/books/Dissertation.pdf

27. K. Thompson, "Reflections on Trusting Trust." *Communication of the ACM*, Vol. 27, No. 8, August 1984, pp. 761-763. Available: http://cm.bell-labs.com/who/ken/trust.html. Assessed on: May 6, 2014.

28. Fuzzing is a security test where engineers monitor applications while sending random or invalid data to the application. An application running an error routine, crashing, or reacting unexpectedly may signal the presence of a bug.

29. Hackers may discover vulnerabilities in the system and simply not report them. Instead they could sell the information to other hackers so they could break into the system, or use the knowledge to target other organizations.

30. Moore's Law, created by the co-founder of Intel Corporation Gordon Moore, states that computing power expressed as the number of transistors in an integrated circuit, doubles approximately every two years. Kryder's Law, created by the senior vice president of research and chief technology officer of the digital storage company Seagate, Mark Kryder, states that the density of hard drive storage doubles every thirteen months. Nielsen's Law created by web usability consultant Jakob Nielsen states that a high-end user's home network connection speed doubles every 21 months.

31. Computer scientist Robert Metcalf, co-inventor of the Ethernet standard for connecting computers over short distances proposed that the value of an information network is proportional to the square of the number of connected users in the system. More accurately, "As systems and users (n) are added to a network the value of the network increases between n log n to n^2." We define 'utility' as the relative benefit people receive from a system or network.

32. C. Stoll, *The Cuckoo's Egg – Tracking a Spy Through the Maze of Computer Espionage*, New York, NY: Pocket Books, 1990.

33. See http://www.ic3.gov/media/annualreport/2013_IC3Report.pdf

Chapter 3:

1. C. Stoll, *op. cit.*

2. A. Toffler, *The Third Wave*, New York, NY: Bantam Books, 1980.

3. To read the account of the 1990 hackers see U.S. General Accounting Office, *Information Security - Computer Attacks at Department of Defense Pose Increasing Risk*, Washington, D.C., 1996; U.S. General Accounting Office, *Hackers Penetrate DOD Computer Systems - Statement of Jack L. Brock, Jr*, Washington D.C., 1996. Available: http://archive.gao.gov/t2pbat7/145327.pdf

4. Associated Press, *Computer Security Experts: Dutch Hackers Stole Gulf War Secrets*. Mar 24, 1997. Available: http://www.apnewsarchive.com/1997/ Computer-security-experts-Dutch-hackers-stole-Gulf-War-secrets/id-9bdfd653327fc9c17e643090f08d1d04. Accessed: Sept 12, 2015.

5. G. W. Bush. *A Period of Consequences*. Sept 23, 1999. Available: http://www3.citadel.edu/pao/ addresses/pres_bush.html

6. Richard Clarke and Robert K. Knake confirm the attack in their book *Cyber War: The Next Threat to National Security and What to Do About It*. Others argue that this story started as an April Fools joke in the April 1, 1991 *InfoWorld* magazine, and took on a life of its own, making its way into books and numerous print and television articles.

7. U.S. General Accounting Office, *Hackers Penetrate DOD Computer Systems - Statement of Jack L. Brock, Jr.*, Washington, D.C., 1996. Available: http://archive.gao.gov/ t2pbat7/145327.pdf.

8. U.S. General Accounting Office. *Information Security - Computer Attacks at Department of Defense Pose Increasing Risk, Washington, D.C.*, 1996. Available: http://www2.gwu.edu/~nsarchiv/ NSAEBB/NSAEBB424/docs/Cyber-010a.pdf

9. B. Graham, *Hackers Attack Via Chinese Web Sites*, Washington Post, Aug 25, 2005. Available: http://www.washingtonpost.com/wpdyn/content/article /2005/08/24/AR2005082402318.html. Accessed: Feb. 4, 2014.

10. W. J. Lynn III, "Defending a New Domain, The Pentagon's Cyberstrategy," *Foreign Affairs*, Sept/Oct 2010. Available: http://www.foreignaffairs.com /articles/66552/william-j-lynn-iii/defending-a-new-domain.

11. *Ibid.*

12. S. Gorman, Y. J. Dreazen and A. Cole, "Insurgents Hack U.S. Drones," The Wall Street Journal, Available: http://www.wsj.com/articles/ SB126102247889095011

13. J. McCurry. "North Korean Hackers May Have Stolen US War Plans," *Guardian*. Dec. 18, 2009. Available: http://www.theguardian.com/world/2009/ dec/18/north-south-korea-hackers. Accessed: Jan. 3, 2014.

14. N. Hodge, "Chinese Jet Spurs Interest in U.S. F-35," *USA Today*, Jan 18, 2011, p. A13.

15. *ibid.*

16. Lockheed Martin, *Patriot Advanced Capability-3 (PAC-3)*. Available: http://www.lockheedmartin.com/us/products/PAC-3.html

17. E. Nakashima, "Confidential report lists U.S. weapons system designs compromised by Chinese cyberspies," *Washington Post*, May 27, 2013. A Available: http://www.washingtonpost.com/world/national-security /confidential-report-lists-us-weapons-system-designs-compromised-by-chinese-cyberspies/2013/05/27/a42c3e1c-c2dd-11e2-8c3b-0b5e9247e8ca_story.html

18. Department of Defense, Defense Industrial Base Cyber Incident Reporting & Cyber Threat Information Sharing Portal. Available: http://dibnet.dod.mil/

19. Snowden's story is challenging to investigate. It's difficult to openly confirm or deny the content of the information Snowden has posted.

20. J. R. Clapper. *Statement for the Record Worldwide Threat Assessment of the U.S. Intelligence Community, Senate Select Committee on Intelligence*, March 12, 2013. Available: http://www.odni.gov/files/documents/ Intelligence Reports/2013 ATA SFR for SSCI 12 Mar 2013.pdf. Accessed: Sept 17, 2013.

Chapter 4:

1. F. Cohen, "Computer Viruses: Theory and Experiments," *Computers and Security*, vol 6, 1987, pp 22-35.

2. D. Yadron, "Symantec Develops New Attack on Cyberhacking," The Wall Street Journal, May 4, 2014. Available: http://www.pcworld.com/article/2150743/antivirus-is-dead-says-maker-of-norton-antivirus.html

3. This is a generalization. Organizations may have other security services that protect systems outside the enterprise firewall.

4. U.S. Department of Defense, *Defense in Depth — A practical strategy for achieving Information Assurance in today's highly networked environments.* Available: https://www.nsa.gov/ia/_files/support/defenseindepth.pdf. Accessed: Dec. 28, 2014.

5. C. von Clausewitz, M. Howard, and P. Paret. *On War.* Princeton, NJ: Princeton UP, 1984.

6. U.S. Government. NIST Special Publication 800-53A helps decision-makers determine if security controls meet their intended goals. For example, the document stated that for "Wireless Access" a manager should "Determine if the information system protects wireless access to the system using authentication and encryption." Unfortunately, the policy doesn't provide guidance as to the cost and impact of implementing authentication and encryption or if the specific technologies are effective at deterring or preventing attacks.

7. S. Frei, *Correlation of Detection Failures*, NSS Labs, 2013. Available: https://www.nsslabs.com/news/press-releases/are-security-professionals-overconfident-%E2%80%9Cdefense-depth%E2%80%9D. Accessed: Feb 1, 2014.

8. The is an analysis of 9,000 publicly available malware samples that included exploits, worms, bots, viruses and flooding tools. See P. Zatko, "If you don't like the game, hack the playbook...," *DARPA Cyber Colloquium*, Nov 7, 2011.

9. See http://threatpost.com/groundbreaking-cyber-fast-track-research-program-ending-030613/77594

10. Feng Xue, *Attacking Antivirus.* Available: http://sebug.net/paper/Meeting-Documents/syscanhk/AttackingAV_BHEU08_WP.pdf.

11. H. Kelly, "The 'Heartbleed' security flaw that affects most of the Internet," *CNN.* Available: http://www.cnn.com/2014/04/08/tech/web/heartbleed-openssl/

12. The MITRE Common Vulnerabilities and Exposures (CVE) provides a fairly comprehensive database of vulnerabilities, including those in security controls. Available: https://cve.mitre.org

13. Verizon, "Verizon Data Breach Investigation Report," 2013, p6. Available: http://www.verizonenterprise.com/resources/reports/rp_data-breach-investigations-report-2013_en_xg.pdf?r=72

14. B. Sullivan, "Exclusive: Millions of printers open to devastating hack attack, researchers say," *NBC.* Available: http://www.nbcnews.com/business/consumer/exclusive-millions-printers-open-devastating-hack-attack-researchers-say-f118851

[15.] G. Shipley, "Outgunned: How Security Tech Is Failing Us," *Dark Reading*. Available: http://www.darkreading.com/vulnerabilities-and-threats/outgunned-how-security-tech-is-failing-us/d/d-id/1093153?

Chapter 5:

[1.] U.S. military policy states that the goals in cyberattacks are to destroy, deny, degrade, disrups, deceive, corrupt, and usurp.

[2.] R. Clark and R. Knake, *Cyber War: The Next Threat to National Security and What to Do About It*, New York, NY: Harper Collins, 2010.

[3.] For a fascinating and very detailed discussion of apparent Chinese government sponsored hacker activities and the steps they used see http://intelreport.mandiant.com/

[4.] For more on the hacker mindset, see P. Zatko, "Psychological Security Traps" in A. Oram and J. Viega, *Beautiful Security*: O'Reilly Press, 2009.

[5.] Exploiting some targets may require multiple vulnerabilities and steps, and each step may be complex. For example, exploiting a modern operating system may require one exploit to break out of a browser, another to gain access to the operating system, and another to gain administrator access to the computer.

[6.] T. Ryan, "Getting in Bed with Robin Sage." Available: http://media.blackhat.com/bh-us-10/whitepapers/Ryan/BlackHat-USA-2010-Ryan-Getting-In-Bed-With-Robin-Sage-v1.0.pdf, Accessed: July 11, 2015.

[7.] C. Stoll, *op. cit.*

[8] ████████████████████████████████████

[9.] T. A. Wadlow, *The Process of Network Security*. Reading, MA: Addison-Wesley, 2000.

[10.] Verizon, "Verizon *2010 Data Breach Investigations Report*," Available: http://www.verizonbusiness.com/go/2010databreachreport/

[11.] N. Shachtman, "Military Networks 'Not Defensible,' Says General Who Defends Them," *Wired*. January 12, 2012. Available: http://www.wired.com/2012/01/nsa-cant-defend/. Accessed: Jan 17,2014.

[12.] See https://www.nsa.gov/careers/career_fields/netopps.shtml. Accessed: 10 Nov 2015.

[13.] See https://www.nsa.gov/about/faqs/about_nsa.shtml. Accessed: 10 Nov 2015.

[14.] NIST, *Continuous Monitoring Frequently Asked Questions*. Available: http://csrc.nist.gov/groups/SMA/fisma/documents/faq-continuous-monitoring.pdf. Accessed: May 15, 2015.

[15.] D. Guido, *EIP Revisited – Exploitation and Defense in 2013*. Presented at BruCon Sept 26, 2013.

Chapter 6:

[1.] Kaspersky Laboratory, *Kaspersky Lab provides its insights on Stuxnet worm*. Russia. Available: http://www.kaspersky.com/about/ news/virus/2010/Kaspersky_Lab_provides_its_insights_on_Stuxnet_worm. Accessed: 24 Sep 2010.

2. J. Markoff and D. Sanger, "In a Computer Worm, a Possible Biblical Clue" *New York Times*, Sept. 29, 2010, Available: http://www.nytimes.com/2010/09/30/world/ middleeast/30worm.html. Accessed: 17 November 2015.

3. W. Broad, J. Markoff, and D. Sanger, "Israel Tests on Worm Called Crucial in Iran Nuclear Delay," *New York Times*, Jan15, 2011. Available: http://www.nytimes.com/aponline/2010/09/25/world/middleeast/AP-ML-Iran-Cyber-Attacks.html?_r=0. Accessed: Nov 17, 2015

4. "China says sanction cannot resolve Iran nuclear issue," *Xinhua News Agency*, Apr 13, 2010. Available: http://news.xinhuanet.com/english2010/china/ 2010-04/13/c_13249560.htm. Accessed: Nov 17, 2015.

5. J. R. Clapper, *Statement for the Record Worldwide Threat Assessment of the U.S. Intelligence Community, Senate Select Committee on Intelligence*, Mar 12, 2013. Available: http://www.odni.gov/files/documents/ Intelligence Reports/2013 ATA SFR for SSCI 12 Mar 2013.pdf. Accessed: Sept 17, 2013.

Chapter 7:

1. In the United Kingdom the Government Communications Headquarters (GCHQ) is responsible for signals collection. See http://www.gchq.gov.uk.

2. M. Davis, *The Universal Computer: the Road from Leibniz to Turing*. New York: Norton. 2000

3. For more information on cryptography, the study of breaking codes, and the history of code breaking see *The Codebreakers: The Comprehensive History of Secret Communications from Ancient Times to the Internet* by David Kahn.

4. Sun Tzu also knew that placing spies inside an adversary's defenses provides an advantage when it comes time to act — whether through sabotage or assassination. This is discussed in Chapter 9.

5. I. Winkler, *Corporate Espionage: What it is, why it's happening in your company, what you must do about it*. 1997. Rocklin, CA: Prima Publishing. Although dated, this book provides insights into traditional and cyber related industrial espionage.

6. Providing credit card companies with a different and incorrect matriarch name can be an effective way to catch someone using the above technique. This is an example of a "false flag."

7. See Chapter 10 regarding the Farewell Dossier.

8. See http://fbo.gov, http://usaspending.gov, and http://www.defense.gov/contracts/

9. In Chapter 7 we discuss impacting a social network by eliminating specific nodes in the network.

10. Matta Security Limited. *Internet-based Counterintelligence*. Available: http://www.trustmatta.com. Accessed: Nov 10, 2015.

11. In the analysis community this is often stated, "Correlation doesn't imply causation."

12. More information in TIA can be found in S. Harris, *The Watchers: The Rise of America's Surveillance State*. New York, NY: Penguin Press, 2010.

13. G. Greenwald, "NSA collecting phone records of millions of Verizon customers daily," *The Guardian*. June 6, 2013. Available: http://

www.theguardian.com/world/2013/jun/06/nsa-phone-records-verizon-court-order. Accessed: Nov 17, 2015

[14.] J. Miller, "NSA speaks out on Snowden, spying," *CBS/60 Minutes*. Dec 15, 2013. Available: http://www.cbsnews.com/news/nsa-speaks-out-on-snowden-spying/

[15.] J. Ball, "Verizon court order: telephone call metadata and what it can show," *The Guardian*, 6 June 6, 2013. Available: http://www.theguardian.com/world/2013/jun/06/phone-call-metadata-information-authorities

[16.] S. J. Freedberg Jr, "Top Official Admits F-35 Stealth Fighter Secrets Stolen," *Breaking Defense*, June 20, 2013. Available: http://breakingdefense.com/2013/06/top-official-admits-f-35-stealth-fighter-secrets-stolen/2/

[17.] W. J. Lynn III, *op. cit.*

[18.] "Pentagon Warns of Internet Incursion by Chinese Cyber-Terrorists," *Government Computing News*, Aug 25, 2006.

[19.] B. Krekel, G. Bakos, and C. Barnett, *Capability of the People's Republic of China to Conduct Cyber Warfare and Computer Network Exploitation*. Washington, DC: The US-China Economic and Security Review Commission. 2009.

[20.] U.S. intelligence is composed of numerous subcategories including Human Intelligence (HUMINT) involving collecting using persons, Electronic Intelligence (ELINT) concerned with non-communication signals such as radar, and Communications Intelligence (COMINT) concerned with signals that carry information like radio transmissions.

[21.] J. Bamford. *The Puzzle Palace – Inside the National Security Agency, America's Most Secret Intelligence Organization; Body of Secrets – Anatomy of the Ultra-Secret National Security Agency; The Shadow Factory – The NSA From 9/11 to the Eavesdropping on America*. These three books represent an entertaining read of the history of the National Security Agency.

[22.] D. Popkey, "Idaho's Frank Church has posthumous TV debate with Rick Santorum," *Idaho Statesman*, Aug 5, 2013; "Sen. Frank Church Warns of How Easily Government Can Abuse Expanding Surveillance Capabilities," *Grabien - The Multimedia Marketplace*, Aug 17, 1975; J. Bamford, "Post-September 11, NSA 'enemies' include us," *Politico*, Sept 13, 2011.

[23.] For more information on Echelon and legal restriction on collecting on U.S. citizens see J. Bamford, *Body of Secrets*, New York, NY: Anchor, 2002; S. Harris, *The Watchers: The Rise of America's Surveillance State*. New York, NY: Penguin Press, 2010.

[24.] N. Hager, *Nicky Hager Appearance before the European Parliament Echelon Committee*, Apr 2001. Available: http://cryptome.org/echelon-nh.htm. Accessed: March 2011

[25.] G. Schmid, *On the existence of a global system for the interception of private and commercial communications (ECHELON interception system)*, July 11, 2001. Available: http://www.fas.org/irp/program/ process/europarl_draft.pdf. Accessed: Mar 10, 2011.

26. D. Francis, "Spies Like Us: German Spies on Allies, Too," *Foreign Policy*, Aug 18, 2014. Available: http://foreignpolicy.com/2014/08/18/spies-like-us-germany-spies-on-allies-too/. Accessed: Jan 2, 2014.

27. See R. Singel, "Point, Click ... Eavesdrop: How the FBI Wiretap Net Operates," *Wired*, Aug 29, 2008. Available: http://www.wired.com/politics/security/news/2007/08/wiretap?. Accessed: Sept 14, 2014

28. See https://www.eff.org/document/nsa-transition-2001

29. See http://www.nsa.gov/about/mission/index.shtml.

30. ███████████████████████████████████████

31. ███████████████████████████████████████

32 Protocol I, Article 46 declares military personnel captured in uniform while gathering intelligence are combatants and treated as prisoners of war. However, the act explicitly withholds these protections from undercover operatives, agents captured while conducting espionage, and mercenaries. Similar provisions exist in the Geneva Conventions. Nations can treat the later groups as illegal combatants and prosecute them for espionage. If a spy is a citizen of the country of which they are spying they may be indicted for treason, which is a capital offense in many nations.

33. See http://www.fbi.gov/news/news_blog/five-chinese-military-hackers-charged-with-cyber-espionage-against-u.s

34 Department of Justice. *Chinese National Who Conspired to Hack into U.S. Defense Contractors' Systems Sentenced to 46 Months in Federal Prison.* July 13, 2016. Available: https://www.justice.gov/opa/pr/chinese-national-who-conspired-hack-us-defense-contractors-systems-sentenced-46-months. Accessed: Nov 5, 2016.

35. ███████████████████████████████

Chapter 8:

1. See A. C. Brown, *Bodyguard of Lies*, New York: Harper Row, 1975 and F. Hinsley, C. Ransom, R. Knight, and E. Thomas, *British Intelligence in the Second World War - Its Influence on Strategy and Operations* (Vol. I). London: Stationery, 1979.

2. See F. H. Hinsley, and A. Stripp, *Code Breakers - The Inside Story of Bletchley Park*, London: Oxford University Press, 1993; and T. Burnett, *Conspiracy Encyclopedia*, Collins & Brown, 2006. Another version is that the Royal Air Force intercepted the German directional beams and assumed the Germans were going to bomb the city of London, then mistakenly provided the wrong frequencies to jammers, thus vectoring the Germans into Coventry.

3. The London Times referred to Coventry as the "Martyred city" see M. Farquhar, *A Treasury of Deception: Liars, Misleaders, Hoodwinkers, and the Extraordinary True Stories of History's Greatest Hoaxes, Fakes and Frauds*, New York: Penguin, 2005.

4. R. Reagan. *President Reagan's Address to the Nation on U.S. Air Strike against Libya - 4/14/86*, Available: https://www.youtube.com/watch?feature=player_embedded&v=13xx1J5FdNE. Accessed: Nov 5, 2015.

5. The U.S. government uses 'equities' to refer to sharing resources across competing government goals. Should the governments try to ensure spending is equally distributed across agencies, or determine what is important and then spend resources effectively regardless of agency equities?

6. J. Rogin, "Cartwright: Cyber warfare strategy 'dysfunctional'," *Federal Computing Week*, Feb 09, 2007. Available: http://fcw.com/articles/2007/02/09/cartwright-cyber-warfare-strategy-dysfunctional.aspx

7. J. Rogin, "NSA Chief: Cybercrime constitutes the 'greatest transfer of wealth in history'," *Foreign Policy*, July 9, 2012. Available: http://thecable.foreignpolicy.com/posts/2012/07/09/nsa_chief_cybercrime_constitutes_the_greatest_transfer_of_wealth_in_history

8. Government Accountability Office. *Progress Made but Challenges Remain in Defining and Coordinating the Comprehensive National Initiative*. Mar 2010. Available: http://www.gao.gov/new.items/d10338.pdf. Accessed: Nov 18, 2015.

9. The White House. *The Comprehensive National Cybersecurity Initiative*. Available: https://www.whitehouse.gov/issues/foreign-policy/cybersecurity/national-initiative. Accessed: Oct 1, 2015.

10. NSSs are "Information systems operated by the U.S. Government, its contractors, or agents that contain classified information or that: involve intelligence activities; involve cryptographic activities related to national security; involve command and control of military forces; involve equipment that is an integral part of a weapon or weapons system(s); or are critical to the direct fulfillment of military or intelligence missions (not including routine administrative and business applications)." See *Committee on National Security Systems*. Available: https://www.cnss.gov/CNSS/about/faq.cfm.

11. Government Accountability Office. *Progress Made but Challenges Remain in Defining and Coordinating the Comprehensive National Initiative*. Mar 2010. Available: http://www.gao.gov/new.items/d10338.pdf. Accessed: Nov 18, 2015.

12. The NSA website defines the tasks cyber forces perform: *"Cyberwar is a very real threat and could cause widespread problems. That is why the National Security Agency needs to be prepared with Computer Science professionals who are highly-skilled in Computer Network Operations. Our Computer Network Operations mission involves three major functions: Computer Network Attack (CNA): Includes actions taken via computer networks to disrupt, deny, degrade, or destroy the information within computers and computer networks and/or the computers/networks themselves. Computer Network Defense (CND): Includes actions taken via computer networks to protect, monitor, analyze, detect, and respond to network attacks, intrusions, disruptions, or other unauthorized actions that would compromise or cripple defense information systems and networks. Computer Network Exploitation (CNE): Includes enabling actions and intelligence collection via computer networks that exploit data gathered from target or enemy information systems or networks."* Available: https://www.nsa.gov/careers/career_fields/netopps.shtml. Accessed: Sept 4, 2014.

13. D. Sanger, "N.S.A. Leaks Make Plan for Cyberdefense Unlikely," *New York Times*. Aug 12, 2013. Available: http://www.nytimes.com/2013/08/13/us/nsa-leaks-make-plan-for-cyberdefense-unlikely.html?_r=0. Accessed: Sept 15, 2015.

14. See *Greetings from the Orient* in Chapter 2 for information on the first detected Chinese intrusions into military networks.

15. Comments made during a presentation by General (ret) Michael Hayden, *Cyberinsecurity*, Washington DC, May 6-7, 2010.

16. "Attack, Sensing, Warning, and Response: This focus area seeks to increase the ability of the U.S. to defend its critical networks through detection and response. Our research includes development of effective methods for detecting and responding to cyber attacks including: intrusion detection systems, malicious code detection, attack attribution (also known as traceback), visualization, data reduction and analysis, and alert correlation." Available: https://www.nsa.gov/research/ia_research/research_areas/. Accessed: Dec 1, 2015.

17. U.S. Government. *Security. Memorandum of Agreement Between the Department of Homeland Security and the Department of Defense Regarding Cybersecurity.* Available: http://nsarchive.gwu.edu/NSAEBB/NSAEBB424/docs/Cyber-037.pdf

18. U.S. Department of Homeland Security. *Preventing and Defending Against Cyber Attacks*. Nov 2010. Available: http://www.dhs.gov/xlibrary/assets/defending-against-cyber-attacks-november-2010.pdf. Accessed: Nov 15, 2015.

19. M. I. Kellner, and J. J. Jaime, *The CENTAUR System: Helping to Protect the NIPRNet*, 2005. Available: http://resources.sei.cmu.edu/asset_files/WhitePaper/2005_019_001_51510.pdf. Accessed: Nov 12, 2015.

20. M. Ravindranath. *Committee Grills DHS Official Over Einstein's Failure to Prevent OPM Attack*. June 24, 2015. Available: http://www.nextgov.com/cybersecurity/2015/06/house-committee-grills-dhs-official-failure-einstein-cdm-prevent-opm-attack/116242/. Accessed: Aug 16, 2015.

Chapter 9:

1. An insider can do other damage to an organization, such as subverting an organization from the inside, however this discussion will limit itself to taking and exposing sensitive organizational information.

2. Verizon, *Verizon Data Breach Investigation Report*, 2016. Available: http://www.verizonenterprise.com/DBIR/

3. J. Garside, "Panama Papers: inside the Guardian's investigation into offshore secrets," *The Guardian*, April 16, 2016. Available: https://www.theguardian.com/news/2016/apr/16/panama-papers-inside-the-guardians-investigation-into-offshore-secrets.

4. J. Miller, "NSA Speaks Out on Snowden Spying," *CBS News*, Dec 15, 2013. Available: http://www.cbsnews.com/news/nsa-speaks-out-on-snowden-spying/

5. The author admits that it is challenging to confirm or deny the validity of information Snowden has posted using open sources. There may be no means to confirm or deny information Snowden posts using open sources.

6. M. Riley, "U.S. Agencies Said to Swap Data With Thousands of Firms," *Bloomberg,* June 15, 2013. Available: http://www.bloomberg.com/news/2013-06-14/u-s-agencies-said-to-swap-data-with-thousands-of-firms.html

7. F. Johannès, "Revelations on the French Big Brother," Société, July 4, 2013. Available: http://www.lemonde.fr/societe/article/2013/07/04/revelations-on-the-french-big-brother_3442665_3224.html

8. C. Freeze, "Data Collection Program Got Green Light From Mackay in 2011," *The Globe And Mail,* June 10, 2013. Available: http://www.theglobeandmail.com/news/national/data-collection-program-got-green-light-from-mackay-in-2011/article12444909/

9. See: http://www.thesmokinggun.com/documents/woman-arrested-for-obama-bloomberg-ricin-letters-687435

10. N. Anderson, "Spy Games: Inside the Convoluted Plot to Bring Down WikiLeaks," *Wired,* Feb 14, 2011. Available: https://www.wired.com/2011/02/spy/

11. The White House, *The Comprehensive National Cybersecurity Initiative.* Available: http://www.whitehouse.gov/issues/foreign-policy/cybersecurity/national-initiative

12. C. Cooper, "Intelligence Chief Offers Dire Warning on Cyberattacks," *Cnet,* Mar 12, 2013. Available: http://www.cnet.com/news/intelligence-chief-offers-dire-warning-on-cyberattacks/

13. D. E. Sanger and E. Schmitt, "Snowden Used Low-Cost Tool to Best N.S.A.," *NY Times,* Feb. 8, 2014. Available: http://www.nytimes.com/2014/02/09/us/snowden-used-low-cost-tool-to-best-nsa.html?_r=0

14. The White House, *The Comprehensive National Cybersecurity Initiative.* Available: http://www.whitehouse.gov/issues/foreign-policy/cybersecurity/national-initiative
"CNCI Initiative #7. Increase the security of our classified networks. Classified networks house the Federal Government's most sensitive information and enable crucial war-fighting, diplomatic, counterterrorism, law enforcement, intelligence, and homeland security operations. Successful penetration or disruption of these networks could cause exceptionally grave damage to our national security. We need to exercise due diligence in ensuring the integrity of these networks and the data they contain."

15. The White House, *Executive Order 13587 -- Structural Reforms to Improve the Security of Classified Networks and the Responsible Sharing and Safeguarding of Classified Information,* Oct 07, 2011. Available: https://www.whitehouse.gov/the-press-office/2011/10/07/executive-order-13587-structural-reforms-improve-security-classified-net

16. NSA National Computer Security Center, *National Insider Threat Policy,* Available: http://ncsc.gov/nittf/docs/National_Insider_Threat_Policy.pdf. Accessed: Dec 10, 2015.

Chapter 10:

1. Georgia, *Russian Invasion of Georgia - Russian Cyberwar on Georgia*, Nov 10, 2008. Available: http://www.mfa.gov.ge/files/556_10535_798405_Annex87_CyberAttacks.pdf. Accessed: Jan 1, 2014.

2. It should be noted that on August 14, 2008 the U.S. Joint Forces Command, the U.S. military entity responsible for the U.S. military warfighting doctrine, issued a memorandum terminating the use of the term and concept 'effects based operations.'

3. C. M. Kyle, *RMA to ONA: The Saga of an Effects Based Operation*, U.S. Army Command and General Staff College, 2008. Available: http://www.dtic.mil/cgi-bin/GetTRDoc?Location=U2&doc= GetTRDoc.pdf&AD=ADA499725. Accessed: July 21, 2013.

4. The Pentagon notes five effects: *Disrupt, Deny, Degrade, Destroy,* and *Deceive.* Disrupt is preventing something from occurring over a short period of time. Deny is preventing something from occurring over long period of time. Degrade is limiting the effectiveness of something. Destroy is damaging a target so badly that it can neither function as intended nor be restored to a usable condition. Deceive is manipulating someone to believe something that is false to cause them to do something, not do something, or distract them.

5. C. W. Williamson III, "Carpet bombing in cyberspace," *Armed Forces Journal,* 2008.

6. D. Waller and M. Thompson, "Onward Cyber Soldiers," *Time,* Aug 21, 1995, Col 146, No. 8. Available: http://www.csm.ornl.gov/~dunigan/timemag.html. Accessed: Jan 1, 2015.

7. G. Weiss. *Farewell Dossier - Duping the Soviets.* Available: https://www.cia.gov/library/center-for-the-study-of-intelligence/csi-publications/csi-studies/studies/96unclass/farewell.htm. Accessed: Aug 24, 2013

8. S. Kostin, and E. Raynaud, *Farewell,* 2nd Ed, Las Vegas, NV: Amazon Crossing, 2011.

9. G. Weiss. *op. cit.*

10. Kostin and Raynaud state that the explosion occurred in December 1983, while others claim June or October 1982.

11. F. A. Castro Ruz, "Deliberate Lies, Strange Deaths and Aggression to the World Economy," *Global Research,* Sept 23, 2007. Available: http://www.globalresearch.ca/deliberate-lies-strange-deaths-and-aggression-to-the-world-economy/6861. Accessed: Aug 24, 2013.

12. W. Safire, "The Farewell Dossier," *New York Times,* Feb 2, 2004. Available: http://www.nytimes.com/2004/02/02/opinion/the-farewell-dossier.html. Accessed: Jan 26, 2014.

13. B. Krebs, "ZeusTracker and the Nuclear Option," *The Washington Post,* May 7, 2009. Available: http://voices.washingtonpost.com/securityfix/2009/05/zeustracker_and_the_nuclear_op.html

14. President's Information Technology Advisory Committee. *Report to the President - Cyber Security: A Crisis of Prioritization.* Feb 2005. Edited by M. R.

Benioef, and E. D. Lazowska. Available: https://www.nitrd.gov/Pitac/ Reports/20050301_cybersecurity/cybersecurity.pdf

[15.] M. Thompson, "U.S. Cyberwar Strategy: The Pentagon Plans to Attack," *Time*, Feb. 2, 2010. Available: http://content.time.com/time/nation/article/ 0,8599,1957679,00.html.

[16.] R. Rosenbaum, "A Real Nuclear Option for the Nominees," *Slate*, May 9, 2008. Available: www.slate.com/id/2191104/pagenum/all/

[17.] C. Cooper, *op. cit.*

[18.] Vice Admiral William Studeman public statement at the *Cyber Metrics Meeting*, Draper Laboratory, Cambridge Massachusetts, 28-31 October 2013

[19.] An attack that affects a financial system may cause others to doubt the integrity of the international financial market — a system that manages trillions of dollars daily using only 1's and 0's, creating catastrophic consequence to international finance.

[20.] D. Waller and M. Thompson, *op. cit.*

[21.] W. J. Lynn III, *op. cit.*

[22.] D. Waller and M. Thompson, *op. cit.*

Chapter 11:

[1.] B. Brodie, *Strategy in the Missile Age*, Princeton NJ: Princeton University Press, 1959.

[2.] B. Brodie (editor), *The Absolute Weapon: Atomic Power and World Order*, New York, NY: Harcourt, 1946.

[3.] Later, others came up with additional policies such as Nuclear Utilization Theory (NUTs) that advocated limited use of nuclear weapons (reality is so much stranger than fiction).

[4.] T. C. Schelling, *Arms and Influence*, Yale University Press, 1966.

[5.] A clear "line in the sand" trigger is needed to prevent the target from gradually escalating events to eventually achieve their goals, called *salami tactics*.

[6.] Advances in technology enabled tactical, battlefield weapons such as nuclear artillery and "backpack" nuclear weapons. Tactical nuclear weapons eventually included short and mid-range missiles, including the U.S. Honest John and Lance, and the Soviet Frog and Scud. These could be safely controlled through advances in communications. However, effective use of tactical nuclear weapons required deployment close to a potential threat, often in an allies' country. This created political issues for both sides as they deployed weapons in Cuba, Germany, and Turkey.

[7.] Based on *Deterrence and Dissuasion for the 21st Century*, Ryan Henry, Principle Undersecretary of Defense for Policy, IFPA-Fletcher Conference, Dec 14, 2005

[8.] M. Libicki, *Cyberdeterrence and Cyberwar*, RAND Corporation, 2009. Available: http://www.rand.org/content/dam/rand/pubs/monographs/2009/RAND_M G877.pdf

[9.] J. R. Clapper. *Statement for the Record Worldwide Threat Assessment of the U.S. Intelligence Community, Senate Select Committee on Intelligence*, Mar 12, 2013. Available:

http://www.odni.gov/files/documents/Intelligence Reports/2013 ATA SFR for SSCI 12 Mar 2013.pdf. Accessed: Sept 17, 2013

10. I directed this block and directed the block lifted several weeks later. Unfortunately one organization delayed lifting this block, and this happened to be the organization that hosted the FVAP system. We lifted the block on the FVAP when we were notified people couldn't access the system from overseas.

11. S. Baker, *Cybersecurity, retribution, and empowering the private sector,* Sept 18, 2012. Available: http://www.volokh.com/2012/09/18/cybersecurity-retribution-and-empowering-the-private-sector/

12. U.S. Government, *Cyberspace As A Warfighting Domain: Policy, Management And Technical Challenges To Mission Assurance, Hearing Before the Terrorism, Unconventional Threats And Capabilities Subcommittee of the Committee on Armed Services, House Of Representatives,* May 5, 2009. Available: http://www.gpo.gov/fdsys/pkg/CHRG-111hhrg57218/html/CHRG-111hhrg57218.htm

13. M. Arnold and T. Brathwaite, "Davos 2015: Banks call for free rein to fight cyber crime," *Financial Times.* Jan 22, 2015. Available: http://www.ft.com/cms/s/0/d94e855c-a209-11e4-bbb8-00144feab7de.html#axzz3tBiTisXY. Accessed: Dec 2, 2015.

14. The White House, *National Strategy for Combating Terrorism,* Feb 2003. Available: https://www.cia.gov/news-information/cia-the-war-on-terrorism/Counter_Terrorism_Strategy.pdf. Accessed: Nov 15, 2015.

15. U.S. Department of Defense. Joint Publication 1-02, *DoD Dictionary of Military and Associated Terms* (12 April 2001, as amended through April 2010). Available: http://www.dtic.mil/doctrine/jel/new_pubs/jp1_02.pdf

16. There is a distinction between a preemptive war and a preventive war. A preemptive war aims to repel or defeat a perceived invasion before the invasion occurs. A preventive war aims to defeat a force when an attack is not imminent or known - it's done to throw the balance of power in the favor of the nation before the threat obtains too much strength.

17. W. J. Lynn III, *op. cit.*

18. M. Thompson, 2010, *op. cit.*

19. *Ibid.*

20. The government has updated FISMA numerous times including the Federal Information Security Modernization Act of 2014. Available: http://www.natlawreview.com/article/fisma-updated-and-modernized-federal-information-security-management-act#sthash.6eKDMXIR.dpuf. In 2010 the government began requiring a *continuous monitoring* approach to FISMA, which a more complex and time-consuming implementation of the program.

21 T. Carper, *Opening Statement: 'More Security, Less Waste: What Makes Sense for our Federal Cyber Defense.' Testimony before Subcommittee on Federal Financial Management, Government Information, Federal Services, and International Security,* Oct 29, 2009. Available: http://carper.senate.gov/public/index.cfm/otherstatements?ID=4e4123f9-4742-4f1b-a18f-515fbb9d6d85.

22. E. Nakashima, "Hacks of OPM databases compromised 22.1 million people, federal authorities say," *The Washington Post,* July 9, 2015. Available: http://www.

washingtonpost.com/blogs/federal-eye/wp/2015/07/09/hack-of-security-clearance-system-affected-21-5-million-people-federal-authorities-say/
23 Office of Personnel Management, *Cybersecurity Incidents*. Available: https://www.opm.gov/cybersecurity/cybersecurity-incidents/. Accessed: Aug 6, 2016.
24. S. Gallagher, "OPM director on security issues: We're trying very hard." *ARS Technica*, Jun 24, 2015. Available: http://arstechnica.com/information-technology/2015/06/opm-director-on-security-issues-were-trying-very-hard/
25. J. Rogin, "Cyber Officials: China Hackers Attack 'anything and everything'," *Federal Computer Weekly*, Feb. 13, 2007.
26. S. Baker, S. Waterman, and G. Ivanov. *In the Crossfire, Critical Infrastructure in the Age of Cyber War*, 2010. Available: http://www.govexec.com/pdfs/012810j1.pdf

Chapter 12:

1. The USA Patriot Act of 2001 defined critical infrastructure as "systems and assets, whether physical or virtual, so vital to the United States that the incapacity or destruction of such systems and assets would have a debilitation impact on security, national economic security, national public health or safety, or any combination of those matters."
2. E. Nakashima, "Foreign Hackers targeted U.S. water plant in apparent malicious attack, expert says," *Washington Post*, Nov 18, 2011. Available: http://www.washingtonpost.com/ blogs/checkpoint-washington/post/foreign-hackers-broke-into-illinois-water-plant-control-system-industry-expert-says/2011/11/18/ gIQAgmTZYN_blog.html. Accessed: Sept 11, 2013.
3. K. Zetter, "Comedy of Errors Led to False 'Water-Pump Hack' Report," *Wired*, Nov 30, 2011. Available: http://www.wired.com/threatlevel/2011/11/water-pump-hack-mystery-solved/. Accessed: Sept 11, 2013.
4. The DHS defines 16 critical infrastructures: (1) Chemical - production, storage, and transportation of chemical products; (2) Commercial Facilities - private facilities for the general public, such as stadiums, casinos, hotels, amusement parks, movie studios, offices, and retail shopping facilities (3) Communications - such as satellite, wireless, and wireline telecommunications providers, (4) Critical Manufacturing - crucial to national economic prosperity such as manufacturing metals, machinery, electrical equipment, transportation equipment (5) Dams - dams, hydroelectric, navigational locks, levees and water control facilities (6) Defense Industrial Base - delivery and maintenance of military weapon systems (7) Emergency Services - first responders to man-made incidents and natural disasters (8) Energy - power generation, transmission and distribution; (9) Financial Services - protection of funds, credit, liquidity, investments, and transfers of wealth (10) Food and Agriculture - oversight of farms, restaurants, and food manufacturing, processing and storage (11) Government Facilities - government buildings; (12) Healthcare and Public Health - protection form terrorism , infectious diseases and natural disasters; (13) Information Technology - hardware, software, and information technology systems and services; (14) Nuclear Reactors, Materials, and Waste - nuclear power, reactors and radioactive materials(15) Transportation Systems - aviation,

highways infrastructures, maritime , mass transit, pipeline rail, postal and shipping; (16) Water and Wastewater Systems - fresh water production and transport, and sewage treatment. These are paraphrased from http://www.dhs.gov/critical-infrastructure-sectors.

5. Department of Homeland Security. Available: http://www.dhs.gov/what-critical-infrastructure. Accessed: Sept 11, 2013.

6. B. Woodward, *Obama's Wars*, New York, NY: Simon & Schuster, 2010. pp. 10.

7. U.S. Government, *Senate Financial Crisis Report, 2011*. Available: http://www.hsgac.senate.gov/public/_files/Financial_Crisis/FinancialCrisisReport.pdf

8. Pew Charitable Trusts, *The Impact of the September 2008 Economic Collapse*, Apr 28, 2010. Available: http://www.pewtrusts.org/our_work_report_detail.aspx?id=58695

9. "Suspicion has no place in our interchanges; it is a shield for ignorance, a sign of fear, uncertainty, and doubt." Caesar Augustus Yarbrough, The Roman Catholic Church Challenged, p. 75. The Patriotic Societies of Macon, 1920.

10. See: http://www.boozallen.com/about/leadership/executive-leadership/McConnell. Mike McConnell retired from Booz Allen Hamilton on June 30, 2014.

11. http://www1.salary.com/booz-allen-hamilton-hldg-cp-Executive-Salaries.html

12. U.S. Government. *Homeland Security Presidential Directive 7: Critical Infrastructure Identification, Prioritization, and Protection*. Available: http://www.dhs.gov/homeland-security-presidential-directive-7. Accessed: Sept 11, 2013.

13. For an interesting documentary on U.S. electrical power, see: The History Channel, Season 11, Episode 30. Available: http://www.history.com/shows/modern-marvels/episodes/season-11; Also see P.F. Schewe, *The Grid: A Journey through the Heart of Our Electrified World*. Washington, D.C.: J. Henry, 2007.

14. See http://www.ferc.gov/legal/maj-ord-reg.asp

15. The Aurora experiment has created much consternation across the power and security communities. Some argue it demonstrated that an attack is possible and others argue it was a farce. Arguably, many generators have physical controls that would prevent a similar attack from being successful. However, as a proof of principle, the Aurora experiment did open eyes to the possibilities.

16. E-ISAC and SANS. *Analysis of the Cyber Attack on the Ukrainian Power Grid*. March 18, 2016. Available: http://www.nerc.com/pa/CI/ESISAC/Documents/E-ISAC_SANS_Ukraine_DUC_18Mar2016.pdf. Accessed: Sept 1, 2016.

17. Helen Dewar, et al, *Ground War Not Imminent, Bush Says: Allies to Rely on Air Power 'for a While,'* Washington Post, February 12, 1991: A14

18. J. R. Clapper, *Statement for the Record Worldwide Threat Assessment of the U.S. Intelligence Community, Senate Select Committee on Intelligence*, March 12, 2013. Available: http://www.odni.gov/files/documents/ Intelligence Reports/2013 ATA SFR for SSCI 12 Mar 2013.pdf. Accessed: Sept 17, 2013.

19. *Ibid.*

Chapter 13:

1. A. Sipress, "An Indonesian's Prison Memoir Takes Holy War Into Cyberspace: In Sign of New Threat, Militant Offers Tips on Credit Card Fraud," *Washington Post*, Dec 14, 2004; pp. A19. Available: http://www.washingtonpost.com/wp-dyn/articles/A62095-2004Dec13.html

2. It is always dangerous to generalize about any group or set of groups. Terrorist groups range from domestic skinheads and the Klu Klux Klan to Islamic fundamentalists, and everything in between.

3. W. Reich, "The Logic of Terrorism." *Origins of Terrorism: Psychologies, Ideologies, Theologies, States of Mind*. Washington, DC: Woodrow Wilson Center, 1998. 15.

4. G. Weimann. "www.terror.net - How Modern Terrorism Uses the Internet," United States Institute of Peace, Mar 2004. Available: http://www.usip.org.

5. A. al-Zawahiri, *Letter to Abu Mus`ab al-Zarqawi*, Released by the Office of the Director of National Intelligence, Oct 11, 2005. Available: https://www.ctc.usma.edu/posts/zawahiris-letter-to-zarqawi-english-translation-2

6. Readers should be wary searching for terrorist websites. They may gather the attention of the terrorists or the government agencies that monitor the terrorists and those that support them. Note: it is illegal in the U.S. to provide any support to U.S. State Department designated terrorist organizations.

7. The Arabic word jihad means, "to struggle, strive, or exert oneself." It is typically used to mean religiously approved fighting on behalf of Muslims and Islam. Islamist can be thought of as a group who support a political role for Islam through implementation of Islamic law by the state. Fundamentalism is strict adherence to orthodox theological doctrines.

8. In should be noted that this is not intended to imply that Islamists are the only terrorist group that use cyberspace. Other terrorist groups include but are not limited to the Basque ETA Movement, Irish Republican Army (IRA), Shining Path (Sendero Luminoso), Armed Revolutionary Forces of Columbia (FARC), and the Ku Klux Klan.

9. Deputy Assistant Secretary of Defense Garry Reid, in testimony before the Senate Armed Services Subcommittee on Emerging Threats and Capabilities, hearing on U.S. government efforts to counter violent extremists, Mar 10, 2010.

10. Possession of some of the materials listed here may be illegal in some regions.

11. A. Sipress, *op. cit.*

12. Paisley, "al-Qaeda's Top Cyber Terrorist," *Defense Tech*, Jan 26, 2008. Available: http://defensetech.org/2008/01/26/al-qaedas-top-cyber-terrorist/

13. U.S. Department of Defense. *Donald Rumsfeld's Message – DOD Web Site Opsec Discrepancies*. Jan 14, 2003. Available: http://www.defense.gov/webmasters/policy/rumsfeld_memo_to_DOD_webmasters.html. Accessed: 1 July 2015.

14. http://www.cbc.ca/fifth/torontoterror/timeline.html

15. Check Point. *Volatile Cedar, Threat Intelligence and Research*, Mar 30, 2015. Available: https://www.checkpoint.com/downloads/volatile-cedar-technical-report.pdf

16. W. Reich, *op. cit.*

17. *Statement of Steven Chabinsky, Deputy Assistant Director, FBI Cyber Division, before the Senate Judiciary Committee Subcommittee on Homeland Security and Terrorism, at a hearing entitled Cybersecurity: Preventing Terrorist Attacks and Protecting Privacy Rights in Cyberspace,* Nov 17, 2009.

18. C. A. Theohary and J. Rollins, *Terrorist use of the Internet: Information Operations in Cyberspace,* Congressional Research Service, Mar 8, 2011

19. http://www.thefiscaltimes.com/Articles/2013/03/11/The-Coming-Cyber-Attack-that-Could-Ruin-Your-Life#sthash.o6RZ7EWq.dpuf

Chapter 14:

1. For more information on the history of U.S. classification and government secrecy see D. P. Moynihan, *Secrecy: The American Experience,* New Haven, CT: Yale University Press, 1998.

2. The White House, *Executive Order 8381 - Defining Certain Vital Military and Naval Installations and Equipment,* Mar 22, 1940.

3. The National Security Act of 1947, signed by President Harry S. Truman, also created the Secretary of Defense, National Security Council, U.S. Air Force, and ratified the creation of the Central Intelligence Agency.

4. National security involves actions a government takes to protect it and its citizens from harm. Security from conventional threats may require traditionally forms of power including political, economic, and military power. Security from unconventional threats to national security, such as non-state actors, drug cartels, multinational corporations and non-governmental organizations (NGOs) require law enforcement and other national elements. The U.S. definition of national security is "the national defense or foreign relations of the United States." *Executive Order 13526 - Classified National Security Information,* President of the United States, Dec 29, 2009. Available: https://www.whitehouse.gov/the-press-office/executive-order-classified-national-security-information. Accessed: Jan 4, 2014.

5. *Executive Order 13526 - Classified National Security Information,* President of the United States, Dec 29, 2009. Available: https://www. whitehouse.gov/the-press-office/executive-order-classified-national-security-information. Accessed: Jan 4, 2014.

6. *Ibid.*

7. *Ibid.*

8. Office of the Director of National Intelligence. Information Security Oversight Office. Report for Fiscal Year 2011.

9. *Ibid.* The report noted 127,072 original classification decisions and 92,064,862 derivative classification decisions. The document does not define a "classification decision," or the quantity of information this entails. It is unclear if a decision means a decision in a security classification guide, the classification of a paragraph, document, or set of documents.

10. Office of the Director of National Intelligence. *Intelligence Community Classification Guidance Findings and Recommendations Report,* ODNI CIO, IC

Technology Governance, Jan 2008. Available: https://fas.org/sgp/othergov/intel/class.pdf. Accessed: Jan 4, 2014.

[11.] *Ibid.*

[12.] U.S. Government, *Redefining Security: A Report to the Secretary of Defense and the Director of Central Intelligence*, Joint Security Commission, Feb 28, 1994.

[13.] Director of National Intelligence. *Creation of New Information Staring Steering Committee for the Intelligence Community*, ODNI News Release No. 06-07, Mar 6, 2007.

[14.] Today government and military schools teach acronyms like DIME (Diplomatic, Informational, Military or Economic) and PMESII (Political, Military, Economic, Social, Infrastructure and Information Systems) as mnemonics for the elements of national power.

[15.] M. Gannon, *Operation Drumbeat: The Dramatic True Story of Germany's First U-Boat Attacks Along the American Coast in World War II*. New York: Harper & Row, 1990.

[16.] D. Sanger, "A Washington Riddle: What Is 'Top Secret'?" *NY Times*, Aug 3, 2013. Available: http://www.nytimes.com/2013/08/04/sunday-review/a-washington-riddle-what-is-top-secret.html

[17.] For an example of an automated tool see http://scan4you.biz.

[18.] C. Mundie, *A Matter of National Security: Microsoft Government Security Program Provides National Governments with Access to Windows Source Code*, Jan 14, 2003. Available: http://news.microsoft.com/2003/01/14/a-matter-of-national-security-microsoft-government-security-program-provides-national-governments-with-access-to-windows-source-code

[19.] D. Priest and W. Arkin, "Top Secret America," The Washington Post, July 18, 2010. Available: http://projects.washingtonpost.com/top-secret-america/articles/a-hidden-world-growing-beyond-control/

[20.] Information Security Oversight Office, *Report on Cost Estimates for Security Classification Activities for Fiscal Year 2011*, 2011. Available: http://www.archives.gov/isoo/reports/2011-cost-report.pdf. Accessed: Jan 20, 2015

[21.] Moynihan. *op. cit.*

Chapter 15:

[1.] The White House, *Remarks by the President on Securing Our Nation's Cyber Infrastructure*, May 29, 2009. Available: https://www.whitehouse.gov/the-press-office/remarks-president-securing-our-nations-cyber-infrastructure.

[2.] C. Whitlock and G. Jaffe, "Obama announces new, leaner military approach," The Washington Post, Jan 5, 2012. Available: https://www.washingtonpost.com/world/national-security/obama-announces-new-military-approach/2012/01/05/gIQAFWcmcP_story.html

[3.] R. S. Bolia, "Overreliance on Technology: Yom Kippur Case Study," *Parameters*, Summer 2004. Available: http://www.army.mil/professionalWriting/volumes/volume2/september_2004/9_04_4.html#24. Accessed: Oct 2, 2014

4. R. Scales and P. Van Riper, "Preparing for War in the 21sy Century," *Strategic Review*, Summer 1997, 15.

5. The contemporary meaning of Luddite is a person opposed to new technology, specifically the electronic technology spreading through society. The term originally referred to "a member of any of the bands of English workers who destroyed machinery, especially in cotton and woolen mills, that they believed was threatening their jobs (1811–16); a person opposed to increased industrialization or new technology." Compact Oxford English Dictionary at AskOxford.com retrieved September 15, 2013.

6. Air gapping a network means to create an information network not connected to any other network. While this is not a perfect solution, air gapped networks may significantly hinder hackers.

7. J. Lewis, speech to Center for Strategic and International Studies, Washington, D.C., Jan 2, 2010.

8. This concept is similar to the concept of air superiority on a conventional battlefield. Air supremacy occurs when one side of a conflict possesses complete control of the skies. Air superiority is a lesser state, where a side is in a more favorable position than their opponent.

9. The Pentagon defines information superiority as "The operational advantage derived from the ability to collect, process, and disseminate an uninterrupted flow of information while exploiting or denying an adversary's ability to do the same." *Joint Publication 3-13, Information Operations*, Nov 27, 2012 incorporating change 1, Nov 20, 2014. Accessed: http://www.dtic.mil/doctrine/new_pubs/jp3_13.pdf. Accessed: June 19, 2015.

10. Author's discussions with Office of the Director of National Intelligence Chief Information Office staff – May 8, 2013.

11. Sun Tzu, T. Cleary (translator), *The Art of War*, Boston, MA: Shambhala Publications, 2004.

Glossary

Administrator Access — A privileged account permitting a higher level of authority and unrestricted freedom in what the account holder can perform on systems.

Active Defense — The employment of limited offensive actions and counterattacks to temporarily disable an imminent and impending attack.

Advanced Persistent Threat — Hackers who establish a stealthy and continuous presence on a victim's network using sophisticated capabilities and/or tradecraft.

Assurance — Actions or measures to facilitate trust in the quality of a system or process. This term creates a great deal of misunderstanding since there is no requirement quality is achieved, only steps taken to attempt to achieve quality.

Asymmetric — An out of balance or unequal situation. An asymmetric advantage is an advantage providing a much greater benefit then the costs to achieve the benefit.

Asymmetric Warfare — A conflict where the resources of two combatants differ and each attempts to exploit the other's weaknesses.

Attack Surface — The collection of all vulnerabilities a hacker may use to achieve their goals.

Attack Vector — A specific means to deliver malware or commands to a target.

Attribution — The ability to definitively identify and assign responsibility for any actions to a machine or individual on a network.

Backdoor — Any method permitting the bypass of normal access controls in a system.

Backlash — The impact from an enemy or victim because of an action. For example, in response to a hacker penetrating a system, a victim may counterattack the hacker and damage the hacker's systems. See blowback.

Beacon — Software repeatedly transmitting messages indicating it is active. Hackers install beacons to call out of compromised hosts to the hacker, who can then accept the connection and bypass security controls.

Best Security Practices — A list of guardian processes that work in the general case. Examples include knowing what is installed on a network, limiting control and access to information and systems, maintaining systems with the latest patches and updates, monitoring everything, and having a practiced response plan.

Blowback — The impact to an aggressor (those performing an action) as the result of an action. For example, a hacker deactivates a foreign financial system and causes the world to mistrust electronic commerce, resulting in the loss of all electronic sales in the hacker's nation. See backlash.

Botnet — A set of compromised (zombie) computers controlled by a master.

Brick — An inoperable computer.

Bug — an error in computer code.

Coventry Argument — Deliberately sacrificing a third party to preserve intelligence sources or methods.

Certification and Accreditation — A time consuming and expensive process to document best security practices so management can protect themselves from subsequent criticism or legal penalties when hackers compromise their networks.

Cloud Computing — Outsourcing information services.

Collateral Damage — Unintentional or incidental injury or damage to persons or objects that would not be lawful military targets in the circumstances ruling at the time. (US Department of Defense Joint Publication 3-60)

Common Criteria Evaluation — A government program encouraging lucrative vendors to bring products to market with serious design flaws that undermine security and reliability, but who could pay for the evaluation. The program then encouraged the government to only purchase the insecure products that successfully passed the vendor-defined tests.

Computer Network Attack (CNA) — "Actions taken through the use of computer networks to disrupt, deny, degrade, or destroy information resident in computers and computer networks, or the computers and networks themselves." (US Department of Defense)

Computer Network Defense (CND) — "Actions taken to protect, monitor, analyze, detect, and respond to unauthorized activities within DoD information systems and computer networks" (US Department of Defense). Operations a government operator is forced to perform, responding to poor decisions to purchase and field fundamentally insecure systems to conduct mission critical actions.

Computer Network Exploitation (CNE) — "Enabling operations and intelligence collection capabilities conducted through the use of computer networks to gather data from target or adversary automated information systems or networks." (US Department of Defense)

Controls — Any manual or automated (security) tool meant to ensure the quality of a state or process.

Cracker — Some use the term to refer to Script Kiddies. Others use the term to refer to malicious hackers who damage, degrade, or destroy information and systems.

Critical Infrastructures — "The systems and assets, whether physical or virtual, so vital to the United States that the incapacity or destruction of such systems and assets would have a debilitation impact on security, national

Glossary

economic security, national public health or safety, or any combination of those matters." USA Patriot Act of 2001.

Cut-Out — Compromised third-party computers that are unwitting intermediaries between a hacker and their victim. These are often used as hop-off points to attack a victim, or drop-off points to send exfiltrated information.

Cyber Hygiene — A buzzword to mean anything to someone trying to justify additional funding. See Best Security Practices.

Cyberconflict — Human struggle and ambition projected onto cyberspace. It is the actions of belligerents in cyberspace where conflicting agendas have transformed information and information systems into the targets, weapons, and battlefield.

Cyberspace — The set of computers and people interconnected by communications systems to enable them to achieve their goals.

Default Passwords — The passwords that come installed on systems by the vendors and are easily found by hackers. See Owned.

Defense-in-Depth — Redundant security controls placed in series in the hope one detects and/or prevents malicious activities.

Defense Industrial Base — A nation's manufacturing assets of direct or indirect importance to their armed forces.

Demarche — Formal notifications or written protests issued by the Department of State against other nations.

Denial of Service (DOS) — An attempt to make a machine or network system unavailable by overwhelming its processing, storage, or network resources.

Drive-by-Attack — A means to deliver malware to a victim by the victim visiting a website.

Egress Filtering — Removing potential malware or other malicious activity as it leaves a network.

Elite — A talented or skilled hacker with advanced knowledge and experience, and is often the true innovators within the field of hacking. Elite hackers are often those responsible for creating new capabilities, tools, and discovering zero-day vulnerabilities. Also called a wizard.

False Flags Operations — Deliberately using untrue information to mislead victims as to a perpetrator's identity. This phrase goes back to the days of sailing ships, where a captain would fly the flag of another country to deceive another ship captain, then 'strike' that flag and raise their national flag when it was too late for their victim to react effectively.

Geolocation — Assigning a geographic location to a person, device, or activity.

Hardening Paradox — When government networks created from commercial technology becomes more secure, their adversary's networks also created using this technology becomes more secure.

Heartbeat — See Beacon.

Honeypot/Honeynet/Honeymonkey — A honeypot is data and/or systems that appear legitimate but that guardians use to bait and/or observe hackers.

A honeynet is a set of honeypots. A honeymonkey is an automated system that visits websites searching for sites that infect visitors with malware.

Hyperwar — The fusion of warfare and technology that results in a vastly more intense and destructive battlefield.

Information Dominance — "The operational advantage gained from fully integrating information functions, capabilities, and resources to optimize decision making and maximize warfighting effects." U.S. Navy

Insider — Any member of a group (e.g. current or former employee or contractor) who has taken a hacker role such as voyeur, spy, or saboteur.

Intelligence — Activities to collect, analyze, and disseminate information so decision makers can grasp what is occurring or about to occur and make informed decisions.

Intelligence Community (IC) — In the U.S. it is a collection of sixteen government agencies that perform intelligence activities on behalf of the U.S. Government. The IC is led by the Director of National Intelligence (DNI).

Malware — Malicious software. Any software that a hacker may use to create a desired effect. See Trojan Horse, Virus, and Worm.

Mark — Intended victim.

Metadata — Data about data.

Mobile Code — Software transferred between systems (e.g. transferred across a network or via a USB flash drive) and executed on a local system without explicit installation or execution by the recipient.

Network Centric Warfare — Military doctrine that translates an information advantage, enabled in part by information technology into a competitive advantage. Also called Network-Centric Operations and Net-Centric Warfare.

Obfuscate — To change a file or application format or structure, to make its functionality unclear or unintelligible.

One-and-Done — see Zero-Day Vulnerability

Open Source Intelligence — Collecting publicly available information.

Originator Controlled (ORCON) — A U.S. government information sharing notice indicating the information may not be shared or disseminated without the authorization of the government agency that classified the information.

Owned — Hacker slang for having complete control of a victim's computer.

Patch — Computer code that fixes an error or adds new functionality in an application or operating system.

Perverse Effect — A situation that occurs when as the result of an action an environment evolves into a situation contrary to the original action's intent.

Phishing — A method to acquire sensitive information by masquerading as a trustworthy entity in electronic communications.

Protocol — A set of rules for communicating.

Pyrrhic Victory — A military victory that is so costly to the "winning side" that they are worse off.

Glossary

Rendition — Forcefully apprehending people in foreign nations that are suspected of being criminals or terrorists and transporting them to another country for interrogation and/or punishment.

Resilient Systems and Networks — A term used once it is impossible to hide that hackers repeatedly compromise a system. Strategies are then used to quickly restore the systems when they break or are compromised.

Retrospective Analysis — The progression from failure, detection, investigation, and update that most security controls require to defend against new attacks.

Reverse Engineering — Analyzing systems structure, function and operation of computer code and hardware to determine how a system operates.

Risk Management — Wishful thinking taught to guardians since they can't know all of their vulnerabilities, adversaries' capabilities, effectiveness of security controls, or impact of an attack, but they make a best guess to make management feel good.

Script Kiddie — Less sophisticated hackers that make up for their lack of technical understanding by collecting and reusing tools developed by sophisticated hackers.

Sneaker Net — Moving data between networks using removable media.

Social Engineering — Conning, defrauding, and misleading.

Spam — Unsolicited or unwanted messages.

Spills — A government euphemism for the loss of a nation's sensitive government information.

Spoof — To imitate.

Spycraft — See Tradecraft.

Super User — See Administrator Access.

Superiority — A condition when a side has a more favorable position than their opponent in an environment. See Supremacy.

Supply Chain Attack — Compromising a system typically by entering malware or counterfeit components into products during the design, manufacturing, handling, distributing, and installation stages of the manufacturing process.

Supremacy — A condition when a side of a conflict has complete control over an environment. See Superiority.

Tradecraft — The techniques and activities used to achieve a goal. In the Intelligence Community this term is associated with activities by human intelligence agents to enable the gathering of intelligence information, rather than other more technical intelligence collection.

Tragedy of the Commons — A situation where each individual's pursuit of their own best interest results in a situation that is worse off for the population.

Trojan Horse — Malware that appears to be a useful application or data but contains malicious content, similar to the wooden horse of Greek mythology. When the recipient accesses the file or program the Trojan payload is activated.

Trusted System — A system that has some security properties that causes decision-makers to believe their system is secure or safe. Decision-makers should evaluate a trusted system by asking, "trusted against what threats?"

Vet (Vetting) — A careful and critical examination or investigation of a person, technology, or process.

Virus — Malware attached to a legitimate program or file. When someone accesses a program or file infected by a virus the virus infects the computer with the virus payload commands. A virus spreads when a human or program shares the infected program or file with another machine.

Watermark — Unique sets of characters or images hidden in files.

Weaponization — The process of converting bugs and vulnerabilities into effective and efficient offensive tools.

Worm — Malware that uses a system's existing communications features to spread to other machines.

Zero-day Vulnerability — A vulnerability that has not been publically announced, and therefore is most likely not defended against.

Zombie — A compromised computer controlled by a hacker. See botnet.

Glossary

Index

Index

Index

About the Author

Dr. Michael VanPutte (Lieutenant Colonel, U.S. Army, retired) is an award-winning expert on cyber warfare, and a decorated combat veteran. He began his career as an elite U.S. Army Airborne Ranger, and led troops in combat in Iraq. He taught computer security and cyber warfare at the U.S. Army War College. He then ran offensive and defensive strategic cyber warfare operations, working side-by-side with U.S. cyber experts, law enforcement officers, and intelligence officers at the Joint Task Force – Computer Network Operations, and Joint Task Force – Global Network Operations, the predecessors to U.S. Cyber Command.

From 2006 to 2010 he was a government program manager at the Defense Advanced Research Projects Agency (DARPA), where he led high-risk, high-payoff research and development projects. He's currently a co-founder at Provatek LLC, which conducts research and development of advanced computer network operations (CNO) and intelligence, surveillance, and reconnaissance (ISR) and industrial control systems (ICS) capabilities to improve national security.

Dr. VanPutte received numerous decorations during his 24-year military career. These awards culminated in the Secretary of Defense recognizing his cyber warfare expertise with the highest award for public service — the Secretary of Defense Exceptional Civilian Service Award, and three Secretary of Defense Awards in cyber warfare, culminating in the Secretary of Defense Cyber, Identity, and Information Assurance Individual Award.

Dr. VanPutte received a BS from The Ohio State University, an MS in Computer Science from the University of Missouri - Columbia, and a Ph.D. in Computer Science from the Naval Postgraduate School.

Dr. VanPutte and his wife Linda live in Tampa Florida.

Find out more about Mike at www.mvanputte.com or email him at michael@mvanputte.com.

Made in the USA
Middletown, DE
14 December 2018